BROKEN PLEA

BROKEN PLEA

THE EXPLOSIVE SEARCH FOR TRUTH BEHIND THE IDAHO MURDERS

CHRISTOPHER WHITCOMB

Broken Plea

Published by Harper Select, an imprint of HarperCollins Focus LLC, 501 Nelson Place, Nashville, TN 37214, USA.

ISBN 978-1-4002-5716-4 (audiobook)
ISBN 978-1-4002-5715-7 (ePub)
ISBN 978-1-4002-5714-0 (HC)
ISBN 978-1-4002-6051-5 (ANZ)

HarperCollins Publishers, Macken House, 39/40 Mayor Street Upper, Dublin 1, D01 C9W8, Ireland (https://www.harpercollins.com)

Library of Congress Cataloging-in-Publication Data application has been submitted.

Art Direction: Belinda Bass and Grace Cavalier
Cover Design: David Fassett
Interior Design: Kait Lamphere

Printed in the United States of America
26 27 28 29 30 LBC 5 4 3 2 1

To my father, for his lifelong devotion to truth, justice, and the rule of law.

Contents

Author's Note

An FBI colleague once told me justice is a moving target. I found that odd from a man who had dedicated his life to the battle between good and evil, but after fifteen years in the Bureau, I began to understand his wisdom. Many believe the American legal system to be the best in the world, but few would argue it is perfect. Cops err, technologies fail, and witnesses falter, placing the burden of proof on lawyers who win or lose based on how much a defendant can afford to pay.

When I first heard Bryan Kohberger's name, he was preparing for trial with the death penalty on the line. Prosecutors were claiming DNA and cell tower pings linked him to the scene, but they had no weapon, witnesses, or motive. Kohberger's team seemed to dismiss the case as flawed and predicted exoneration. I paid little attention, thinking experts would sort it all nicely.

But then, two things happened almost simultaneously. Kohberger changed his plea to guilty, and a colleague called to say he'd seen the file—terabytes' worth of lab reports, autopsy photos, and forensic analysis. In his opinion, something was wrong. DNA on the knife sheath had seemingly been mishandled; the crime scene appeared to have been cleaned and altered; timelines didn't seem to add up; witness statements were confusing. Looking deeper, I came to believe he was right.

Whatever happened that terrible Sunday morning at 1122 King Road will likely never be revealed through a slow drip of FOIA requests and police disclosures. We know that Bryan Kohberger has pled guilty to the 2022 murders of four University of Idaho college students and is serving four life terms in prison without the possibility of parole. No other individuals have been implicated or charged with the crimes, and the individuals discussed in this book have denied any involvement. All, of course, are innocent under the law. But, I leave it up to the reader to decide if the file raises questions about the guilty plea for you as it does for me. In such multilayered situations, truth and justice may appear to be moving targets, but together, perhaps we can pin them down.

Throughout the book, you will read actual police reports and interviews, included verbatim. The only changes made were to periodically correct the misspelling of someone's name, so as not to confuse the reader.

The quest begins here.

Key Individuals

Victims

Kaylee Goncalves, 21, University of Idaho student, resident 1122 King Road

Madison Mogen, 21, University of Idaho student, resident 1122 King Road

Xana Kernodle, 20, University of Idaho student, resident 1122 King Road

Ethan Chapin, 20, University of Idaho student, resident 1122 King Road

Survivors

Dylan Mortensen, 19, University of Idaho student, resident 1122 King Road

Bethany Funke, 19, University of Idaho student, resident 1122 King Road

Convicted

Bryan Kohberger, 27, PhD student at Washington State University

Law Enforcement

Officer Mitch Nunes, Moscow Police Department
Officer Eric Warner, Moscow Police Department
Sergeant Shaine Gunderson, Moscow Police Department
Detective Lawrence Mowery, Moscow Police Department
Sergeant Dustin Blaker, Moscow Police Department
Detective Brett Payne, Moscow Police Department
Detective Jeffory Talbott, Idaho State Police
Detective Jake Schwecke, Idaho State Police
Lieutenant Darren Gilbertson, Idaho State Police
Rylene Nowlin, forensic manager, Idaho State Police Laboratory

Prosecution Team

William Thompson, Latah County Prosecuting Attorney
Jeff Nye, Idaho Deputy Attorney General
Ashley Jennings, senior deputy prosecuting attorney
Paulette Sutton, expert witness (forensic criminologist)

Defense Team

Anne Taylor, court appointed public defender
Bicka Barlow, attorney and DNA forensics expert
Elisa Massoth, attorney with death penalty expertise
Dr. Brent Turvey, expert witness (forensic criminologist)
Christopher Holland, former FBI agent (forensic criminologist)

Prologue

Most stories do not begin at the end. But here we find ourselves, July 2, 2025, in an Idaho courtroom, with a pronouncement of guilt in a case that will never go to trial.

•

"All right, this is CR012431665," the judge says. "Defendant is present."

•

The presiding justice, Steven Hippler, is a fifty-nine-year-old former partner at a law firm best known for defending doctors against claims of malpractice. At this point in his career, he is a highly regarded jurist, assigned by Governor C. L. "Butch" Otter to the state's Fourth Judicial District. Today he is focused on a hastily arranged change of plea in the matter of *State of Idaho v. Bryan C. Kohberger.* It is a death penalty prosecution of capital murder. Theories run rampant.

•

"In custody, with counsel."

•

It has been over two years since Kaylee Goncalves, Madison Mogen, Xana Kernodle, and Ethan Chapin were found dead at a three-story house in a town called Moscow. This is one of the most sensationalized crimes this century, and everyone from Reddit bloggers to legacy media have covered the case in heavy rotation. In a last-minute legal maneuver to avoid the death penalty, Kohberger has agreed to a plea deal that will land him in prison for the rest of his life. As in most cases of this nature, emotions run high, with four separate families trying to make sense of incomprehensible evil. Gag orders have made facts of the case hard to come by.

•

"Miss Thompson, Miss Jennings, and uh, pardon me . . ." Judge Hippler stumbles over names in his hastily prepared notes. "Miss Taylor, Miss Massoth, and Miss Barlow."

•

The courtroom is small, crowded, quiet. The prosecution sits five-wide, below and to the judge's left. The defense sits stage right, a team of four, with the defendant in the middle. Bryan Kohberger looks focused, attentive, staid. He is wearing a crisply pressed shirt and a matching paisley tie. His hair looks neatly groomed, his eyebrows trimmed, his hands folded on the table in front of him, as he sits bolt straight in his chair.

•

"The state's present with Mr. Thompson," Judge Hippler says with a nod. He is known for fair and measured opinions in a broad array of cases. Records suggest that only one of his rulings has been overturned in twelve years on the bench. "Mr. Hurwit, Miss Jennings, and um . . . Mr. Nye is here as well. Did I miss anybody?"

•

He looks directly at the woman seated to Mr. Thompson's left.

•

"Miss Allen is here as well," the lead prosecutor advises. She is one of four members of his team but apparently not on the judge's list.

"Miss Allen is here as well . . . very well, thank you."

•

Perhaps the oversight makes sense considering the speed and shocking nature of this turn of events. Just weeks before jury selection was slated to begin, with a trial date set for August, Bryan Kohberger is said to have changed his mind. After thirty months of a steadfast denial, the defense apparently wants to make a deal, and for those wondering if the defense might try some kind of nolo contendere argument to avoid a firing squad, that will not happen today. The State of Idaho does allow for an "Alford plea," where the defendant maintains innocence while acknowledging evidence sufficient to convict, but this is a case of capital murder; Kohberger's only option is to cop to all counts and throw himself upon the mercy of the court.

•

"All right, we are here today to entertain a change of plea," Judge Hippler says, stating one of the few known facts of the case. His gag orders have reduced disclosure to nuanced interpretation of motions from the defense.

"Before we start, I want to address some issues of concern . . ."

•

It seems important we pause here to point out that everyone in the courtroom has issues of concern. True crime is the hottest genre in entertainment, and this is the crime of the century, meaning America is hooked with prurient interest on the tragedy of vibrant youth cut down in the middle of the night by a PhD student in criminology. There has already been a book written by a journalist from *The New York Times* and another by a famous author best known for fiction. Amazon Prime has released a documentary that many criticize for relying on family photos and haunting music in lieu of facts. Peacock has one, too, as does *Dateline*.

•

"First," Hippler states, "I appreciate everyone in attendance today being on their best behavior. Please, no outbursts or demonstrations."

•

The families have questions also, more than a dozen mothers and fathers connected to the victims via marriage and divorce. Even Bryan Kohberger's parents have flown in from Pennsylvania, which might seem awful to some, but they have lost a child too.

•

"I want to point out that there have been calls by some for the public to contact me and my office in an attempt to influence my decision-making in this case," Hippler scolds the courtroom. "The court is not supposed to, and this court will never, take into account public sentiment in making an opinion regarding its judicial decisions in cases."

•

This, of course, is a direct reference to reports of outrage among a wide spectrum of interested parties. The families of Xana Kernodle and Kaylee Goncalves say they were not notified of an agreement until after the whole thing had been arranged. Witnesses hang in limbo regarding dates and details of testimony. Law enforcement officials who have spent years mired in the investigation will later state that they were not advised. Consultants, experts, and criminologists hired by the defense know only what they have heard on the news, and the news knows nothing. Maybe worst, we live in a social media age where opinion can flame to rage with one keenly worded post. The algorithm has been triggered. Disgust is going viral; the internet is losing its mind.

•

"Courts should, and I always will, make decisions based on where the facts and the law lead me. Period," Hippler states. He sounds angry. "I have not read any of the numerous messages nor listened to any of the various voicemails sent to me and my staff. Those have all been forwarded to security and, where appropriate, to law enforcement."

•

Though Judge Hippler has offered many hours of opinion in dozens of rulings, it seems important to quote him here for two reasons. The first is that these will be the last words he utters before the accused becomes the guilty. The second is that Hippler knows that a plea agreement may forever seal details of an investigation already blurred opaque. The moment Kohberger's sentence is pronounced, the killer will disappear into the anonymity of a life behind bars. There, the truth will die with him. No one will ever find the murder weapon; there will be no revelations of motive or means, no real sense of how or why.

•

"Will the defendant please stand."

•

All heads turn toward Kohberger as he rises. Gone, somehow, is the blank stare that has plagued him in news accounts since that first hearing where his lawyer, Anne Taylor, spoke on his behalf.

•

"You've heard the plea agreement that I talked about today," Judge Hippler confirms. "Do you agree with that plea agreement?"

"Yes."

"And do you understand the nature of the charges that are . . . that you've been charged with, that I understand you're going to plead guilty today to?"

"Yes."

"As I indicated, I'm not bound by the plea agreement, but the plea agreement is for the maximum on each count. Do you understand that I'm not bound by the plea agreement?"

"Yes."

•

At this point the judge asks Kohberger if anyone has promised him leniency. Kohberger says no, which may be a stretch because the prosecution has offered life in prison instead of death, certainly a reduction. Next, Kohberger affirms to the judge that no one has threatened him, promised him anything, offered a reward. He waives future rights to appeal.

•

"All right. I want you to understand what the state would've had to have proven, at trial, had you—as to the crimes that you're pleading guilty to—had you, if you didn't plead guilty. Let me find the document. Hang on a second here. So as to count one, burglary, the state would have to have proven that on or about November 13, 2022, in Latah County, Idaho, you unlawfully entered a residence located at 1122 King Road in Moscow, Idaho, with the intent to commit the felony crime of murder."

•

Though this is technically a charge of burglary, the impact feels seismic. Whatever happened at 1122 King Road that fateful night, events began with a killer standing outside a house in the dark, likely clad in a balaclava, possibly holding a knife. We can all imagine the scene. It's a nightmare.

•

"As to count two, the state would've had to have proven that on or about that same date in Latah County, Idaho, you did willfully, unlawfully, deliberately, with premeditation and malice of forethought, kill and murder Madison Mogen, a human being, by stabbing Madison Mogen, from which she died."

•

Calling her a "human being" somehow makes the nightmare worse.

•

"As to count three, the state would've had to have proven that on that same date in Latah County at that same address, you did willfully, unlawfully, deliberately, with premeditation and malice of forethought, kill and murder Kaylee Goncalves, a human being, by stabbing her, from which she died."

•

Kaylee was attacked with savagery. Stabbing might have been the least of it.

•

"As to count four, the state would've had to have proven that on or about that same date in Latah County, Idaho, you did willfully, unlawfully, deliberately, with premeditation and malice of forethought, murder Xana Kernodle, a human being, by stabbing her, from which she died."

•

What the judge does not tell the world is that Xana fought violently for her life, wrestling with her killer on the floor of her room in a pool of blood. In this hearing, details about valor in the face of horror somehow fade, muffled beneath legal jargon and statutory prose. Here, only the butcher wins.

•

"And then to count five, also murder in the first degree, that on or about November 13, 2022, in Latah County, Idaho, you did willfully, unlawfully, deliberately, with premeditation and malice of forethought, kill and murder Ethan Chapin, a human being, by stabbing him, from which he died. Do you understand those things the state would've had to have proven?"

"Yes," Kohberger states.

"And do you understand that by pleading guilty, the state no longer has to prove those things, because you're admitting those things are true?"

"Yes."

•

At this point, the judge mentions a plea form and some paperwork, then goes through the whole thing again. Did Kohberger go to the house? Yes. Did he intend to commit murder? Yes. Did he kill each of the four young humans, each identified by name? Yes, Kohberger says, yes, he did it all. And then Judge Hippler turns the whole thing over to the prosecution.

•

"Thank you, Your Honor," Thompson says, standing. He is an imposing figure: bearded, avuncular, stern. This is his last case, after decades on the job, a capstone achievement in an admirable career. "The state's evidence as an overview would show that back in March of 2022, when the defendant was residing at his parents' residence or was residing back in Pennsylvania, in his home state, he purchased online a KA-BAR knife and sheath with an Amazon gift card that he had purchased shortly prior to the purchase of the knife, sheath, and sharpener."

•

And here is where we suspend the narrative long enough to ask an obvious question: What could be the point in writing a book about a story we already know?

The answer begins with a 1963 Supreme Court decision titled *Brady v. Maryland*, in which the federal government ruled that prosecutors must disclose all evidence to the defense. This means Bill Thompson had to hand his files to Kohberger's lawyer, Anne Taylor, who in turn farmed them out to experts for exculpatory opinion. As fate would have it, two of those experts, seeking transparency, provided me with a large chunk of Thompson's "Brady disclosure," a cache of fifty-nine thousand files, containing more than two hundred thousand largely unredacted exhibits. From autopsy photos to the contents of Kohberger's phone, I have reviewed it all in my research for this book.

•

"Jumping ahead," Thompson says, "at the end of June of that year, the defendant, Mr. Kohberger, moved from Pennsylvania to Pullman, Washington, which is right across the state line from Moscow, Idaho, for the purpose of pursuing a PhD in criminal justice at Washington State University."

•

This much is true.

•

"The state's evidence would indicate that beginning July 9, 2020, Mr. Kohberger's phone began connecting to a cell tower that serves the area of the 1122 King Road residence in Moscow, Idaho. Now, I will acknowledge for the court and all present that there are many residences in that area. It's a dense population of mostly college-related occupants. Between July 9, 2022, and November 7, the defendant's phone connected to that particular tower during late night, early morning, approximately twenty-three times.

"Now, I will acknowledge, also, we do not have evidence that the defendant had direct contact with 1122 or with residents of 1122, but we can put his phone in that area on those times. In the interim, on August 22, 2022, Latah County Sheriff's Deputy Darren Duke conducted a traffic stop in the early morning hour or late evening hours, about eleven p.m., on the west side of Moscow, on the Moscow-Pullman road. This was the traffic stop of Mr. Kohberger's car."

•

It's difficult to see where this is going, but as it is a plea hearing, there are no objections.

•

"We then move to the early morning hours of November 13, 2022. The state's evidence would show that early morning hours on that day, Mr. Kohberger's phone left his Pullman residence. That phone was then subsequently turned off at approximately 2:54 a.m. and remained off until approximately 4:48 a.m. on Sunday, the 13th of November. The state's evidence includes, or would include at trial, a video surveillance of a business on the Moscow-Pullman Highway, just across the state line from Moscow that would show a vehicle matching the description of the defendant's Hyundai Elantra entering Moscow at approximately 3:02 a.m."

•

Circumstantial evidence is perfectly admissible in a murder case, but a vehicle "matching the description of the defendant's Hyundai" seems a bit less than proof beyond reasonable doubt.

•

"Compiled surveillance that the investigators put together from businesses and residences then show the defendant's car, the white Elantra, circling the 1122 King Road area, that neighborhood, starting around 3:30 or so in the morning. And approximately 4:05 that morning, the defendant's car had entered that area, was leaving, stopped at the intersection of King and Queen Road, did a U-turn, and the state's evidence would show that defendant's car came back and parked behind and above the 1122 King Road residence."

•

Nothing in the files I reviewed show anything of the kind.

•

"The state believes that its evidence would then show that the defendant entered the residence of 1122 through the kitchen sliding door on the backside of the residence, which is the side of the residence that would face the area above, where the defendant's car was parked. Defendant entered the residence, went to the third floor, and with a knife, killed Madison Mogen and Kaylee Goncalves."

•

The courtroom hangs on every word as the narrative builds, but there is no mention of the fact that Kaylee was asphyxiated to the point of petechia, beaten so severely, her skull, palate, and orbital bones were fractured. Her throat was slashed ear to ear, twice, postmortem. This was a crime of rage.

•

"The defendant, as he left that room, for whatever reason, ended up leaving . . . or the sheath for a KA-BAR knife was left on the bed next to Madison Mogen's body. That sheath was tested by the Idaho State Police forensic lab, and single source male DNA was found on the snap of that sheath."

•

Thompson does not mention seemingly significant flaws in this part of his case, including FBI laboratory reports that the state's DNA sample may have comprised less than ten human cells. He does not mention the fact that the DNA sample was first sent to a private genetic genealogy lab in The Woodlands, Texas, where it was traced to "four brothers," none of whom were named Kohberger. He does not mention a potentially catastrophic chain of custody issues or the fact that handwritten Idaho State Police evidence retention forms note the sheath was found not on the bed but on the floor. As this is a plea hearing and not a trial, the prosecution is not bound to present any particular point of evidence, only what they choose to present in their statement at the hearing.

•

"The state's evidence would show that Xana Kernodle was still awake at this time. Her room was not on the third floor; it was on the second floor on the west side. As the defendant was either coming down the stairs or leaving, he encountered Xana, and he ended up killing her also, with a large knife."

•

Thompson does not explain that Xana died thirty feet from where she was first attacked. He does not explain the forensically impossible trail of apparently altered evidence Xana left along the way, including blood spatter that was diluted "with an unknown substance." He does not explain how two survivors inside the house did not notice her screams, though the audio recording from a surveillance camera down the street did. He does not explain how Xana's boyfriend, a six-foot-four, 228-pound football player, never got out of bed to help her as she fought for her life just three feet away.

Thompson does not mention that Ethan's undiluted blood was found at the top of the stairs leading down to the first floor, other stains somehow hidden under a box of White Claw beverages.

He does not mention apparently overwhelming forensic evidence of crime scene alteration, a cleanup of the house's common spaces, or the highly likely involvement of a second assailant.

•

"Ethan Chapin, Xana's boyfriend, was asleep in their bedroom, in her bedroom, and the defendant killed him as well with a large fixed-blade knife. Each victim suffered multiple wounds. I will state for the record that there is no evidence there was any sexual component or sexual assault on any of the victims."

•

Thompson does not address the fact that Ethan's naked body was covered with a blanket sometime after he was dead. He does not divulge evidence showing that despite a trail of blood from Maddie's room on the third floor to Xana's on the second, not a drop was found in the bed where Ethan supposedly died at the hands of a lone offender. There is no mention that a clump of hair was discovered in Ethan's closed fist, presumably pulled in a fight with his killer. There is no citation of laboratory evaluation, because there was none. The hair, labeled "debris," was never examined beyond color and length. There was no attempt to identify its source using DNA.

•

"There were two other roommates in the house, and they were already asleep. During the course of this, one of those roommates awoke, looked out her door not knowing what was going on, and saw the defendant, who was dressed in black with a black belt, holding some sort of container in his hand. And she saw him leave the house through the direction of the kitchen where that sliding door is, that I mentioned before."

•

This is interesting.

Thompson is talking about reports attributed to surviving witness Dylan Mortensen. Body camera footage recorded by MPD officer Mitch Nunes proves that Dylan never mentioned the belt or the container in her first interview Sunday afternoon standing outside the house. She did not mention it during her second interview, later that afternoon, with Officer Lawrence Mowery at the Moscow police station. She did not discuss the belt or the container until days later, in the presence of her lawyer, during a November 17 interview with ISP detective Vickie Gooch. When asked what she remembered, police reports show Mortensen said she did not remember much of anything. Instead of pressing the issue, Gooch reassured Mortensen that she was a witness, not a suspect, and asked very little of probative value.

•

"At approximately 4:20 that morning, defendant's car is seen on a surveillance camera for 1112 King Road, leaving the area at a high rate of speed."

•

White car, yes. Defendant identified as the driver? No.

•

"The evidence would show that following that, the defendant in his Elantra drove south of Moscow. We know that he drove on the back roads because there are surveillance cameras on the main highways, Highway 95, that would've picked up the defendant's car if he'd gone that route."

•

Meaning no one knows anything at all about where the car actually went.

•

"About 4:48 that morning, the defendant's phone comes back on, and the evidence will show that that phone was located south of Moscow, likely at a side road intersection with Highway 95. From there, the defendant's phone activity tracks heading back north towards Pullman, Washington, where the defendant lived. About 5:26, starting approximately 5:26, various surveillance cameras in Pullman, Washington, pick up the defendant's vehicle as he enters Pullman from the south and heads north and slightly west towards his apartment where he arrived at approximately 5:30 in the morning."

•

This assertion is slightly more accurate, though in my opinion, misleading. Analysis by the FBI's Cellular Analysis Survey Team (CAST) shows tower connections to Kohberger's phone, but their graphically animated courtroom presentation only claims accuracy to within thirteen miles. Despite prosecution assertions, cell pings place Kohberger nowhere near the scene.

•

"Later that morning, Mr. Kohberger's phone returned to the area of King Road. It's about nine o'clock in the morning, was there for about ten minutes and then returned to his Pullman residence. About nine thirty, the state's evidence will show evidence taken from the defendant's phone, that he took a selfie of himself on his phone in what appears to be the bathroom of his Pullman apartment with a thumbs-up."

•

In fact, such a photo was not out of character or in some way unique. Kohberger's phone was filled with a large number of selfies, photos of hiking, eating dinner with his family, or petting his dog. He seemed to like baseball, especially the Yankees, had numerous socially awkward selfies, and had googled porn a grand total of three times. Among 3,509 text messages he sent or received in the four months leading up to the crimes, all but a few were to his family. Nothing suggests premeditation.

•

"The defendant's phone then went to the Lewiston–Clarkston valley, approximately thirty miles south of Moscow and Pullman, and the defendant is actually seen with his car at various businesses down there. This area is the confluence of the Clearwater River and the Snake River. Lewiston is Idaho's seaport, large bodies of moving water down there."

•

Thompson's insinuation is unclear. Perhaps he thinks this is where Kohberger tossed the knife?

•

"In addition to tracing the defendant's activities . . . the state's evidence will show that following Sunday, November 13, 2022 . . . the defendant began searching for a KA-BAR knife and KA-BAR knife sheath, as the state believes, to replace the one that was left at the scene of the murders. The evidence also will suggest that there were at least attempts by the defendant to delete or alter his purchase history on Amazon, where all these transactions had occurred."

•

Based on careful analysis of all prosecution files, these claims seem highly dubious, but once again, there is no cross-examination in a change of plea hearing.

•

"Later that week, the state's evidence will show that Mr. Kohberger went to what we would call DMV motor vehicle licensing here in Idaho to change his car registration from Pennsylvania to Washington. That's of note because Pennsylvania cars do not require a front license plate. The vehicle seen on the surveillance cameras of defendant's car showed it didn't have a front license plate on it."

•

Of the five white cars captured on camera, only one shows a missing plate.

•

"Mr. Kohberger proceeded to finish his semester of studies at Washington State University and returned to Pennsylvania for the holidays. Law enforcement located him in Pennsylvania, and they conducted what's called a trash pull."

•

The FBI did not simply "locate" him in Pennsylvania. They surveilled him more than twenty-five hundred miles as he drove home from school with his father. A trash pull is a warrantless search. It would have been contested at trial.

•

"Working with the sanitation department back in this neighborhood in Pennsylvania, we took trash that had been set out on the street for collection, sent the contents of that from the Pennsylvania residence of the defendant's parents to the Idaho State Forensic Laboratory, where the lab experts there were able to identify DNA on a Q-tip as coming from the father of the person whose DNA was found on the knife sheath that was next to Mogen's body in the bed."

•

FBI guidelines for DNA submission to the Combined DNA Index System (CODIS) require a minimum sample for short tandem repeat (STR) identification. The DNA sample obtained from the knife sheath was determined to be significantly less than what the FBI required to make a forensic match.

•

"I can tell the court, public, the weapon itself, the knife, has not yet been recovered. I can tell the court that the defendant's apartment in Pullman was searched as well as his office. Nothing of evidentiary value was found."

•

Nothing of evidentiary value was found? *Nothing?* This is a death penalty case.

•

"In Pennsylvania, the defendant's car was seized, and it was actually pretty much disassembled internally, and it also had been cleaned. There was a bucket of cleaner right beside it. I think we can all look to our own cars, you know, when those compartments in the doors, we try to keep them clean where you put stuff. There's always some degree of crud in there."

•

"Some degree of crud" in the places "where you put stuff." That's what he told the judge.

•

"The defendant's car had been meticulously cleaned inside, and the state would present to the jury that that was part of the defendant's plan in covering up this. The defendant has studied crime.

In fact, he did a detailed paper on crime scene processing when he was working on his predoctorate degrees, and he had that knowledge and skill."

•

Kohberger's predoctoral degrees were in psychology. When police searched his car, they found empty wrappers, a Band-Aid, empty water bottles, miscellaneous receipts, spare change, and the hotel room card holder from when he drove cross-country with his dad.

•

"So, Your Honor, at the end, the state submits that the evidence would show that on November 13, 2022, Mr. Kohberger entered the residence at 1122 King Road in Moscow, Idaho. He did that with the intent to kill. We will not represent that he intended to commit all of the murders that he did that night, but we know that that is what resulted, and that he then killed intentionally, willfully, deliberately, with premeditation and with malice and forethought, Maddie Mogen, Kaylee Goncalves, Ethan Chapin, and Xana Kernodle. Thank you."

•

Thompson takes his seat. You can hear a pin drop.

•

"Thank you," Judge Hippler says. "All right. Based on the state's proffer and importantly, based upon defendant's explicit admission to committing these crimes, the court finds there is a factual basis. Therefore, with respect to count one, burglary, felony, how do you plead, Mr. Kohberger? Guilty or not guilty?"

•

And, here, the whole nightmare apparently comes to a close. Kohberger stands.

•

"Guilty," he says.

"As to count two, murder in the first degree as it relates to the murder of Madison Mogen, how do you plead? Guilty or not guilty?"

"Guilty."

"As to count three, as it relates to murder in the first degree for the murder of Kaylee Goncalves, how do you plead? Guilty or not guilty?"

"Guilty."

"As to count four, the first-degree murder of Xana Kernodle, a human being, how do you plead? Guilty or not guilty?"

"Guilty."

"As to count five, the first-degree murder of Ethan Chapin, a human being, how do you plead? Guilty or not guilty?"

"Guilty."

"All right." The judge nods. "The court will find that the defendant understands the nature of the charges and each offense, and the possible consequences to him of his guilty plea. The court finds that there is a factual basis for the plea, and finds the defendant believes the plea to be in his best interest. I find that the plea was given freely, voluntarily, and was intelligently made."

•

The judge then runs through a checklist of formalities, mandated by the Constitution, because all Americans are presumed innocent until found guilty in a court of law. The checklist is long, but no one seems to mind because Kohberger has saved the State of Idaho months at trial, saved family members the trauma of disclosures, saved witnesses the toll of recollection.

•

"I accept the plea," Judge Hippler says. "I direct that it be entered."

•

Here, in this moment, the end becomes our beginning.

What the world actually knows after two and a half years of investigation comes down to a few undisputed facts. Within the walls of the three-story structure at 1122 King Road, four young students were cut down in the prime of life. On the third floor, Kaylee Goncalves lay beaten, smothered, and slashed, with Maddie Mogen cuddled beside her, posed as if napping. On the second floor, Xana Kernodle was found spread-eagle in a sprawl of coat hangers and shoes, with her boyfriend murdered in bed just a few feet away.

What the world does not yet know is that Bryan Kohberger's guilty plea may have negligently whitewashed one of the great travesties of modern jurisprudence. In lieu of a trial, no one will ever know how a lone assassin, with no ties to any of the victims, entered the house on King Road in the middle of the night, committed four murders in around four minutes, and escaped without a trace. What were his motives? Who was his target? Why did he not kill two witnesses who waited eight hours before calling police?

In order to answer these questions and truly accept Kohberger's plea, we must go back to that awful night in Moscow and reexamine the case for ourselves. Yes, justice remains the realm of lawyers and courts, but we are now all a jury of Kohberger's peers with every right to weigh the evidence as presented. Truth beyond reasonable doubt is our objective.

We begin with a song.

PART 1

THE COMMUNICATION

10.09.2023

Dear Scout,

Earlier, you and I, unbeknownst to you, "communicated"

I have no doubt that your Heart was conscious of what I intended . . .

Always of your Pack, Brother

Bryan C. Kohberger
Letter to his dog
Latah County Jail

CHAPTER 1

Suicide, French Fries, Silver Sedan

Odd as it might sound, everything we truly know about the Idaho murders starts with the song "My Only Enemy," during the middle section that sounds old-school country, after Jelly Roll's opening but before Struggle Jennings jumps in on rap.

"My only enemy is me . . ."

And though some will wonder how a murder investigation begins with a song, we should consider the soundtrack to be a crucial part of a case that plays out like a made-for-TV movie. Despite three years of gag orders and obfuscation, the truth about what police found on November 13, 2022, at 1122 King Road unfolds in documentary fashion, with fifty-six minutes of body camera video. Unlike the officially redacted version, the actual tape reveals details that will prove critical in a forensic search for the truth. If we want to understand Kohberger's plea, we need to fully reconstruct the case against him.

•

"911, location of your emergency?"

Police involvement starts Sunday at 11:56 a.m. with Bethany Funke's call for help.

"Something is happening," she is heard saying in a widely scrutinized recording. "Something happened in our house, and we don't know what."

Funke, of course, is one of two surviving roommates in the house at the time of the crimes. Investigators would later conclude that Kohberger left the house around 4:17 a.m., which means Funke waited almost eight hours before calling for help.

"What is the address of the emergency?" Whitcom 911 operator Carolina Calvin asks.

"1122 . . ." Funke tries to answer, through tears. "Oh . . . King Road."

"And is that a house or an apartment?"

"It's a house."

Calvin tries to follow up with basic questions about the location and nature of the emergency, but Funke hands the phone to another female, later identified as Emily Alandt.

"I'll talk to you guys," Alandt says. "We live at the Whites, so we're next to them."

"Okay," Calvin prods, "tell me exactly what's going on."

"Um, one of our, one of the roommates is passed out and she was drunk last night and she's not waking up. Oh, and they saw some man in their house last night."

At that point, Funke returns to the phone, distraught.

"Okay, I need someone to keep the phone," Calvin scolds. "Stop passing it around."

"Can I just tell you what happened pretty much?"

"What is going on currently? Is someone passed out right now?"

Funke tries to provide context, but Calvin wants current information, and things go back and forth until Funke hands the phone to a male, later identified as Hunter Johnson. He can be heard breathing heavily in the background as chaos ensues.

"She's not waking up," Funke says, returning to the phone a third time.

Calvin calmly states, "Okay, one moment. I'm getting help started that way."

She switches to emergency response protocols, and in a single transmission launches what will be the biggest criminal investigation in Idaho history.

"Dispatching Moscow law, ambulance, unconscious female, 1122 King Road," the 911 operator says. "Units responding, RP's advising the patient is not conscious, not breathing."

We cut back to body cam video of Officer Mitch Nunes behind the wheel of his SUV as the audio kicks in.

"I'm up against something I can't beat . . ."

He is listening to his "good times" radio in the background as the Motorola two-way chirps squelch between ten codes. It's the very same AM/FM system you'd listen to in your own Ford Explorer if it were not marked POLICE. Many cops will tell you a little music comes in handy in the middle of a long shift where boredom poses the biggest threat to officer safety. In this case, the shift is Sunday morning after a home game weekend in which the University of Idaho football Vandals took a shellacking from UC Davis. Much of the campus is sleeping off a night of bar hops and house parties. The campus is quiet. Reports have been filed, patrol vehicles gassed up. It's too late for coffee, not yet time for lunch.

"Multiple people at the scene are advising that a roommate at the scene is passed out." A woman's voice breaks through the Jelly Roll song. "Not waking up."

"Moscow 170 en route," Nunes responds, using his badge number as a call sign.

"Copy that, twenty-year-old female unconscious, trying to get further."

Officer Nunes hits the gas, without employing his siren, and pulls up in front of 1122 King Road at 12:00:08. He shuts down his engine, goes around to the rear of marked unit MPD-5, and retrieves a blaze orange EMS bag.

"Where's she at?" he calls out, walking briskly toward the house. There are three women standing outside: Dylan Mortensen, Bethany Funke, and Emily Alandt. They look visibly distraught.

"Where's she at?"

"Do you have a defibrillator?" Funke asks, still on the phone with Calvin.

"Yup. Where's she at? Where's she at?"

Hunter Johnson is standing in the open doorway wearing shorts and a blue-green hoodie.

"Where at?" Nunes asks, entering the house.

"Up here, up here," Johnson responds, leading the officer up a staircase to the second floor. "We got a call from them this morning, that something wasn't okay, that something really wasn't normal, and I just came in here to check in here and somebody's down."

Johnson leads Nunes through the living room, past the edge of a white table set up for beer pong. The place is a mess from recent parties, but Nunes is focused on what appears to be a female on the floor at the end of a hallway. Even from the top of the first-floor stairs, he can tell that she is lying face up in a dried stew of mayhem. This is not a passed-out coed.

"Fuck," Nunes says.

Hunter leads him down the hall to what now is obviously a lifeless body.

"And I checked to see if she's breathing," he says, stepping into Xana's room. He stands over the body of a young woman clad in underwear and a hoodie. "And she's dead hard."

Nunes sweeps the room with the beam of his flashlight, trains it on an adult male lying sprawled across a queen-size bed. The man's legs stick out from under a fawn-colored comforter, naked except for socks. A blue blanket covers his torso and head.

"And I didn't check him yet," Hunter says, "but I'm pretty sure he's—"

"Thirteen," Nunes interrupts, speaking into his radio. "I think we have a homicide."

The shock of realization is obvious. Nunes pauses, trying to make sense of things: furniture bloodied and violently displaced, Ethan in bed, Xana's legs splayed toward the door.

"Okay, get back," Nunes tells Johnson.

The room is cluttered with items one might expect to find in a college student's bedroom, but they are scattered: shoes, a coat hanger, a plate of food near a fan. There's laundry in a bin, a water bottle, a cell phone near Xana's left hand, french fries between her feet. There is blood on the walls, the door, the sheets, a nightstand, the floor. It's carnage.

"I don't know if they are still in here or not," Hunter says, walking back down the hallway, toward the folding table set up for beer pong. "I grabbed this knife—"

"Thirteen, seven-zero," Nunes interrupts, turning back to the bedroom for a second look.

"This is the knife I grabbed—"

"Okay, stay back there, please."

Nunes seems somewhat overwhelmed, slow to process the gravity of the situation.

"Fuck."

•

Which provides the perfect opportunity to pause for context. As a 2019 University of Idaho graduate himself, Nunes was no stranger to college life, and though he was only twenty-five years old with barely two years on the job, it would be hard to consider him a rookie. He had joined the police department in May 2020 after five years volunteering with the Moscow fire department, where he gained plenty of exposure to violence by misadventure. Just months earlier, on April 28, 2022, he received the Pullman, Washington, police department's Meritorious Lifesaving Award for his efforts responding to a September 2021 shooting in the town's College Hill area. According to the citation and local reports, Officer Nunes provided "immediate life saving measures" on two gunshot victims, one of whom died.

•

"Let's slow down . . ." are the next words we hear him speak.

He has walked back through the living room to the top of the stairs leading down to the open front door. Officer Eric Warner has arrived as backup, with no clue what he's walking into.

"Just come here," Nunes tells him. "There's two . . . looks like two fatalities."

Nunes pulls on a pair of black nitrile gloves as the two officers move to the bedroom, where Nunes pauses for a deep breath, surveys the scene for the third time, and says again, "Fuck."

He's trying to make sense of things that make no sense at all. You can hear it in his voice.

"Dude . . ."

Nunes focuses the beam of his flashlight on the bed as Warner looks on.

"I think he might have killed himself."

"How'd you get there?" Warner asks.

"I don't know, I just see blood. I haven't . . ."

Nunes turns to his radio.

"Thirteen, seven-zero," he reports. "For your information, there's two college-aged people appearing both to be deceased. Lots of blood."

Through the lens of his body camera, we see Warner pulling on his own black nitrile gloves. He seems almost unnaturally calm and collected, the consummate professional.

"Yeah," Nunes affirms, using police jargon to describe the two victims. "They're DRT."

•

Moscow dispatch would know *DRT* means "dead right there," but that is where clarity ends. From the moment Nunes makes his initial assessment, everything we think we know about this case starts to devolve. Despite all the countless reports and interviews and laboratory analyses, the first moments of this investigation are captured veritas-style on fifty-six minutes of body cam video. Before we continue, we need to look at why and how it seemed to be ignored.

On November 13, 2022, Moscow Police officer Mitchell Nunes filed a report titled Supplemental 3, detailing the initial investigation at 1122 King Road. Prior to the release of body camera footage three years later, it was the origin story of all we knew about the case. Nunes's report is here transcribed verbatim:

> On 11/13/2022, at approximately 1156 hours, I responded to an unconscious subject at 1122 King Road in Moscow, Idaho. Upon my arrival, I found a large gathering of people in the parking lot immediately north of the 1122 King Road residence. 1122 King Road is a white, three story, single family residence with multiple bedrooms. The "1122" designation is located directly above the front door, facing north. I was directed to a bedroom on the second floor by Hunter I. Johnson in the northwest corner, to locate the unresponsive female.
>
> Upon entering the room, I observed a female laying supine on the floor, next to a bed. According to Dylan M. Mortensen, this female was likely Kaylee J. Goncalves. Dylan also lived at 1122 King Rd. I observed dried blood surrounding Kaylee's body and signs of cutting trauma to her face. Kaylee was covered in so much blood I wasn't able to immediately discern

where any additional injuries would have likely been. Kaylee was apparently deceased due to her pale skin color, rigid body tone and apparent blood loss.

On the bed, in the same room I observed Kaylee, I observed a male lying supine on the bed. According to Dylan, the male was likely Ethan J. Chapin. Dylan said Ethan was commonly at the residence. I observed blood covering portions of Ethan's legs, surrounding his body into the bed sheets, and drops of blood on the wall near Ethan's head. As I backed out of this room, Hunter showed me a kitchen knife and said he had it in his possession. I told Hunter to leave the knife and go back down the stairs to the front entrance.

Ofc. Warner and I moved to visually clear the residence for any suspects or additional victims. On the third floor, Ofc. Warner and I found two additional apparently deceased females, both laying supine in a bed. This bedroom was on the southwest corner of the third floor. According to Dylan, these two females were likely Xana A. Kernodle and Madison M. Mogen. One female showed an apparent traumatic injury to her face due to the basic facial structure being unrecognizable. Both females showed very pale skin. Both females were covered in dried blood and apparently deceased. After the residence was deemed safe, Ofc. Warner and I exited the residence to secure it and the immediate area, to include the parking lot immediately to the north of the residence.

I walked outside and began interviewing Dylan. Dylan told me at approximately 0400 hours she heard a voice scream and believed it to be Kaylee's. Dylan said she heard Kaylee scream and announce there was "somebody" inside the residence. Dylan said she could hear Kaylee run from the third floor, down the stairs to the second floor, into the northwest bedroom. Dylan said she locked herself in her bedroom and continued to hear a commotion. Dylan said eventually she stopped hearing a struggle and heard a male voice say, "you're gonna be fine. I'm gonna help you." Dylan said she did not recognize the male's voice. Dylan said after a few minutes, she peeked out of her bedroom and observed a male described as approximately 6-feet tall, slim build, with a black ski mask leave the second-floor patio area. This door was likely left open as it was found open upon my arrival.

I interviewed an additional roommate, Bethany G. Funke, who told me she was at the residence during the commotion. Bethany said she was on the second floor, in the living area, watching Vampire Diaries with Dylan, and an additional person named Lakelynn. Bethany said at approximately 0200 hours on 11/13/2022, Madison and Kaylee came home from a night out at the Corner Club bar, located at 202 N Main Street in Moscow, Idaho. Bethany said she also believed Madison and Kaylee went to the Grub Wandering Kitchen truck that was commonly located in the 300 Block of South Main Street. Bethany said she and Madison let Madison's dog out, "Murphy," sometime between 0200 hours and 0230 hours. Bethany said she went to bed around 0230 hours. Bethany said Madison came into her bedroom sometime after 0230 hours to ask if she knew where Murphy was. Bethany said she told Madison no and Madison left. Bethany said she woke up in her bedroom, which was located on the first floor, to a sound she described as a firecracker and a flash. Bethany said she initially thought the sound was a prank.

According to Bethany's phone log she showed me, Bethany called Xana at 0421 hours, Ethan at 0422 hours, Madison at 0422 hours, Madison again at 0430 hours, and then Kaylee at 0431 hours. Bethany said she never received an answer on each phone call. Bethany said she went back to sleep and woke up around 1156 hours, when 911 was called.

Initially, I was told Kaylee was likely located on the second floor bedroom, with Ethan. After comparing Dylan's initial statement with other investigations officer's observations, it appeared to actually be Xana that was located on the floor of that bedroom room. And Kaylee was one of the other females located in the third floor room.

I was originally assigned to identify all of the people in the area. However, I was reassigned by Sgt. Gunderson to begin the search warrant application process. I provided the above information in the search warrant application.

In the 1960s, an MIT mathematician named Edward Lorenz was studying weather patterns when he discovered that small variations in the initial condition of a system could turn into huge and unpredictable outcomes further down the line. He coined the term *butterfly effect*, arguing that a monarch flapping its wings in Brazil could create a tornado in Texas, an analytical model that has become the foundation of everything from biology to stock market investing. And though chaos theory is not often taught in law enforcement academies, nothing could more accurately describe what seems to have gone wrong in the prosecution of

Bryan Kohberger for the murders of the Idaho Four. To make sense of his plea, we have to look closely at apparent missteps made long before any of us knew his name.

One issue, in my view, is Nunes. As first officer on scene, he recorded the initial condition of the scene in high-resolution audio and video, but because paperwork is the bulwark of investigation, he also filed a written report, and there, things seem to fall apart. Video proves that many of the statements he later made on paper were in apparent contradiction to what was on the video. And because other steps were taken *based on the paper report*, these seeming mistakes may have been compounded as additional agencies joined the hunt. Just as the MIT mathematician predicted, small mistakes at the beginning can snowball into outcomes no one could have predicted.

In order to make sense of things, one must compare what Nunes wrote with what his video shows. And though detailed exegesis should start with the crime scene itself, Nunes's report begins with identification of the first victim, so we will start there as well.

•

"Upon entering the room, I observed a female laying supine on the floor, next to a bed," Nunes wrote in the second paragraph of his report. "According to Dylan M. Mortensen, this female was likely Kaylee J. Goncalves."

•

Female supine on the floor? Yes. Kaylee? No. The butterfly flaps its wings.

•

"We woke up last night at four a.m. . . ." are the first words of explanation Dylan actually offers. Nunes's camera captures her talking to Kaylee's ex-boyfriend Jack Ducoeur as he arrives at the house. It seems clear that she wants Nunes to hear her because she looks right at him.

"In the main room . . . pretty much in the main room, and I heard them dancing and laughing. Kaylee went upstairs, and she screamed 'cause someone's in the room and she ran down the stairs, and I kept calling her name, but she wouldn't answer, and then I saw the guy. And I just locked the door, and I ran downstairs to Bethany, and we don't know what's going on."

•

Those who have followed this case will immediately realize this is not part of the prosecution's narrative. What Mortensen actually said and what Nunes wrote down differ in material ways. Her timeline, physical description, interaction with the suspect, and other recollections sound clear on tape but devolve like a game of telephone as events unfold.

•

"Can you come over here with me, please?" Nunes asks Mortensen at 12:10:01. They step toward MPD-5 as Jack Ducoeur talks with Bethany Funke near an overflowing dumpster. Mortensen, who has vacillated between hysteria and relative calm, stands barefoot while Nunes retrieves a clipboard and some standardized forms.

"Okay, how much have you seen in there?" Nunes asks after a painfully long delay. Instead of gathering time-critical facts, he spends the first seven minutes on administrative questions about names, dates of birth, and phone numbers. The clock is ticking, but he seems distracted.

"Not . . . I don't really know," Dylan tells him. "I just saw my friend laying like that when I called Hunter, 'cause we were so scared, we were like, 'Hunter, can you please come help us?' and that's all I saw because Hunter told us not to go in there."

"Who is Hunter?"

•

Nunes does not document, in his written report, that Dylan said she actually saw Xana's body, apparently prior to calling Hunter. This apparent oversight would prove crucial.

•

"That man right there," she says, pointing toward the house. "That helped show you around."

Cars drive by. Visitors arrive. People huddle under blankets, weeping.

"So, Hunter did go in there."

"Yeah, and that's when he told us, 'You need to call the cops right now,' and we did."

Jack Ducoeur steps in with a question but is told to wait, and then Nunes says, "Okay, when, now I overheard you talking about last night."

"Yeah."

"Okay, um, you don't have to. The more we know right now, the better. But we gotta start this process. Somebody will probably be revisiting this interview with you very soon."

"Yeah, that's fine."

"So, just . . . you're probably going to have to retell this story quite a bit."

"That's fine."

"Okay, what do you remember seeing? What started . . ."

"I remember, um, I was in my room, and I was trying to go to bed, and I heard Kaylee, who . . . Jack's ex-girlfriend, who has a dog, Murphy."

Nunes clarifies that Jack is Jack Ducoeur, the man standing a few feet away, then follows with questions that seem to have little to do with the murders. He verifies things like parents' names and the location of Mortensen's room before getting down to details about what she witnessed.

•

These are our first witness statements about the crimes; Dylan's exact words matter. They are quoted directly from the police report.

•

"All I heard was I heard her going upstairs and go, 'Okay, I'm gonna go to sleep right now,' 'cause she's going upstairs."

"Heard who go upstairs?"

"Kaylee, and the dog, Murphy."

"And upstairs to the very top?"

"Yeah. That's where her room is."

"Okay."

"And then also, I heard her walking up, I heard her scream, and she ran downstairs 'cause she saw someone, that's when I'm pretty sure she said, 'Someone's here' and she screamed and just ran downstairs and I called her name, but I jumped up and locked my door because I was so scared. Um, and then I heard someone in the bathroom, I heard her crying and I heard some guy say that 'you're going to be okay, I'm going to help you.' And I kept calling her name, but she wasn't answering, and then I opened up for a second and I saw this guy and he was not insanely tall, but he was wearing all black and like a mask that was covering his forehead and his mouth. And then I locked the door, and I called Bethany, and I didn't know what to do."

"This was at four a.m."

"Four a.m., yes, and so I ran down."

"You left here?"

"Yeah, I left my room down to Bethany's room but she's that one"—Mortensen points at the house—"the one with the white shades at the bottom . . . I ran down there and we talked and we just locked the door, we didn't think anything of it, we're like, 'Nothing happens in Moscow,' so we just tried to go to bed and we woke up and it was weird because none of our roommates were up and we called all of them and they were not waking up and me and Bethany were like this is weird so I called Emily and Hunter to come over and then that's when all this happened."

•

Instead of asking for clarifications of seemingly contradictory statements, such as Mortensen expressing terror over an incident involving a masked intruder and a screaming roommate followed by, "We didn't think anything of it," he moves on to ephemera.

•

"Who all lives here with you?"

Mortensen names all four victims and describes exactly where they sleep, providing direct contrast to what Nunes later wrote in his report. Nunes even pauses to verify that Xana Kernodle is the woman on the second floor beside Ethan, who is not a roommate but visits often. He takes written notes, pausing to check on spelling and other details.

"All right, describe the guy that you saw."

"I don't think . . . he was a little bit taller than me . . . and, um . . . I couldn't really see much of him but he . . . I'm almost positive he was wearing a full black outfit, and he had this mask that was just over his forehead and over his mouth, and he didn't say anything to me like at all, and I just shut the door and locked it 'cause I didn't know what to do, and I think he went out the side door, the sliding door in the kitchen that goes out to the backyard. And then I didn't know anything else so I called Bethany, and I was like 'I just need to come downstairs because I don't know where anyone else is,' and I called Maddie, I called Xana, I called Kaylee; no one would answer, except Bethany."

"Okay," Nunes says as Mortensen appears to break down emotionally.

•

It's worth noting that in twenty-one minutes of recorded crying, as seen on the video, it does not seem to me that Mortensen shed a single actual tear.

•

"You're doing great," Nunes tells her at one point.

"I'm scared."

"It's all right, I'm asking a lot of you," he responds.

•

He does not ask why she's scared now, with police on scene, after waiting almost eight full hours before calling 911. Yes, she may have just seen Xana on the floor, but she saw the same thing at 4:20 a.m. also.

•

"Okay, let's go back, I just wanna make sure we're getting everything. So you're sure it was about four this morning . . ."

"Yes, it was four, four ten . . ."

"You first noticed a guy."

"Well, I first heard Kaylee go upstairs and scream and run downstairs."

"So, four this morning, Kaylee went upstairs, to the way top."

"Yes, to her room, with Murphy the dog."

"Okay, and then you heard Kaylee scream?"

"I heard her scream and run, like run as fast as she could downstairs, and she said, 'Someone's here.'"

"She ran downstairs?" Nunes asks, taking copious notes.

"Yes, I could hear, you can hear everything, and I'm sure I heard her run downstairs really fast, and then I heard Murphy barking a lot."

•

Dylan's bed on the second floor is directly beneath Madison's on the third. The stairway where she heard Kaylee running abuts her wall. We will return to this later.

•

"And then I heard her go into I think it was the bathroom, and I remember her sobbing, and I just remember hearing this guy's voice, and I didn't recognize it, saying, 'You're going to be okay, I'm going to help you,' but it wasn't in a good way, it wasn't like, I don't know how to explain it. Like it wasn't in a nice way, it was in a weird way, with a weird tone."

•

The spot where Dylan Mortensen stood in her bedroom was two doors and approximately twenty-seven feet away from the only bathroom on the second floor. Perhaps Nunes is not yet familiar enough with the house to question how she could have heard a woman sobbing or assessed the intruder's tone within those constraints.

•

Nunes confirms that she reports the man said, "You're gonna be okay, I'm gonna help you."

"Yeah."

"And you didn't hear anything from Kaylee anymore, at that point?"

"No, I didn't hear anything. So, then I kept calling her name, I called on my phone, I called Xana, Maddie, and Kaylee, none of them answered. So, I opened up my door to look and that's when

I saw the guy pass by. He looked at me, but he didn't come toward me or say anything, which seemed confusing to me. I don't understand that, and then I'm pretty sure he went out the side door. And then I called Bethany; she said she thought maybe there was a fire or like fireworks. We didn't know. She heard this loud noise and a light, I guess?"

"Did you hear like a pop or a bang?"

Dylan turns toward Bethany for clarification, but Nunes brings her back.

"What . . . just what you heard."

"I didn't hear that."

A silver sedan comes up the street, and Nunes interrupts the already disjointed interview to ask the driver where he is going. When he returns to Mortensen, she seems to be searching for reference.

"I don't think I ever heard a bang," she says. "I didn't think anything about fire or fireworks, and I . . . since I called her, I don't think I heard anything of that, but I was also in and out of it because I was so scared and it was really . . . I was really tired . . . um, that's when I called Bethany and I told her, 'I need to come to your room,' because she was the only one who was answering me, so I ran down there and for a second, I stopped and I saw Xana passed out and I thought that maybe she was just sleeping or something, and I think because I was so out of it, I went into Bethany's room and we just fell asleep. And then we woke up this morning, and no one was waking up at all, I mean like no one was answering, which was really weird, because all of us wake up around like nine or ten, and then I called Emily who brought Hunter to come check."

•

Viewing the tape, I wondered why she would ask a female friend for help instead of calling 911. Nunes does not ask. Perhaps more confusing, he does not ask Dylan how she decided the woman he had just seen butchered on the second floor could possibly have been mistaken as sleeping.

•

"Hunter came here first, and I told him what happened, and then he looked in the bedroom and said, 'You need to get out. Call the cops.'"

"Okay, the guy that you saw. I know it was dark, right, or were the lights on?"

"I think there were lights on in the house. I don't really know what he looked like because he had a mask, but he wasn't super tall."

"How tall are you?"

"I'm five ten. I think he was maybe my height, an inch or two higher or lower, I can't really remember."

"So, about six foot."

"I think so, around there."

"Okay, how was he built? Fat, skinny, stocky?"

"More like skinny—but basketball player skinny, but not too skinny, but almost fit skinny in a way, that's what I think, I don't know for sure."

"Okay. And then the voice? You said when he said those words, you just, you didn't recognize that voice before."

"I didn't, no, I didn't recognize him or his voice. I mean I also couldn't see him, but I didn't recognize that voice at all. It didn't even cross my mind who that could be."

"Did you guys have a party last night, too, or . . . ?"

"Not tonight, but there was a Sigma Chi party, and we had like a formal thing beforehand, that was two days ago."

"Okay, is there anything that popped out about that event, anything that was concerning?"

"No, I mean I went to Sigma Chi because Ethan, he is a Sigma Chi, and Xana and him are dating, and Xana went there. I was there for a little bit and then I went to my friend Aly's house down the street, and then I came back home with my friend Lake and Bethany. Everything was fine, nothing weird at all, nothing suspicious, until four a.m."

A red sedan passes on the street as Nunes turns toward Bethany Funke and a group of friends huddled under blankets near the dumpster.

"Okay. All right, um . . . I don't think I have any questions for you right now. Somebody else will be talking to you. So, let's grab that"—he points to the blanket she is standing on. "Let's go back over there."

With that, he moves to the first interview with Bethany Funke.

•

Before we go there, we need to acknowledge the apparent differences between what police body cameras recorded and what is written in reports. If we want to determine when the butterfly wings started gathering momentum, we need to go back inside the house and start matching Dylan's account with what police actually found.

As we will soon discover, there seems to be a wide gap between what the prosecution claims and what the evidence shows. Prosecutor Bill Thompson's narrative and defense attorney Anne Taylor's defense do not seem to be based on the same set of facts.

CHAPTER 2

Vandals Football, Ring Cam Device, Pi Phi Formal

Think about all the times you have gathered with friends and family around a dinner table to reminisce over important moments you have shared in life. Maybe it's a graduation or a wedding or a birthday—some event that starts out with everyone in general agreement, only to suddenly turn sour. Invariably, someone mentions a detail about what they heard or felt or saw, and somebody else disagrees. Before you know it, the rest of the conversation descends into differences of opinion. It's not until someone brings out a photograph or a video that everybody starts to laugh about how often human beings get things wrong.

Crime scenes are no different. Victims forget, witnesses fail, cops falter.

Fortunately for us, Nunes's body camera footage tells an incorruptible story. No matter what he typed in his report, we can now go back and reexamine the differences between what the evidence shows and what seems to have gotten lost in translation.

"I think he might have killed himself" might be a great place to start.

•

This is the point in the investigation where Nunes, an EMT with experience in violent injury, calls out "cause of death" without getting within five feet of the victims. Nunes never checks Ethan for vital signs, never bends down to examine Xana.

"How'd you get there?" Officer Warner asks. It's a legitimate question.

"I don't know, I just see blood. I haven't . . ."

•

And though some might consider Nunes's assumptions understandable under the circumstances, it is important to note that assumptions could lead to bias. Bias leads to speculation. Speculation leads to confirmation, and confirmation bias is the enemy of truth. Yes, 22-MO9903 would eventually become a detailed examination of means, motive, and modus operandi, but there is no escaping the fact that this started with conjecture. When prosecutor Bill Thompson handed Kohberger's legal team their mountain of forensic analysis, it did not mention that Ethan Chapin, one of the first victims, was initially thought to be a suspect.

"Ofc. Nunes advised the female and a male in the bedroom had blood on them and appeared to be beyond help," Warner wrote in his initial report. He made no mention of Ethan dying by suicide, nor anything else about the horrific scene in Xana's room. His report provides no details whatsoever before moving back toward the living room. "I walked out of the bedroom toward Johnson and saw a clean steak knife on a beer pong table."

This, of course, begs discussion of an apparent second critical misstep in the early moments of the investigation. In a quadruple homicide where casual observation suggests death by stabbing, the knife on the beer pong table might be considered important. When Hunter first mentioned the knife, police had not cleared the house for suspects, had not even discovered Mogen and Goncalves on the third floor. They had not checked to find the kitchen door open, had no idea who might or might not still be there. To disregard an edged weapon in plain view of two hacked-up bodies seems difficult to understand, especially watching the video.

Warner wrote in the police report:

> Johnson said he got the steak knife from the kitchen because he arrived and saw the female on the bedroom floor covered in blood and did not know if there was anyone else present in the room. Johnson said he checked the room with the knife for protection.

Nunes's body camera does record Hunter mentioning the knife as the two men leave Xana's room, but Nunes seems not to have heard him. Based on what appears to be the sound of the knife hitting the table, Hunter dropped it after Nunes discovered Xana and Ethan but before he talked to Warner. If Hunter told Warner about the knife, it's not recorded on tape.

This is a problem because the origin of the steak knife and the manner in which it was found are never properly explained. Despite discovery of the KA-BAR sheath on the third floor, we should recall that even the prosecution admitted in the plea appearance that no murder weapon has ever been identified, recovered, or named. Autopsy photographs suggest at least three different edged weapons were used in the four murders, and despite all the hype, no laboratory finding proves that a KA-BAR knife was one of them. Even if Hunter did grab the knife from the kitchen for self-defense, police should have treated it with suspicion.

Nunes's report makes it clear that he did not:

> As I backed out of this room, Hunter showed me a kitchen knife and said he had it in his possession. I told Hunter to leave the knife and go back down the stairs to the front entrance.

Body camera footage also shows this statement seems to be false. Nunes never mentions the knife, does not secure it, does not seem to acknowledge it in any way. This will prove important later in the day when an Idaho State Police (ISP) lab team responds to process the MPD warrant. Here, we add another report, one written by ISP detective Jeffory R. Talbott:

> On November 13, 2022, at about 12:22 p.m., the Moscow Police Department (MPD) requested Idaho State Police (ISP) District 2 investigations to assist with multiple homicides at 1122 King Rd. I . . . was assigned as the lead crime scene investigator.

It is important to note that Detective Talbott did not file this report until December 6, three full weeks after the search. As the person responsible for logging, handling, securing, and establishing chain of custody for all evidence that first day, it would seem as if Talbott should have built a solid procedural foundation under the items he seized, including the KA-BAR knife sheath that would become a cornerstone of the prosecution's case. Looking back, it seems odd that no one questioned the timing or veracity of his recollections, especially the defense. Three weeks is a long time, and as we will soon see, any mistakes he might have made that first day could prove catastrophic down the line.

In this same supplemental, Talbott wrote:

> As you go up the stairs to the second floor you enter a small living room area. There was a folding table set up on the west side of the area, partially blocking the entry to the west hallway. The table had multiple red solo cups on it in game formation (Beer Pong) along with a small steak knife. There were multiple areas of red liquid on the table that appeared to be blood.

Imagine finding a knife directly on top of what is reported to be liquid blood left in the commission of four edged-weapon murders, in a heavily trafficked room. Now imagine that the detective in charge of the search does not cordon, segregate, or secure it. Finally, imagine that crime scene photos, laboratory analysis, and independent blood spatter treatments clearly show *there was no liquid found anywhere* on the white folding table, not even in the cups. Stains beneath and around the steak knife were dry and so faint they do not appear in body camera footage. Lab experts later determined that actual bloodstains had been "diluted with an unknown substance" and were wiped or altered to the point where it was impossible to identify their source.

There is more. Talbott continued in the seven-page document:

> At about 5 p.m., after a search warrant was signed, Sgt Blaker, Det. Payne, Latah County Prosecuting Attorney (LCPA) Bill Thompson, LSCPA Ashley Jennings, and I entered the scene and conducted a walk-through.

According to his timeline, formal crime scene analysis did not begin until about five hours after Nunes arrived. At that point, police logs and video indicate that more than a dozen people had seemingly walked through the house without adhering to the most basic anticontamination protocols. Every law enforcement academy and criminology program in the world preaches that it is impossible to enter a crime scene without tracking contaminants in and evidence out. The fact that police wore nitrile gloves makes little difference, because gloves protect the officers from blood and other potentially toxic substances, but they do not prevent cross contamination. Transference is exactly the same, whether from skin or a thin barrier of latex.

Talbott continued:

> At about 7:05 p.m., Det. Powell, Det. Schwecke and I started marking the evidence with numbered placards, while Det. Roberts photographed the exhibits.

According to this statement, the ISP did not commence their formal search until almost fifteen hours after the crimes occurred. During this time, Dylan Mortensen, Bethany Funke, Hunter Johnson, Emily Alandt, and others are known to have moved through the house with little or no documentation. Although this did not defy any apparent police orders and it was their home, to date, any possible intentional or unintentional alterations of the crime scene have never been fully explained. In thousands of reports, interpersonal dynamics are barely mentioned.

More on that later. For now, it is important to focus on Talbott's work. He wrote on page 5 of his report:

> The following evidence was recorded and/or collected. Steak knife, located on folding table in living room.

The knife is labeled "Exhibit 022," among fifty-five separate items, and before dismissing it as irrelevant to the outcome of this case, we need to consider Talbott's treatment of other potential weapons. He is the one, after all, who documented and entered into evidence the infamous KA-BAR sheath. Though prosecutors would rely upon DNA found on a thumb snap, Talbott's chain of custody log would seemingly turn out to be shockingly flawed.

To fully understand how, we need to consider that chain of custody is a foundation of evidentiary procedure. Every exhibit introduced at trial must come attached to a detailed provenance that shows where the item was found, who touched it, where it was kept, each time it changed hands. When considering DNA found on the knife sheath, two details beg early mention. The first involves origin. Though Talbott's December 6 report glosses over discovery, statements by both Nunes and Warner send up alarms.

Warner wrote in a police report on November 13:

> On the third floor in the southeast bedroom, I saw two clothed females laying on a bed on their backs who appeared deceased. One female on the left side of the bed in relation to the bedroom door had an extreme amount of lacerations to her face and upper body which made her unrecognizable. The other female had multiple lacerations on her upper body and some blood on her face. I walked to the far side of the bed to determine if the female on the right was beyond help. I saw the female's leg was off the edge of the bed and it had lividity. Once I noticed the lividity in the female's leg, I backed out of the room.

Oddly enough, Nunes's body camera records Warner standing no more than eighteen inches from Mogen's lifeless body, shining his flashlight on the bed, the victims, and, specifically, Mogen's leg where it extends out from under a comforter. This is the area where prosecutors allege the KA-BAR sheath was found, *yet neither Warner nor Nunes mentioned the sheath in their reports.* In fact, Nunes returns to the bedroom after Warner has gone downstairs and shines his own flashlight directly where crime scene photographs later show the sheath to have been found. A frame-by-frame analysis of the video, widely available online, shows there is no KA-BAR sheath where the prosecution claims.

Perhaps this could be dismissed as a misleading camera angle or administrative oversight, but what turns up next really starts to feel like a problem. Though Detective Talbott made no mention of it in his December 6 report, he had already composed and logged a separate handwritten inventory, contemporaneous to the search. On November 13, 2022, he filed a four-page Evidence/Property Receipt documenting what he discovered and seized at the house.

This is the form he filled out with a pen as he was bagging and tagging items seized pursuant to the MPD's warrant. Unlike the December 6 supplemental, this form was completed at the scene.

Talbott's November 13 inventory lists dozens of items, from "foot cast on the ground, NW of Residence," and fingerprints lifted from the kitchen, to "Vic #1 female 2nd floor bedroom," meaning Xana, and "Vic #2—male (F2) bed—2nd floor," later identified as Ethan. Each item is listed according to where it was found.

It isn't until we get to page 2 of the report that butterfly wings really start to beat. According to his handwritten receipt, the location where he found Exhibit 14, *the foundation of the prosecution's case*, is not what we have been led to believe.

"Knife (Kbar) sheath," Talbott wrote. "On floor next to Vic #3."

Though never previously disclosed, Detective Talbott here drops a bomb on the prosecution's narrative. If Talbott's handwritten inventory is correct and the sheath was found on the floor, prosecutor Bill Thompson has problems. His Brady disclosure, wherein he handed over every detail, should have handed Kohberger's defense a whole treasure chest of reasonable doubt.

How is it that the Idaho State Police's lead forensic investigator could write that he found a knife sheath on the floor, only to later document that it was found in the bed? Was it moved? If so, when was it moved? What does the ISP chain of custody sheet show, and why did Talbott not file his report until three weeks after the search? Where is the state's explanation of seemingly glaring inconsistencies? The list goes on and on.

To be clear, this is the KA-BAR knife sheath used as a cornerstone of the State of Idaho's case. This is where laboratory examiners claimed to have found DNA on a thumb snap, tying Kohberger to the scene. This is the sheath he supposedly dropped in the bed while murdering Kaylee Goncalves and Maddie Mogen. This is the sheath detectives claim they found lodged beneath Mogen's thigh.

And here is where even the most casual sleuth might ask how a seeming mistake this outrageous could be possible. How could the prosecution's case begin with a handwritten chain of custody that seems irreparably broken? How could defense attorney Anne Taylor have seemingly ignored this? Did she miss it?

The only way to answer those questions is to return to the initial condition of the crime scene itself. We need to understand that Talbott was not the first outsider to enter the house. It was not even Nunes or Warner. It was Hunter Johnson. If we want to get to the bottom of what really happened at 1122 King Road that horrible night in November, we need to look at what Hunter told police.

Despite what you think you know about this case, the storm Lorenz predicted from butterflies flapping their wings is barely yet a whisper.

On November 28, two weeks after the murders, MPD officer Lawrence Mowery filed Supplemental 42 for results of interviews conducted at 1122 King Road. It is here transcribed verbatim:

> Hunter I Johnson DOB: XX/17/1999 PH: 208 XXX 8709
>
> Address: 621 W Taylor Ave Apt 1
>
> Hunter said around 1200 hours on 11/13/2022, Dylan called Emily (Hunter's Girlfriend). Dylan told Emily she

thought something "was not right in her house." Dylan also told Emily she heard or saw a man in her house the night prior. Dylan asked Emily and Hunter to come over and make sure everything was OK because she locked herself in Bethany's room. Hunter said he was the first person to get to the residence. Hunter said he entered the code to the front door where Bethany and Dylan were in Bethany's room on the first floor. Dylan and Bethany were telling Hunter they did not know what was going on.

Hunter said he went up the stairs and immediately went into Xana's room. Hunter said this was the only room he went into. Hunter said when he approached the door it was only partially open. Hunter said when he opened it, he saw Xana and Ethan. Hunter said he initially did not realize all the blood was dried blood in the room. Hunter said he thought at first they had been drunk and left a mess. Hunter said when he stood there for a moment he began to realize what he was seeing. Hunter said Bethany and Dylan were uncontrollably crying. Hunter said he told them to get out of the house and call law enforcement.

Hunter said he then went to the kitchen and grabbed a knife from the drawer. Hunter said he then went into the room and checked the closet to make sure there was not anyone else in the room. Hunter said he checked for a pulse on both Xana and Ethan. Hunter said both of the bodies had rigor mortis and were cold with no breath or pulse. Hunter said he believed the two had been deceased for a while. Hunter said he believed he left the knife on the folding table in the living room. Hunter said Emily, Josie and Linden started to enter the house and come up the stairs. Hunter told them to get out of the residence. Hunter said this was about the time Moscow PD arrived on scene. Hunter said the officer told him to stay where he was at. Hunter said he did not know if anyone else was upstairs as he had not gone anywhere else in the house. Hunter said he had trouble comprehending what he was seeing.

Hunter said he was not at the Sigma Chi party the night prior. Hunter said he and Ethan were texting the night prior (11/12/22) by phone. Hunter said Ethan wanted him to come over, but Hunter chose not to. Hunter said he knew Ethan since Fall of 2021. Hunter said he was in Phi Delta Theta and Ethan was a member of Sigma Chi. Hunter indicated Josie and Emily were in the same sorority and were roommates. Hunter said Linden who was also present was in the fraternity Delta Tau Delta and was currently dating Josie. Hunter said he and Linden stayed at Josie's apartment with Emily and Josie the night of 11/12/22. Hunter was asked when the last time was he was at 1122 King Road.

Hunter indicated he was last at the residence on 11/12/22 where he was "pre-gaming for the Vandals football game." Hunter said he got to the residence at around 1200 hours or 1300 hours and left at about 1430 hours to go to a different party. Hunter said the last time Emily was at 1122 King Road was Friday 11/11/22. Hunter did not know of anyone who had issues with Ethan and Xana dating. Hunter estimated Xana and Ethan were dating for 8 months. Hunter said he knew Xana very well through his girlfriend Emily. Hunter said he was not very familiar with Maddie or Kaylee. Hunter allowed pictures to be taken of his phone of the conversations between him and Ethan.

To begin unraveling clues left inside the house, we need to establish the last moment when the crime scene was still intact. Every homicide detective will tell you there is no way to build a case when you don't trust the evidence, and there is no trust in evidence that has been corrupted. A smoking gun is worthless if you can't prove who left it.

Common sense would suggest that our timeline begins when the crimes occurred. This would be approximately 4:15 a.m., according to the prosecution, just about when Dylan Mortensen claims she first heard Kaylee run down the stairs. This would correlate with what are believed to be screams recorded on a Ring cam device at 1112 King Road. It fits cell and social media communications from women inside the house. It conforms with general facts of the case, as provided by a DoorDash driver named Molly McMichael, witness statements, and neighborhood reports of an aggressively barking dog.

The problem with establishing the initial condition of the crime scene is that there were survivors. Despite numerous interviews with Bethany Funke and Dylan Mortensen, police never fully established where the two women went or what they did between the hours of 4:00 a.m. and 12:00 p.m. Though Dylan claimed to have left her room after spotting the intruder, evidence appears to suggest that may not have been the case. Police files indicate that an Apple Watch she wore that night documented movements that are very hard to explain.

Before we get to Dylan, it makes sense to revisit Hunter. According to Mowery, he was the first person to enter the residence after the crimes. Hunter told police he entered through the locked front door, using a punch code to gain access before finding Bethany and Dylan in Bethany's room. This will become important once police receive an eyewitness account that the front door was open just prior to Hunter's arrival.

On November 17, MPD officer Aaron Morris filed Supplemental 20 detailing information provided by a neighbor named Justin Nadeau. It reads:

> Nadeau stated on Sunday 11-13-22, between 0900 and 1000 hours, he was walking his dog. He stated when he walked by the first time he noticed the front door to 1122 King Rd. on the north side of the building facing campus was wide open. He stated he knew it was a party house so assumed someone was too intoxicated and forgot to close the door the night prior. Nadeau stated he walked his dog up Taylor Ave. to Blake Ave. then down Sweet Ave. He said the walk took him approximately 1 hour. Nadeau stated when he walked back to his apartment around 1100 hours the front door was still wide open.

If the two survivors never left Bethany's room, who closed and locked the door?

More on that shortly.

What first begs inquiry is apparent inconsistencies introduced by Hunter's story. He told Mowery that Xana's room was the only one he entered, though he told Nunes and Warner he went into the kitchen to retrieve a knife. He said the door to Xana's room was partially open when he approached, but that directly contradicts Dylan's statement that she saw Xana lying on the floor as she went downstairs. Hunter said Bethany and Dylan were uncontrollably crying when he told them to get out of the house, implying that they may have gone up to the second floor with him.

Hunter's statement is further complicated by the fact that he told Mowery his girlfriend, Emily, started to enter the house with Linden (later identified as Beck) and Josie, and that he told them to get out. If this is true, it brings to six the number of people who may have tracked evidence into or out of the house before Nunes even arrived.

Perhaps most interesting to crime scene analysts is Hunter's statement that he checked for a pulse on both Xana and Ethan upon first entering the room. If true, this means his initial statements to Nunes may have been false. He told Mowery both of the bodies had rigor mortis and were cold with no breath or pulse, an assessment that seems unusual for a twenty-year-old college student with no medical training. According to Mowery, Hunter said the two victims had been "deceased for a while."

If these contradictions do not seem confusing enough, Mowery's subsequent interviews of other witnesses will prove baffling. We know, for example, that Bethany Funke called Whitcom 911 standing outside the open front door with Dylan Mortensen. We know from Hunter Johnson's preceding transcribed interview with Officer Mowery that his girlfriend, Emily Alandt, was the calm voice who took the phone from Bethany to speak with 911 operator Calvin. What we did not previously know is that another student, Jenna McClure, was there also. Before further analyzing Hunter's statements, it makes sense to consider what Jenna told Mowery. Together, they provide the clearest picture yet of what the house looked like before police arrived.

As Mowery reported on November 13 in Latah County Prosecuting Attorney (LCPA) Supplemental 42:

> Jenna said she texted Bethany at 1120 hours. Jenna asked Bethany if she was awake. Jenna said Bethany called her back at 1149 hours. Bethany told Jenna she and Dylan were in Bethany's room. Jenna said Bethany was freaked out because her roommates were not answering the phone.

Mowery's report indicates that Jenna was already en route to the house when Bethany called back but does not indicate why:

> Jenna said she heard Dylan on the phone in the background saying, "I saw something." Jenna said Bethany asked her to come over to 1122 King Road and pick her up.

Despite a lack of detail, Mowery's report establishes several critical considerations. First, it shows that Bethany wanted Jenna to drive over to 1122 King Road and pick her up, indicating a sense that something was wrong. Whatever Bethany thought about events of the previous eight hours, she called three friends before calling 911.

Second, though forensics would later provide a foundation of physical evidence, police initially had no idea who might have murdered four coeds with a knife. Or why. In order to gain a better understanding of events leading up to the murders, they needed to evaluate the possibility of a broader threat to the community. They needed background on the victims, needed to know who might want them dead. McClure had answers.

She started by establishing a chronology of campus events the night before:

> Jenna said she did not go to the Sigma Chi party, but went to a different one instead. Jenna said Bethany and Dylan came to this other party after she left Sigma Chi. Jenna estimated Dylan left her party at 0030 hours and Bethany left her party at about 0100 hours on 11/13/2022.

Mowery clarified that Jenna was a member of the Pi Beta Phi sorority with Dylan, Lakelynn McComas, Bethany Funke, Xana, and Maddie Mogen, although Xana and Maddie had "dropped out." He determined that Kaylee was a member of the Alpha Phi sorority but had dropped out as well. Though no one knew it at the time, sorority affiliation would prove important down the line, once investigators learned that Kaylee had moved away from Moscow but returned for the weekend primarily to attend a Pi Beta Phi formal as Dylan's plus-one.

Documenting suspicious activity leading up to the murders, Mowery wrote:

> Jenna said she knew Kaylee saw a dark figure staring at her from the tree line when she took her dog Murphy out to pee. Jenna said this occurred about a month ago at 1122 King Road. Jenna said there has been light hearted talk and jokes made about a stalker in the past.

Though Mowery does not go into further detail about the stalker, he does extend his investigation to one last interview of

Linden Beck. Not widely known within the context of this investigation, Beck provided valuable insights. As Mowery wrote in his report:

> Linden said Dylan had called Emily around 1000 hours, and sounded scared. Linden said Dylan told Emily someone had been in her house last night. Linden said Dylan and Bethany ran downstairs and locked themselves in a room.

According to Beck, he had stayed at his girlfriend's apartment on Saturday night. Emily Alandt and Hunter Johnson were there as well. He said Alandt and Johnson came into the room where he was staying sometime before noon that Sunday:

> Linden said Dylan informed them she saw someone in the house and Dylan could only see his nose and his chin. Linden said Dylan was freaking out and wanted them to come over to 1122 King Road.

Though no one knew it at the time, Dylan calling Emily at ten o'clock Sunday morning provides the first apparent contradiction in her story. She had told police she fell asleep with Bethany and did not wake up until shortly before calling 911. As Mowery reported:

> Linden said he walked with Emily, Josie to 1122 King Road from Josie's apartment on Taylor Ave. Linden said Dylan and Bethany walked out of the house crying. Linden said Hunter arrived to the residence first, because he left before them.

> Linden said he went to the downstairs door and Hunter told him not to come up the stairs.

Which brings us to the scene Officer Nunes's body camera recorded as he walked toward the house that Sunday. Based on interviews conducted on scene and in subsequent days, we can establish that the people standing outside included Linden Beck, Hunter Johnson, Bethany Funke, Dylan Mortensen, Josie Lauteren, and Emily Alandt.

Before we reenter the house to start our forensic look at what police found, it is important to discuss one final report. LCPA Supplemental 7 is a statement of investigation filed by Officer John Lawrence. Though the two-page document provides a considerable amount of information, its greatest value at this point is that it records the names, ranks, and affiliations of law enforcement personnel at the scene November 13:

> I called Det. Vargas and was informed she was out of town and would be back in Moscow on Monday morning. I called Det. Mowery, and he informed me he would be on his way shortly. I called ISP Lt. Mike Mooney and told him I need assistance from ISP detectives in processing the crime scene. Lt. Mooney put me in contact with Sgt. Gilbertson. I briefed Sgt. Gilbertson on what I knew, and he told me he would start to assemble his team. MPD Cpt. Roger Lanier, MPD Sgt. Dustin Blaker, Det. Payne, and multiple other MPD officers providing scene security.

What stands out is the speed with which Moscow police sought help from outside agencies. This might surprise some who think all crime is local, but it is important to understand how agencies work. First, there are more than eighteen thousand law enforcement organizations in the United States, ranging from one-badge sheriff departments in Utah to monoliths like the NYPD, which dwarfs the FBI. America divides its law enforcement functions among local, state, and federal jurisdictions, and as one might expect, resources are distributed accordingly. A small town might find it burdensome to buy a single cruiser, while the FBI this year will spend more than $10 billion.

It seems clear that police started out at a disadvantage and that apparent flaws in early reporting have grown each time the story was told. For almost three years, everyone from prosecutors and the defense to *Dateline* on NBC based their narratives on what Officer Nunes wrote in his initial report, but body camera footage shows he was shaken and at a loss for words, which may have contributed to statements that could be seen as judgmental and premature.

Lawrence's report makes that obvious:

> Det. Blaker provided me with the following briefing: When officers entered the house they found two deceased residents (KERNODLE and CHAPIN) inside a bedroom on the 2nd floor. The officers also found two more deceased residents (GONCALVES and MOGEN) in a bedroom on the 3rd floor.

We now know Nunes and Warner left the house for approximately one minute and seven seconds before returning and deciding to "clear" it from the first floor to the third. Only then did they find Mogen and Gonclaves. As Lawrence reported:

> All the victims appeared to have multiple stab wounds. The sliding glass door located in the kitchen (2nd floor, rear of house) was open and there was a set of footprints in the melting snow leading into and away from the residence. There was one shoeprint near the western edge of the property leading west into a neighbor's yard. In front of the residence (north) were five vehicles belonging to the deceased residents.

We know the five vehicles were Kaylee's silver 2015 Land Rover Range Rover, registered to Jazmine D. Sumner; Xana's blue 2010 Honda Civic, registered to Jeffrey K. Kernodle; a white 2014 Chevrolet Cruze, registered to Maddie's mother, Karen M. Laramie; and a red 2011 Jeep Wrangler and a black 2017 Ford Explorer, registered to James E. Chapin.

Lawrence continued:

> Sometime in the early morning hours, Mortensen was awoken and opened her room door (2nd floor) and heard a male say, "It's ok Kaylee, I'm here for you," and crying. She then shut the door. A short while later she opened the door again and saw someone approximately 5'10" tall, dressed all in black with a ski-mask standing in the kitchen. She made eye contact with the person and could see they were Caucasian through the cut-outs for the eyes.

What seems to be apparent is the speed and extent to which police began their arguably circular reporting of confusion. In body cam footage, Mortensen describes the assailant as one or two inches shorter or taller, making him anywhere between five feet eight and six feet tall. She did not claim to have seen him in the kitchen and, at that point, had not described him as white, let alone Caucasian. Nunes did not even ask. Lawrence wrote:

> She shut her door, again, and texted FUNKE, whose bedroom is on the east end of floor 1. FUNKE told her to join her in her room and MORTENSEN ran down the stairs to FUNKE's room where they fell asleep.

Though the elements of this narrative match what Nunes heard, it would turn out to be much more involved than that.

CHAPTER 3

Princess Pose, White Claw, Stain 26

Whoever said a picture is worth a thousand words did not work in law enforcement. Despite a staggering cache of photographs and hours of body camera video in prosecutor Bill Thompson's file, there are few written documents offering summation.

Some might argue that this is a good thing, because the Supreme Court's 1964 *Brady v. Maryland* ruling mandates discovery of all evidence given to the defense but does not require assistance in sorting it out. Prosecutors are allowed to dump huge caches of information at the last possible moment, with no formal organization or reference, forcing defendants and their attorneys to play catchup all the way to trial.

This is a distinct advantage for the state, of course, because they control the timeline and the narrative. Prosecuting attorneys typically have huge resources at their disposal, everything from local, state, and federal agencies with high-tech labs to subject matter experts and grand jury secrecy laws that shield their work from prying eyes until the moment they make arrests.

The accused in the Kohberger case was an indigent student with a public defender who left her Latah County position to avoid what appeared to be conflict-of-interest restrictions due to a client list that may have included two of the victims' mothers. Yes, Kohberger had taxpayer-funded access to expert witnesses, but in my eyes Anne Taylor and her assistants did not seem to be a dream team. Much of her experience involved low-level drug charges, DUIs, and the occasional assault, because Latah County, Idaho, has one of the lowest crime rates in a state with one of the lowest crime rates in the nation. She had never defended a death penalty case.

As if that were not enough of a thumb on the scale of justice, media interest did not make Taylor's job easier. Judge Hippler's gag order handed the prosecution strategic advantage because it limited what the world knew about their case. Constant pressure from a sea of reporters led to a steady stream of leaks, which only sowed confusion within the defense. Anne Taylor received fifty-one terabytes of Brady disclosure material, which may seem like fair play until you realize that the bulk of it arrived just months before trial, and she had to go through it by herself. Bill Thompson's team enjoyed broad discretion in how they submitted their files. I discovered a great deal of exculpatory evidence in mislabeled folders, for instance.

The reason I mention this here is that almost all evidence presented at Bryan Kohberger's change of plea hearing was limited to what the world already knew. Bill Thompson focused on cell tower pings, knife sheath DNA, and remote sightings of what is alleged to have been Kohberger's white Hyundai Elantra, but he offered nothing in terms of revelation. What remains unresolved, to this day, is why so little mention was made of evidence found inside 1122 King Road, or why almost none of it was cited in affidavits or filings made available to the defense. Though police have now released hundreds of documents and photographs, they have withheld tens of thousands more, limiting outside scrutiny of what the prosecution may have known, what the defense may have missed.

As it turns out, the defense may have missed a lot.

As I looked through the massive amount of information, it appeared to me that the majority of the prosecution's work was on hard drives that still have not adequately been probed. Even the most experienced criminologist would find it daunting to know that Anne Taylor's workload included files containing hundreds of thousands of cell phone calls, social media feeds, text chains, selfies, email and Snapchat entries, motor vehicle registrations, and other intimate details subpoenaed from dozens of persons of interest who may or may not have had anything to do with the case.

Thompson's files include a digital wilderness of esoteric DNA analysis protocols, Amazon purchases, Google searches, financial record inventories, and data dumps from what seems like a bottomless pit of anonymous sources. Police went so far as to analyze the computer modules of the victims' cars, grocery receipts from Kohberger's trash, and hundreds of tips involving a rogue gallery of potential suspects (none of whom were ever charged). If Anne Taylor had the time and the staff, perhaps she could have built a proper defense from what she was handed, but even reading one page a minute, it would have taken years just to peruse it.

The magnitude of this investigation and Thompson's claims would have been open to scrutiny at trial, of course, but there never was a trial.

Not only was the public denied access to exculpatory evidence, as is standard when there is a plea deal, but they were never even told it existed.

Fortunately, all that has changed. Based on leaks from conscientious sources, we now know that on September 27, 2023, Bill Thompson's office reached out to a Memphis-based criminologist named T. Paulette Sutton for help with forensic analysis. What Sutton found saves us months of investigation, because she lays out the strengths and flaws of the prosecution's case in a single, well-organized précis. As Sutton wrote in the introduction to her sixty-four-page report, which was a part of the Brady file in the case:

> On November 06, 2023, I received a Seagate 1 TB portable storage device from Latah County Prosecuting Attorney's office via FedEx Ground. The storage device was password protected, and the password associated with this hard drive was sent via a separate email from Ms. Jennings on October 31, 2023.

We know from her report that the Seagate drive included imagery taken in and around 1122 King Road within hours of the murders, as well as autopsy photos, surveillance video, drone camera recordings, selfies, social media pics, and screenshots downloaded from a wide selection of phones and devices. We know that information provided to Sutton forms a detailed composite of what police found in the aftermath of the crimes. It forms the blueprint of their investigation; it is the spine of their case.

Sutton also indicated in her report that she personally examined the crime scene:

> On December 21, 2023, I traveled to Idaho and examined the residence at 1122 King Road, Moscow, Idaho. At the time of my examination, all physical contents and all areas of bloodstaining had been removed.

Dismissing, for the moment, that the prosecution's primary criminologist likely never got access to actual physical evidence, we will focus on nine individual caches of photographs taken exclusively by the Moscow Police Department and Idaho State Police. Files listed in Sutton's report contain approximately 3,280 crime scene photos, as well as the body camera video from Officer Nunes. She lists 1,471 autopsy photographs of Chapin, Goncalves, Mogen, and Kernodle, as well as 1,697 photographs specifically related to Bryan Kohberger.

Though Sutton's report summarizes what police found at the crime scene between November 13, 2022, and January 27, 2023, it represents a relatively small sampling of the entire file. The most important thing is that the report offers us a glimpse into the information Thompson had access to in the months leading up to Kohberger's change of plea, and what Anne Taylor apparently did not.

Before we get into the particulars, we should revisit the concept of confirmation bias. At the time Sutton was hired to evaluate critical forensic evidence, Kohberger had already been charged and arrested. By the time she filed her report on August 29, 2024, a date had been set for trial. If the intention among prosecutors was to seek objective truth, Sutton's appearance seems a bit late in the game. One might surmise this report was more about validating Bill Thompson's narrative than looking for unresolved leads.

Whatever his intention, we now have his files, meaning we can assess them with zero bias in terms of guilt. Authors are not bound by gag orders or any of Judge Hippler's onerous rulings. Amateur sleuths do not have to comply with rules of criminal procedure, voir dire, the Idaho bar, or esoteric case studies of constitutional law. All that matters, here, is the evidence, and Sutton's sequential analysis lays it out clearly.

"The building at 1122 King Road, Moscow, Idaho is a multi-level house with six (6) bedrooms," she wrote, because you have to start somewhere, and the house would be a likely choice.

> Two (2) bedrooms are located on the first floor as one enters from the parking area depicted in ISP 4519. The front entrance door depicted between the silver vehicle and the blue vehicle in this image is located on the North side of the building.

Sutton is referring to a widely distributed still photograph taken Sunday night by the Idaho State Police. The silver car is the Range Rover recently purchased by Kaylee Goncalves; the blue vehicle is the Honda Civic registered to Xana Kernodle's father.

> There are two (2) ways to access the second level of the residence. Either by entering the door on the north side of the building depicted in ISP 4519 and then traveling up the staircase from the first floor up to the second floor, or by entering directly via a sliding glass door located at the back (south side) of the residence.

Though this information is widely known, Sutton's report will expose seeming oversights that change the entire nature of this case. To me, they are extraordinary. We need to lay the groundwork of what she and the prosecution believed in order to discover the extent of what they arguably got wrong.

> This sliding glass door on the south side of the building is depicted in ISP 4554 and enters directly into the kitchen on the second level. This level also includes a living area with a sofa and a beer pong table; a bathroom, the bedroom of Xana Kernodle on the west end of the building; and the bedroom of an additional resident on the east end of the building.

Few would argue that the killer or killers entered or exited the house by any other means. As Nunes's body camera demonstrates, the sliding glass door was open when police arrived, and there were no signs of forced entry. Whether or not the front door was open also, as one witness remembered, has never been resolved.

> The upper-most level of the residence is accessible via an internal stairway from the 2nd level and contains two (2) bedrooms. One bedroom on the third level was reportedly assigned to Kaylee Goncalves, and the other bedroom was assigned to Madison Mogen. The bodies of Kaylee Goncalves and Madison Mogen were reportedly discovered in the bedroom assigned to Madison Mogen as depicted in ISP 4856. Ms. Mogen was located on the south side of the bed (closest to the closet opening), and Ms. Goncalves was located on the north side of the bed (closest to the wall). Both are covered with a beige

> comforter. A white fleece item, which appears to be a blanket, is lying at the foot of the bed.

Here, we move from Sutton's summary to what photos show.

Though blurred in redacted images released by police, Kaylee Goncalves and Maddie Mogen were found lying on their backs in a full-size bed, partially covered with a beige comforter. Kaylee was lying atop Maddie's right arm, shoulder, and torso, with her left hand folded adjacent to her chin. Numerous observers have stated that Maddie was placed in a "princess pose," and that the two bodies appeared to have been staged as if they were cuddling.

Offering her expert opinion, Sutton wrote:

> The posture and proximity of the bodies of Kaylee Goncalves and Madison Mogen can best be visualized when the comforter is removed. No blood is noted on the bottoms or tops of their feet, indicating they were not upright or moving about the area after their bloodletting injuries were inflicted.

She used a series of gruesome images to make her point. Kaylee was found in tartan pajama bottoms with her legs spread, wearing an athletic sock on her left foot and a second sock beneath her right calf. Mogen was rolled slightly to her side, with her left leg hanging off the edge of the bed and her foot on the floor.

> The blood visible on the bottom sheet is limited to the upper portion of the bed sheet at approximately chest level. According to their respective autopsy reports, no blood-letting

> injuries were reported below the waist or on the backs of either Ms. Goncalves or Ms. Mogen. It should be noted that there were no drip trails of blood noted on the bedroom floor.

Though many of Sutton's observations seem straightforward, there is no escaping the fact that she furnished her report nearly two years after the crimes, just months before the original date set for the trial. She was hired by the prosecution with funds provided by the State of Idaho, which had charged capital murder with death penalty intentions. At this point in the judicial process, no one on Bill Thompson's team was looking for surprises.

But, here, we find several.

> Drip stains, spatter stains, transfer stains and saturation stains are visible on the comforter and on the exposed bed sheets. Apparent strands of hair are also visible on the comforter.

Though not otherwise discussed in Sutton's report, ISP crime scene analysts photographed two separate deposits of unidentified human hair in Maddie Mogen's bed. The first sample includes five separate clumps, dark brown or black in color, slightly curly, approximately two inches in length. They lie scattered over an area that appears to be eight inches in diameter, between Kaylee's right leg and the wall.

The second hair sample is visible atop the beige comforter on Maddie's side of the bed, roughly between her knees. This lock of hair is several inches in length, shorter than any of the women's hair in the house and markedly darker. Unlike the other samples, this "strand" appears to include bloody roots. One does not need a PhD in laboratory sciences to speculate that it was torn from someone's head.

Sutton's report moves past the hair without speculation or explanation.

> A large pool of blood has accumulated at approximately the thigh region of Kaylee Goncalves even though, referring to the autopsy report, no injuries are reported in this area to account for this pool of blood. For this large pool of blood to accumulate, a source of blood had to be above this area while bleeding occurred.

Officer Nunes's body camera as well as photographs taken within the first two hours of investigation show this pool of blood to be liquid. For blood not to dry after approximately ten hours in a porous barrier like a bed comforter, it would have to be significant in volume. Although that volume was never measured, it seems obvious that Kaylee Goncalves suffered one or more significant "bloodletting" injuries directly above this deposit. The only possible explanation was that she was sitting up at one point during the attack, before moving or being moved to the position where police found her against Mogen.

Sutton agrees.

> The distribution of the bloodstains on the face and upper body of Kaylee Goncalves, the bloodstain on the south wall beside the bed and the pool of blood at Ms. Goncalves thigh region on the comforter indicate that her posture and position did change during the event.

From there, Sutton's report provides very basic assessments of blood spatter, which photos indicate on numerous vertical and horizontal surfaces.

> The directionality of the spatters closer to the doorway is from right to left and downward . . . The area of convergence of this spatter pattern indicates they originated from a spatter producing event(s) that occurred above the level of the bed. Two patterns of cast-off blood indicated. Cast-off is created by the movement of a bloodied object(s).

Meaning a knife.

Based on police disclosures, however, we know that Kaylee Goncalves was asphyxiated and beaten as well, suffering blunt force injuries to her face and skull. At this point, all we have is Sutton's report for reference, but critical evaluation of photos, autopsy reports, search warrant inventories, and laboratory analysis will soon uncover a very different set of facts.

Before we move on to other parts of Sutton's report, we must understand what she suggests about the unusually violent mechanism of the crimes. According to this report, Mogen and Goncalves were not just murdered; they were butchered in a violent rage by an assailant fixated on what police refer to as "overkill." The directionality, proliferation, and spread of blood spatter created during the attack exceeds what seasoned homicide detectives would expect to encounter even in violent crimes of this nature.

> Image ISP 5122 depicts spatter stains associated with impact on the door casing and on the exterior surface of the bedroom

> door belonging to Madison Mogen. This is consistent with these spatter stains having originated due to an impact delivered to a source of exposed blood on the bed.

Sutton documented blood spatter dripping down walls, staining furniture, stuck to the underside of shelves. She noted blood patterns on the comforter, the sheets, the mattress, two pillows, on the doorjamb, and on the door itself. What she did not say is that the distance from Mogen's head to the exterior of the door was approximately ten feet. A trajectory like this would suggest force beyond what one would normally expect in a stabbing.

"The larger stains which culminate with flow stains . . . are indicative of cast-off stains created by a bloody object in motion," she wrote, adding that "spatters associated with impact" were found on the "underside of the shelf above the headboard of the bed."

There was no headboard on Mogen's bed.

Oversights matter in an analysis of this kind, and we will revisit many, but before moving on, we should pause to consider the differences between what Sutton found on the third floor and what Dylan Mortensen, our only witness, remembered hearing. Physical evidence is important, but so is context.

According to crime scene analysis, Mortensen's bed on the second floor was directly below Mogen's on the third, a physical separation of approximately nine feet. According to her initial interview, Dylan said she heard Kaylee and her supposed assailant talking in a bathroom, a distance of almost ten yards. Although she remembered hearing Kaylee on the stairs, Dylan makes no mention of noise one would expect from the violent murders of two housemates directly above where the report says she was lying.

Whatever happened on the third floor of 1122 King Road in the early morning hours of November 13, one might assume that it made plenty of noise.

On November 13, 2022, at 1:49 p.m., Officer Lawrence Mowery summoned Dylan Mortensen to the Moscow Police Department with the intention of interviewing her regarding the murders of Xana Kernodle, Ethan Chapin, Madison Mogen, and Kaylee Goncalves. Though Mortensen had provided information to Officer Nunes earlier in the day, this interview was her first formal representation of facts. Labeled Supplemental 42 in the MPD file, it is here transcribed verbatim:

> Dylan said she was a resident of the house where the incident occurred. Dylan said she was at a Sigma Chi party, at around 1030 hours on 11/12/2022, where she was drinking. Dylan said she went to "Ally's house." Dylan said she believed she arrived home between 0030 hours and 0100 hours on 11/13/2022. Dylan said she thought Bethany arrived home at around 20 minutes after she arrived.
>
> Dylan said she believed Maddie and Kaylee arrived home at around 0130 or 0200 hours on 11/13/2022. Dylan said up to this nothing weird had happened during the night. Dylan said she and her friend "Lake(?)" came home, followed by Bethany from Sigma Chi. Dylan said Lake lived at the Pi Beta Phi house and Bethany was her roommate at the residence. . . . Dylan said when Maddie Mogen and Kaylee Goncalves came home

from the corner club at the same time, and everyone went to bed.

Dylan was asked about the layout of her house. Dylan said Kaylee's room was directly above her room. Dylan said she lived on the 2nd floor and Kaylee lived on the 3rd floor. Dylan said Kaylee and Maddie both live upstairs on the 3rd floor in separate rooms. Dylan said Xana lived closest to the bathroom on the 2nd floor and Bethany lived on the first floor.

When asked about Murphy, Dylan said it was a dog owned in common between Kaylee and her ex-boyfriend Jack. Dylan said there were no apparent issues between Kaylee and Jack. Dylan said Maddie had a boyfriend named Jake Schriger, who was in Boise at the time of the incident.

Dylan indicated Xana was dating Ethan Chapin who was in the room with her at the time of the incident. Dylan did not know of anyone who would want to hurt Ethan, when she was asked. Dylan was asked if she saw any cars in the area that should not be there. Dylan said, "No I was not really looking at that."

Dylan said she woke up at around 0400 hours on 11/13/2022, where she could hear Kaylee and Murphy, the dog, dancing. Dylan said she knew it was Kaylee because she recognized her voice and could hear Murphy barking. Dylan said she heard Kaylee go upstairs and say, "There is someone here." Dylan said she thought she heard Kaylee run back down the stairs. Dylan said Kaylee sounded scared when she made this statement.

Dylan said at this time she jumped up and locked the door because she did not know what else to do. Dylan said she called out Kaylee's name and did not indicate if she got a response. Dylan said she then tried to call Kaylee, Xana and Maddie on their phones. Dylan was asked if she saw anyone come downstairs or heard anything. Dylan said, "No, I don't even know how they got in. We' re usually pretty good about locking doors and never had problems before. It was just really random."

When asked again about the series of events, Dylan said she opened the door when she cried out to Kaylee, then closed the door because she was scared. Dylan said she then opened the door again and heard who she thought was Kaylee, but could have been Xana, crying in the bathroom. Dylan said she then heard a man's voice say, "It's OK I'm gonna help you." Dylan said it was weird because the statement was not in a nice way and the voice was one she had never heard before.

Dylan said she called out to Kaylee again and there was no crying after, and she did not know what happened after that. Dylan said she opened the door again and "the guy" is right there. Dylan described the male as approximately her height (5'10") or a few inches taller, not skinny but athletic build. Dylan said the suspect was wearing all black with a mask that covered just his forehead and goes around his face. Dylan showed with her hands the mask exposed his nose but covered the mouth area.

Dylan said she believed the suspect was white but did not remember eyebrow color or what his eyes looked like. Dylan said when she saw the suspect, he saw her and just left. Dylan said she believed he was holding something near his stomach or belt line. Dylan used both hands to point straight out from her abdomen.

Dylan then moved her hands apart and back together to simulate a bulge. Dylan said this area was black in color and she thought now maybe it was a gun. Dylan said the unknown object had an arrow shape. Dylan seemed really unsure and said she was tired during the event.

Dylan was asked how long she believed it was from the time Kaylee said, "Someone is here", to when she saw the suspect. Dylan said she thought it was about 10 or 20 minutes. Dylan went on to say she was "in and out of it" and she did not fully remember the incident. Dylan was asked where the suspect was at in the residence when Dylan saw him. Dylan said the suspect was between her bedroom door and the kitchen. Dylan said she remembered watching the suspect go out the kitchen door and leave. Dylan said at this time she closed her door and locked it as fast as she could. Dylan said the suspect did not walk toward her or say anything.

Dylan said once the suspect left she immediately called Bethany. Dylan said Bethany informed her she heard a sound that sounded like a firework. Dylan then said she told Bethany she called everyone, and they are not answering. Dylan said she was in and out of it and believed everyone was just asleep. Dylan said she then went to Bethany's room locked the door and went to bed. Dylan said she woke up at around 1100 or 1200 hours and called her roommates and no one answered. Dylan said she called Hunter. Hunter came to the residence, went upstairs and told Dylan they needed to call law enforcement immediately.

Dylan was asked if there was anything else she wanted to share. Dylan said Bethany described the noise as a "loud boom," but Dylan did not hear it.

Dylan was asked if any of her roommates shared any weird experiences in the last couple weeks or calls or texts. Dylan said "No, it's been all normal. Nothing weird at all. Nothing really weird happens in Moscow usually." When asked if there were any altercations at the Sigma Chi party, Dylan said no everything was normal. Dylan mentioned again she was with Ethan and Xana at the party. Dylan was asked if anyone was having sexual relations with anyone they shouldn't be.

Dylan said no.

Dylan brought up an incident which occurred about a month prior. Dylan said she and Bethany remembered Kaylee saw a shadow while she was taking Murphy outside. Dylan said Kaylee also mentioned when she was at Winco 2 or 3 weeks prior, an individual was following her. Dylan also said she arrived home one time and the door to the residence at 1122 King Road was found open. Dylan said she did not believe the slider door was locked the night 11/12/22.

Dylan said she heard Murphy barking a lot around 0400 hours 11/13/22 when Kaylee went upstairs. Dylan said she heard Murphy go outside barking as well. Dylan was unsure if Murphy would chase a suspect outside. Dylan said she did not remember if the suspect who ran left the slider door open.

Consider, for a moment, that everything necessary to prove the guilt or innocence of an offender could be sealed up in a container and protected against contamination forever. We all know that is not possible, because even under the best of conditions, crime scenes are dynamic environments that begin to change the moment investigators enter. To document, seize, and process evidence, things need to be moved, and each time something is moved, the crime scene changes. Even with the best of intentions, there is a point where it becomes impossible to go back to the parts in hopes of reconstructing the whole. This trade-off between documentation and analysis has been the bane of homicide investigations since Cain killed Abel.

Fortunately for us, police now have swabs and digital cameras to bolster recollection. In addition to information provided in Sutton's report, we have objective views provided by other officers, including Nunes, who had a body cam, and ISP technicians with state-of-the-art devices. We also have numerous contemporaneous reports, including those of Detective Jeffory Talbott, the man in charge of the crime scene search. We can glean a great deal by looking at all the different perspectives and using them to ferret out the truth. Let's start with Talbott, who wrote in his December 6 report:

> As you go up the stairs to the second floor you enter a small living room area. There was a folding table set up on the west side of the area, partially blocking the entry to the west hallway.

By comparing his findings with Sutton's analysis, we can really begin to figure out where things seem to have gone wrong. Talbott wrote:

> The table had multiple red solo cups on it in game formation (Beer Pong) along with a small steak knife. There were multiple areas of red liquid on the table that appeared to be blood.

Though he no doubt had plenty of experience interpreting evidence at crime scenes, this seems not to be true at all. Numerous photographs clearly show that potential bloodstains were so faint they were barely visible from a few feet away. These stains had no three-dimensional geometry like one would expect of droplets, suggesting that if blood was present, it had been wiped away. Laboratory analysis would seem to affirm this, based on findings that the stains were unidentifiable because they had been "diluted with an unknown substance." Talbott continued:

> As I walked west from the living room there was a half wall to my right. I could see multiple drops and runs of red liquid along the entire half-wall.

This is confusing. Photographs show there are no drops of any substance whatsoever on the short wall above the staircase leading down to the first floor. Yes, forensic teams would document evidence of staining by what is later determined to be blood, but it looks significantly different from that discovered in Mogen's room on the third floor or Xana's down the hall.

> Across the half wall (north) I saw more red stains on the wall (above the 1st and 2nd floor staircase). The stains and liquid were consistent with cast-off and appeared to be blood.

Again, there is no evidence of any liquid in the common areas of the second floor. Based on photographs and video footage, what Talbott reported is barely visible to the casual observer.

> Continuing west down the hallway there was a bathroom to the left (south) with the hallway ending at a bedroom. On the north wall of the hallway, near the bedroom door, there appeared to be a red-colored transfer mark at approximately my shoulder height.

To explain the importance of this observation, we return to Sutton. Page 32 of her report provides analysis of one highly unusual anomaly, which dovetails with Talbott's observations. Though it might seem that we are skipping ahead here, chronology is not the only matrix in a case this complex. What Talbott and Sutton observed will fit into the larger picture shortly.

> Stain 26 on the half wall of the 2nd floor living room at the end of the beer pong table is depicted in image DSC 4886 and DSC 4685.

This is one of the blood transfers Talbott also mentioned. Sutton wrote:

> Stain 26 was tested for the presumptive presence of blood and was positive. Stain 26 is diluted cast-off with associated flow stains.

The numerical designation was added by Talbott's team Sunday afternoon.

> Cast off is created when blood is released as the result of a bloodied object in motion. The appearance of the bloodstains

> reveal that the blood has been diluted by another liquid. Flow stains as demonstrated in Stain 26 result from gravitational attraction. Additional testing of Stain 26 shows the presence of a mixture of DNA. Kaylee Goncalves matches the major component. Madison Mogen is a potential contributor to the minor component. There is no physical evidence to indicate that Kaylee Goncalves or Madison Mogen was in this location after sustaining their bloodletting injuries.

What Sutton makes clear, and what prosecutors have never disclosed to the public, and are not required to since there was a plea deal, is that liquid blood from the third floor somehow made its way to the second floor, where it was transferred to the half wall leading down to the first floor. This blood, identified through DNA as belonging to Mogen and Goncalves, was diluted with an unknown liquid before drying on white painted Sheetrock with no discernible edges, volume, or mass. These blood spatters, though up to twelve inches in length, appear to have been wiped off the wall.

Altogether, police found and identified fifteen separate areas where blood from victims had been transferred to flat, vertical surfaces on the second floor. Three of these stains were found on floor molding in the hallway leading to Xana's room (two west, one east), and all the rest, except two, on the knee wall or the south wall leading down to the first floor. Every single one of the stains documented by law enforcement laboratories tested positive for blood and was tracked via DNA to Maddie or Kaylee.

Neither Maddie nor Kaylee entered the living room after they were attacked—meaning, the killer or killers may have tracked liquid blood from the third floor and cast it off as droplets while moving from the kitchen, across the living room, then left down the hallway to Xana's bedroom. Oddly, police found a single anomaly that if released to the public could have caused widespread uproar. Documents specify that blood matching DNA from Ethan Chapin was found on the flat wood knee wall at the opposite end of the house, near the top of the stairs leading down. Sutton's report shows that due to being found naked except for unstained white socks, Ethan Chapin never left the room in which he was attacked.

Most important, crime scene photographs appear to document that two of the diluted knee-wall stains were found underneath a box of White Claw beverages. If true, this could prove that someone placed the box on top of the stains after Chapin was murdered. As we will see shortly, these previously undisclosed pieces of evidence alone seem to completely cripple the prosecution's assertions of a lone offender. In my mind, someone almost certainly transferred, via touch, Ethan Chapin's blood to the stairway after he and Xana were murdered. It appears most likely they did so while walking down to the first floor, not fleeing the house via the kitchen.

"Stain E was tested for the presumptive presence of blood and was positive," Sutton wrote in her report, referring to the two stains found on the flat wooden ledge under the White Claw box.

> Stain E consists of two (2) diluted spatter stains. The shape of these spatters show they were traveling from the area of the living room and towards the stairwell opening. The coloration and the edge characteristics of Stain E show concentration around the out periphery indicative of a diluted stain.

For what seems like inexplicable reasons, she notes, "Stain E was not tested further."

Perhaps one might speculate, now, that relative to all other blood spatter evidence in the common areas of the second floor, Stain E represented one significant problem in the case against Bryan Kohberger. If he, in fact, was the lone assailant, why would he take the time to place a White Claw box over bloodstains that were so diluted they were barely visible to the naked eye, far from the path he would have taken in escape?

How did Ethan Chapin's undiluted blood end up at the top of the staircase leading down to the first floor when there is no evidence that anyone except Dylan went down there?

If police were in fact seeking the proverbial "smoking gun" during the early days of their investigation, it would be difficult to imagine anything more compelling than this.

CHAPTER 4

Beer Pong, Two-Dollar Bill, Girl in the Window

Homicide detectives will tell you the first forty-eight hours after a crime are most important, because time is seldom the investigator's friend. Fluids dry, things get touched, furniture is moved, DNA gets wiped away. And yes, this is a murder investigation, not a weather forecast, but if we assume for a moment that Lorenz's predictions are correct and that small changes at the beginning create unpredictable outcomes down the line, we begin to see the apparent problem. From the moment Officer Nunes arrived on-site and labeled Ethan a possible suicide, things started to go downhill. By the time Talbott wrote that he found the sheath on the floor, things seem to have been stumbling toward chaos.

It did not help that the entire process was buried by the courts. On February 25, 2024, Magistrate Judge Megan E. Marshall wrote:

> Based upon the Motion to Seal Search Warrant and Related Documents filed herein, the Court does hereby confirm and

> Order that the Affidavit for Seach Warrant (including any exhibits), Search Warrant, Return of Search Warrant (including any exhibits and inventories of items seized) and Order are confidential, exempt from disclosure and are SEALED pursuant to Idaho Court Administration Rule 32 (g)(1) for the reasons stated in the said motion and until April 1, 2023, or further order of the Court, whichever occurs first.

Some might argue that secrecy is good in a prosecution of this nature, that scrutiny is a taxpayer-funded function of the state. Many would claim that police need time to work, that media only cloud the waters, that investigative journalism is nothing more than directed analysis, a distraction. Perhaps it doesn't even matter, at this point, because the proof is in the pudding. Police have opened their files showing how the case was solved, what they found, who they talked to, when they first made sense of facts. Everything looked copacetic once Kohberger pled guilty.

But even if we agree that justice has been done within the realm of lawyers and courts, maybe we can also agree that occasionally even pros get things wrong. It's easy to recall the apparent wrongful conviction of countless people, from the Central Park Five to Rubin "Hurricane" Carter, the McCollum brothers, and Amanda Knox. Former attorney John Grisham recently published a book called *Framed*, documenting outrageous miscarriages of justice. Well-meaning advocates such as the Innocence Project have logged more than two hundred exonerations based on DNA alone. Incredibly, more than a quarter of these involved initial pleas of guilty.

Some might argue that the problem lies in human error, that

under the best of circumstances, cops are limited to the training and resources at their disposal. No one would claim, for example, that the Moscow Police Department had everything it needed to investigate a quadruple homicide with thirty-five sworn officers and a tax base of twenty-five thousand people. Bill Thompson's office was likely short-staffed and underpaid; we assume that Anne Taylor was state certified to defend murder cases, but that was not her primary responsibility. Even the state police were limited compared to law enforcement in other more populous geographies, with standards that allowed detectives like Talbott to file evidence reports three weeks after collection.

How, then, does one go back, even this early in the investigation, to try to make sense of things like the diluted bloodstains, the posing of Kaylee's and Maddie's bodies, and arguably baffling statements by two surviving witnesses? How does one proceed when on its surface alone, the living room presents a roiling storm of doubt?

The answers lie in scrutiny. In lieu of a trial, we must dig down into the state's assertions in the plea hearing and work to expose apparent contradictions in search of truth. There are secrets buried in Bill Thompson's Brady disclosure; it is our job to reveal them.

Before we delve deeper, several things require stipulation. First, I hold no forensic analysis certification from any accredited association, organization, or school. I have a master's degree from the University of Virginia and fifteen years of investigative experience as a special agent with the FBI, but no training in forensics. My testimony as a court-certified expert in statement analysis helped put a serial killer named Oscar Ray Bolin to death, but I hold no degree in criminology.

Second, cold case investigation is a fast-developing discipline aimed at foisting new techniques upon legacy methods. Whereas homicide investigators focus on acute onset crisis, cold case investigators have the benefit of objectivity and perspective. They face less pressure from media, politicians, or family members, or the strident cries of an outraged public. Oddly enough, time becomes an asset.

Third, chaos theory is now widely taught in the world's finest universities, but police academies eschew it. Concepts like initial condition, nonlinear dynamics, and complex adaptive systems are fundamental to social media developers, game theorists, and financial strategists but anathema to law enforcement. Scientists avoid simple paths like rationale and assumption in favor of logic, but cops do not. If we decide to lean on Lorenz to build new models of inquiry, we need to anticipate resistance from authorities.

Finally, as odd as this might sound to fans of crime and punishment, none of this is new to the United States Department of Justice. When it comes to the antiquated state of crime scene investigations, they agree completely. In fact, they put it in writing.

"The word 'system' is a misnomer, when used in the context of death investigation in the United States," wrote National Institute of Justice Executive Director Dr. Steven C. Clark in the introduction of a 1999 publication *Death Investigation: A Guide for the Scene Investigator.* "There is no 'system' of death investigation that covers the more than 3,000 jurisdictions in this country."

In lieu of standardized methods, we will hereafter refer to and cite the National Institute of Justice's *Death Investigation* (2011 and 2024) as a criminologists' bible. It was composed and peer-reviewed by the DOJ's Technical Working Group for Death

Investigation, a highly accomplished focus group comprised of 144 members. There are no nationally accepted guidelines or standards of practice for individuals performing death-scene investigations. No professional degree, license, certification, or minimum educational requirements exist, nor is there a commonly accepted training curriculum. We cannot even point to a common job title for the thousands of people who routinely perform death investigations in this country.

At the risk of sounding like a shill for the defense, how could it be that the DOJ itself admits such insufficiencies? Most people would assume that America has moved past the days when a bunch of women could be rounded up in a town called Salem and burned at the stake as witches. We live in an age when algorithms predict which clothes you'll buy, songs you'll sing along with, restaurants you might frequent on vacation. Your cell phone uses AI to gather your news, predict social media interactions, guide you from place to place based on data. How is it possible that state-of-the-art technologies like DNA analysis and cell tower triangulation can be used to identify a killer, despite a history of misinterpretation?

Let's blame it on chaos; not the concept, the theory.

In pioneering his models, Edward Lorenz discovered that systems act in predictable patterns no matter where you find them. The world follows rules, those rules govern outcomes, and with proper analysis, those outcomes can be studied as deterministic, not random. According to Lorenz, chaos is not a lack of order; it is a higher degree of complexity. No, he probably never got close to a crime scene, but neither did the guys who invented the D-cell flashlight or started Motorola. A badge and a gun do not impart some magical ability to look at a bloodstain and figure out how it got there. Cops get things wrong, like everybody else.

How, then, do we proceed? How do we accept Kohberger's admissions of guilt while acknowledging facts that seem sufficient to doubt them?

Let's start with the basics of what the file tells us. We know from Dylan Mortensen's first two statements that witness recollections can be sketchy at best. We know that written reports by Officers Nunes and Warner seem to differ significantly from what body camera footage shows. We know that Bethany Funke's delayed call to 911 started the whole thing off on the wrong foot and that statements provided by Hunter Johnson only made things worse. We cannot ignore the fact that Detective Talbott's December 6 report appears to directly contradict the handwritten receipt he filed on November 13. Forensic analysis by the state's blood spatter expert, Paulette Sutton, sows confusion where it was supposed to add science. In my opinion, Bill Thompson's plea hearing summation is rife with half-truths, suppositions, vagaries, and misunderstandings. Anne Taylor promised to mount a defense, but that never happened.

In order to map a path through this chaos, we need to find a beginning, a center, a time and place from which all change flows. Fortunately, we can agree on certain things, including the fact that at 4:00 a.m. on November 13, 2022, there was a three-story house near the middle of the U of I campus. The midpoint of the house was its open second floor. At the center of the second floor was a living room. In the center of the living room stood a white folding table. Everything that happened early Sunday morning had to pass right through it.

Police seem to agree. Numerous reports map the killer's movements through the house, acknowledging that he entered through sliding glass doors in the kitchen before moving upstairs to cruelly attack his victims. Evidence shows that he walked back down to the second floor, leaving a blood trail on the walls and banister, to where he encountered Xana near the door to Dylan's room. He chased her through the living room, turned left down the hallway, killing her within arm's reach of Ethan. Police believe the killer fled the second floor after encountering Dylan just moments before she ran downstairs to Bethany.

Sutton agreed enough to describe the living room in detail.

"Within this area there is a sofa, a television, and a beer pong table," she wrote on page 62 of her forensic analysis. "A metal framed console table is partially visible against the wall opposite the sofa."

If we surmise that the table at the center of the house might be important, prosecutors seem to have ignored it. While acknowledging that it was set up for beer pong in a house that hosted a party the night before the murders, no one questioned its placement. They did not find it odd that ten cups were neatly arranged at one end, with ten others strewn wildly from the other. They did not even try to explain how, after killing Kaylee and Maddie, a six-foot-tall, 185-pound, blood-soaked Kohberger chased a frantic Xana through space occupied by the table without moving it an inch. Bill Thompson himself stated in court that immediately after butchering Xana and Ethan, Kohberger fled back around the table on his way out the door. Throughout this whole ordeal, we are told, the table never budged.

If this all seems unlikely, experts appear not to have cared.

Sutton's report addresses bloodstains on the table but never questions how they got there. She maps blood spatter on the knee wall without calculating trajectories or explaining how blood from "an object in motion" could have lined up precisely with a killer standing where the table was not supposed to be. Officer Nunes's body camera records Hunter and Warner turning sideways to navigate the table, but Nunes never questions how Xana dodged it with a maniacal killer close on her heels, wildly swinging a knife.

Worse, Detective Talbott's evidence collection team documents bloodstains without explaining their odd shape or unlikely placement. Various reports mention the Solo cups without questioning why some stand upright while others lie scattered. Detectives did not find it odd that a Corona Light bottle and a bowl of popcorn somehow escaped disruption. They did not bother to explain how Xana's blood ended up on the table's left side.

How did professionals seemingly overlook such obvious clues? Although Sutton later modified some of her statements due to confusion over placard and intake numbering, she was not shy about offering speculation.

"Stain 39 demonstrates the appearance of diluted bloodstain," she wrote on page 62, referring to dried fluids on the beer pong table that were genetically matched to Kaylee Goncalves. "The presence of an overturned cup in the vicinity of stain 39 is a potential source of the dilution, if the cup contained a liquid at some time or if it was part of the setup for a beer pong game."

Sutton, a professional criminologist, does not explain how she could tell the bloodstains were diluted based on photographs alone. These are the very same stains Detective Talbott noted in his December 6 report as "appearing to be liquid." Neither of the two reports note that the stains were so faint, they do not seem visible in Nunes's body camera footage.

Further, nothing in police files indicates there was liquid in any of the overturned cups. Police found no evidence of any fluid other than blood on the table.

Prosecutors appear not to have questioned how Sutton, their professional analyst, arrived at this conclusion seemingly without any validating evidence. She does not mention that the closest overturned cup was almost two feet from the nearest stain. She does not acknowledge that none of the upright cups contained liquid as police found them, or that none of the sixteen objects found on the table showed any signs of blood. She does not explain why the cups, the bottle, the White Claw can, or the bowl were not tested or even seized as evidence.

This is just the first of many questionable assessments. She continued:

> Spatter Stain F is on the edge of the west side of the table. Presumptive testing of Stain F for blood was positive. This stain revealed the DNA of Xana Kernodle.

The west side of the white folding table was closest to the brass-colored console. Photos indicate the space between them to be approximately eighteen inches.

> The extremely elongated shape of stain F is attributable to an acute angle of incidence between the source object and the side of the beer pong table. Xana Kernodle was injured in proximity to this table.

It should be noted that Sutton later revised parts of this and other findings in a State's Amended Supplemental Disclosure, but she clearly believed Xana was injured "in proximity" to the table. Anyone looking at the photos would wonder how cast-off blood could possibly have landed on the two-inch vertical surface in an elongated pattern. Remember, Xana would have to have been fleeing her killer through the eighteen-inch space, shedding blood from an "object in motion," without disturbing any of the objects to her left or right. That seems virtually impossible, but no one seemed to care.

If the sound of butterfly wings is not yet deafening, remember that the beer pong table sat in the middle of the second floor. Anyone moving through that house prior to the crimes would certainly have had to pass by it. This includes Mogen and Kernodle moving from the front door to their rooms upstairs. It would include Xana and Ethan using the kitchen or the second-floor bathroom, or walking down the hallway to her room. It would include Dylan and Bethany and Lakelynn McComas, when they went upstairs to watch *The Vampire Diaries* after partying Saturday night in neighboring apartments.

Though police never measured distances, Nunes's video makes it clear that adult male officers had to turn sideways, moving between the table and the knee wall, navigating the console, or walking toward the kitchen. Based on known dimensions of similar folding tables (71" x 28"), and the flat wooden ledge (5.75" x 0.75"), one can estimate clearance of no more than eighteen inches.

Why would anyone have placed the beer pong table in that configuration? Guests of the party on Friday night would have had great difficulty getting past it to use the bathroom. Players would have been forced to stand in the open doorway to the kitchen on one end and directly against the knee wall on the other, blocking access to the fridge and launching errant shots down to the first floor. Common sense makes it far more likely that players would have positioned the table 90 degrees in the middle of the wide-open room.

Why is any of this important? Who cares about where someone placed a table? Because police reports place it at the crossroads of the murders. Its position, as police found it, makes no sense at all. Sutton's analysis inadvertently makes that clear.

> Image ISP 4687 depicts the view looking across the beer pong table toward the bedroom assigned to Xana Kernodle. On the right side of this image, one can see a half-wall with a wooden ledge, and the stairs leading from the 2nd level down to the 1st level parking lot entrance on the north side of the residence. Near the middle of the frame, the hallway leading from the living room to the bedroom of Xana Kernodle is depicted.

Sutton has already stated that diluted bloodstains on the top surface of the table were genetically linked to Kaylee Goncalves. The elongated bloodstain on the west side of the table was genetically matched to Xana Kernodle. How is it possible that one cast-off bloodstain would print on the top of the table, while a second somehow printed on its side? Considering the fact that both samples were determined to have been diluted with an unknown substance, sensibility starts to break down.

Moving away from the folding white table, Sutton continued:

> Stain D is located on the north side of the wooden ledge of the half-wall in the living room. Stain D was tested for the presumptive presence of blood and was positive. Stain D is a transfer bloodstain. Subsequent testing of Stain D on the edge of the ledge showed a mixture of DNA, Ethan Chapin being the primary contributor. There is no physical evidence to indicate that Ethan Chapin was ever outside the bedroom after sustaining his bloodletting injuries.

Wait. Ethan? He was murdered in bed, more than twenty feet away. How did his undiluted blood end up at the top of the staircase to the first floor when the killer left through the kitchen? Inexplicably, Sutton moves on without seeming to question the evidence or, worse, what she found right next to it.

> Stain E on top of the wooden ledge is depicted in DSCX 4685 and DSC 4687. Stain E was tested for the presumptive presence of blood and was positive. Stain E consists of two diluted spatter stains. The shape of these spatters show they are traveling from the area of the living room and towards the stairwell opening. The coloration and the edge characteristic of Stain E show concentration around the outer periphery indicative of a diluted stain.

As mentioned in the last chapter, this is the stain discovered under the twelve-pack of White Claw hard seltzers. No one in law enforcement ever asks or explains how it ended up under a box.

Moving east, Sutton wrote:

> Three areas of staining are noted in the stairwell between the 2nd level and the 1st level as depicted in DSC 4430. On the North wall, these stains are labeled as 23 and 24 and Stain 27 is in the area located above the steps.

Like so many other supposed blood transfers found in the common areas of the house, they are difficult to see in photos released by the Moscow PD. They look nothing like blood spatter found in Maddie's or Xana's rooms.

> Stains 23, 24, and 27 were tested for the presumptive presence of blood and were positive. The location and distribution of Stains 23, 24, and 27 are consistent with a cast-off mechanism while their physical appearance is consistent with diluted blood. Cast off is created when blood is released as the result of a bloodied object in motion.

According to the prosecution, this "bloodied object in motion" would have to be the KA-BAR knife. It is the only weapon ever cited or described.

> The appearance of the bloodstains reveal that the blood has been diluted by another liquid. DNA testing of stains from the North wall of the stairwell shows a mixture of DNA. Kaylee Goncalves matches the major components. Madison Mogen is a potential contributor to the minor component.

Moving toward the front wall facing the staircase, Sutton focuses on open space leading down to the first floor.

> Stain 26 on the half wall of the 2nd floor living room at the end of the beer pong table is depicted in image DSC 4886 and DSC 4685. Stain 26 was tested for the presumptive presence of blood and was positive. Stain 26 is diluted cast-off with associated flow stains. The appearance of the bloodstains reveal that the blood has been diluted by another liquid.

As we will see, no diluted bloodstains were found anywhere in Maddie's room or in Xana's. They were found only in common areas of the house, specifically the second floor.

> Flow stains as demonstrated in Stain 26 shows the presence of a mixture of DNA. Kaylee Goncalves matches the major component. Madison Mogen is a potential contributor to the minor component. There is no physical evidence to indicate that Kaylee Goncalves or Madison Mogen was in this location after sustaining their bloodletting injuries.

From there, Sutton moves to the south-facing knee wall at the end of the table. This is where photos show ten red Solo cups standing upright in beer pong formation.

> Stains V and W were tested for the presumptive presence of blood and were positive. Stains V and W represent a second area of diluted cast-off stains with associated flow. The appearance of the bloodstains reveal that the blood has been diluted by another liquid. The flow patterns are the result of gravitational attraction. There is no physical evidence to indicate that

> Ms. Goncalves, Ms. Mogen, Ms. Kernodle, or Mr. Chapin were in this location after sustaining their bloodletting injuries.

Had police or Sutton purchased a white folding table, ten Solo cups, and a small amount of liquid with viscosity similar to blood, they might quickly have found the eighteen-inch gap far too narrow to reconcile the table's position with what we know about the crimes. It seems to have been virtually impossible for an assailant to cast liquid blood against the knee wall from the far end of the beer pong table without hitting the cups, the wooden ledge atop the knee wall, or the floor. Trajectories simply do not match. Gravity does not lie.

If this doesn't ring alarm bells, there's more.

> Image DSC 4704 depicts the stains identified on the baseboards in the hallway between the living room area on the 2nd level and the bedroom assigned to Xana Kernodle. On the left side of the hallway are Stains G and H, and on the right side of the hallway is Stain I.

Though somewhat confusing, Sutton's report documents the presence of cast-off blood spatter on baseboard molding, approximately two inches above the hardwood floor.

> Stains G, H, and I were tested for the presumptive presence of blood and were positive. The physical appearance of Stains G, H and I is consistent with diluted blood. Diluted blood is the result of intermixing blood with another liquid.

Xana was likely bleeding profusely at that point. Her blood, as well as blood from Maddie, Kaylee, and Ethan, was found on horizontal and vertical surfaces throughout the common areas of the second floor. Yet not a single drop was found on the floor itself?

Sutton's report does not mention it.

> Stain 28 is depicted in image DSC 4443 and in closer detail in image DSC 44445 on the North side of the hallway between the living room and bedroom of Xana Kernodle. Stain 28 gave a positive presumptive test for blood. Stain 28 is a swipe stain. Stain 28 appears dark in color and not diluted. An undiluted swipe stain indicates that a bloodied object/surface made contact with this wall while in motion.

Without drawing conclusions or getting lost in the weeds, we need to compare what Sutton wrote in her report with what Officer Talbott stated in his December 6 report. Talbott observed:

> As you go up the stairs to the second floor you enter a small living room area. There was a folding table set up on the west side of the area, partially blocking the entry to the west hallway. The table had . . . multiple areas of red liquid on the table that appeared to be blood.

According to Sutton, the blood spatters were diluted, dried, and faint. Talbott continued:

> As I walked west from the living room there was a half wall to my right. I could see multiple drops and runs of red liquid along the entire half-wall.

Sutton noted no drops of any kind, nothing obviously red. Yet Talbott reported:

> Across the half wall I saw more red stains on the wall (above the 1st and 2nd-floor staircase). The stains and liquid were consistent with cast-off and appeared to be blood.

Photographs dispute this.

> Continuing west down the hallway there was a bathroom to the left with the hallway ending at a bedroom. On the north wall of the hallway, near the bedroom door, there appeared to be a red-colored transfer mark at approximately my shoulder height.

And this would be the exact spot where Bill Thompson's prosecutive narrative, and virtually everything the media have reported, comes to a screeching halt. Anyone looking at the threshold to Xana's room will immediately notice that spatter found inside and spatter found outside look dramatically different. Where the floor inside her room is covered in blood, the floor outside is completely clean.

This contrast screams contradiction.

How is it possible that virtually all bloodstains found in common areas of the second floor were diluted with an unknown substance, while all those found in Maddie's room and Xana's were not? How did the killer slay Kaylee and Maddie on the third floor, then track their blood downstairs to the second, where it mysteriously became diluted? Conversely, how did Xana's blood start out diluted on the beer pong table only to become whole by the time she got to her room? How did Ethan Chapin's undiluted blood end up on the knee wall at the top of the stairs to the first floor if he never left his room?

As we will soon discover, these were just the first whispers of doubt.

On January 10, 2023, Moscow Police Department lead detective Brett Payne filed a report documenting the interview of Molly McMichael regarding a DoorDash delivery made to 1122 King Road in the early morning hours of November 13. The text of Detective Payne's report is here transcribed verbatim:

> On November 23, 2022, at approximately 2039 hours, Molly McMichael came to the Moscow Police Department to be interviewed about her presence in the area of 1122 King Road during the early morning hours of November 13, 2022. McMichael was identified as being in the area through records obtained from Doordash via a search warrant and was confirmed as being in the area based off a Google Geofence warrant which was obtained as a result of this investigation. I was accompanied by FBI Special Agent Alix Skelton during this interview.

McMichael told me she worked for twelve to eighteen hours on the night of November 12th to the 13th and received three orders in the King Road/Queen Road area. Two of the orders were at the 500 Queen Road apartment complex which is immediately to the east of 1122 King Road. McMichael said the delivery at 1122 King Road was her final order for the evening. McMichael said she could not find the 1122 King Road address as the address number was hidden by the porch light which caused her to remain in the area for approximately fifteen minutes. McMichael also stated her Google Maps told her to go to the parking lot immediately behind 1122 King Road.

McMichael stated she initially parked in the front of 1122 King Road and could see a female in the top left window (the third story bathroom). McMichael said she saw the same female a couple more times in the same window and she would duck down when McMichael looked at her.

McMichael then said she drove to the back parking lot behind 1122 King Road and parked. She stated she could see the back "courtyard" area behind the house and noticed all of the lights were on. McMichael stated her map told her to walk into the back of the house, but she did not feel comfortable doing so because there was no path. McMichael said she started to walk down the road which runs north/south immediately to the east of the residence. McMichael stated a tan sedan drove next to her while she was walking.

McMichael said there was a male driver and noticed "he did not look at me". She said he looked "completely zoned" and just drove by her. McMichael later stated the driver was white with blond or red spikey hair. McMichael also noticed the dome light in the car was on when it went by and later told me the male was wearing a light-colored collared shirt.

McMichael stated she walked back up to her car and drove back to the front of 1122 King Road, at which point she saw the address numbers. McMichael said she placed the order at the front door, took a picture, and then left at approximately 0400 hours.

During the time McMichael was in the area of the King Road Residence, the white Elantra can be seen via the 1112 King Road Camera driving back and forth on Walenta Drive and then enter the King Road/Queen Road loop at approximately 0356 hours. At the point McMichael pulled into the front parking lot before she dropped the order off, the white Elantra pulled in behind McMichael's vehicle (a gray Subaru Forester) and then exited the King Road at approximately 0358 hours. McMichael did not mention seeing the white Elantra behind her at any time.

I continued to question McMichael about her time near the residence. She told me she walked down Queen Road at one point with her flashlight out. McMichael can be seen doing so on the footage from 1112 King Road. McMichael also continued to tell me the female she saw in the upstairs bathroom window would duck down when McMichael looked at her. McMichael described her as having long brown hair. McMichael stated she could not identify the girl as one of the victims.

Approximately thirty minutes into the interview, SA Skelton requested McMichael take part in a cognitive interview. McMichael agreed and SA Skelton began the cognitive interview. During this interview, McMichael confirmed much

> of the information she already told us. McMichael was able to remember she had her dog with her during one of her walks in the area but did not clarify much more in the ways of the details of the evening. We thanked McMichael for her cooperation, offered any support she may need, and concluded our interview.
>
> Subsequent investigation of video footage and cellular data showed the "tan sedan" McMichael saw was likely a light-colored SUV which left the area. Moreover, it does not appear McMichael saw the white Elantra at any point during her time near the residence.
>
> I certify (or declare) under penalty of perjury pursuant to the law of the State of Idaho that the foregoing is true and correct.

On December 6, 2022, Detective Jeffory Talbott filed six separate reports.

The first, as discussed earlier, details the methodology, inventory, and timeline he conducted on November 13. The second report, Supplemental 0033, functions as a two-page addendum, noting that on November 14, at 11:24 a.m., "ISP D2 personnel returned to 1122 King Rd., Moscow, Latah County, Idaho for further processing."

Though he does not list reasons for his return, it seems plausible that he was called back to document things found after the fact. No matter the reason, Talbott assigned ISP detective Jake Schwecke to "start a pre-evidence processed video" of the entire property.

According to files delivered from Bill Thompson's office to Bryan Kohberger's defense, this video is broken up, either through editing or in discrete stop-start segments, into four distinct tapes.

The first three, labeled "Pre Search 1," "Pre Search 2," and "Pre Search 3," document interior spaces, as well as the parking lot out front, all vehicles, and the curtilage comprising the exterior of the house. Along with photographs, these tapes provide objective, real-time documentation of what police found upon arrival. At least that was the intention. He wrote:

> At about 11:28 p.m. Det. Powell, Det. Schwecke and I started marking the evidence with numbered placards while Det. Roberts photographed the exhibits.

Those exhibits included four items: two blood swabs, "rolled two-dollar bills, located on desk along north wall of floor 2, west bedroom," and "blue-colored powder" (later determined to be crushed Adderall) in the same location.

At first glance, it seems impossible to tell if time stamps 11:24 a.m. and 11:28 p.m. indicate a typographical error or a twelve-hour gap between the pre-search videos and the actual search itself, but photographs appear to indicate the latter. Talbott's timeline resumes later in his report with a notation that Schwecke conducted a post-search video at 2:12 p.m. but immediately states that "the front door was resealed, and ISP personnel left the scene" at "12:18 a.m."

Stepping past these anomalies for a moment, we need to focus on the fact that Talbott's December 6 reports document crime scene searches conducted three weeks earlier. Exhibit 059, according to Talbott's second report, is a "blood swab, collected from west wall of the living room."

This stands out immediately, because although Sutton's analysis mentions three blood transfers on the west wall, all of them appear to the right of the second-floor hallway leading to Xana's room. What seems to have been overlooked by Talbott's team is a pattern of bloodstains below and to the right of the metal console table. According to close examination of the photographs taken by Detective Roberts, Exhibit 059 was swabbed just above the floor, in a gap of approximately twelve inches between the north end of the console and the corner of the wall. This is the one and only cast-off blood spatter found on the left side of the hallway leading from the living room to Xana's room.

Looking at photographs from the top of the first-floor staircase, which are now widely available online, it appears obvious that while swinging a blood-laden instrument from right to left, the killer must have been standing in the exact space where police found the table. In my opinion, there is no other way to explain a blood transfer with those characteristics.

How is this possible? How could the killer have been chasing and stabbing Xana, moving from the kitchen, across the living room, through the table as she fled screaming toward her room? A possible answer is that the table was not there.

Back to criminologist Sutton's report. On page 61 she wrote:

> DSC 4781 depicts the upper portion of Xana Kernodle's bedroom door. The bloodstains depicted indicate a cast-off pattern composed of diluted blood and associated flow patterns. Cast-off is created when blood is released as the result of a bloodied

> object in motion. The appearance of the bloodstains reveal that the blood has been diluted by another liquid. The mouth and nose injuries of Xana Kernodle as noted in the autopsy report are potential sources of diluted blood.

There is no logical way to make sense of this assertion. Though Xana is found lying in a pool of blood, with blood on the bottoms of her feet, there are no trails whatsoever outside her room, meaning she did not go back to the living room after suffering injuries to her nose and mouth. That did not happen. Laboratory reports show zero samples of diluted blood anywhere inside her room.

Further, Sutton did not address or explain how bloodletting trauma to Xana's nose and mouth would produce volumes sufficient to wash bloodstains off her door. On page 62, she continued:

> DSC 4784 shows the lower portion of Xana Kernodle's bedroom door (exterior surface). Stain 36 indicates diluted flow stains on the exterior surface of the bedroom door. The appearance of these stains indicates that the blood has been diluted with another liquid altering their appearance. The mouth and nose injuries of Xana Kernodle as noted in the autopsy report are potential sources of diluted blood.

Again, how could injuries inflicted upon Xana's nose and mouth, inside the room, dilute blood found outside? How would these injuries explain dilution of blood from Maddie and Kaylee found throughout the second floor?

Even more perplexing, photos showing blood on the upper part of the door do not match photos of blood on the bottom.

The upper door stains are washed out and difficult to see, with no distinct edges, no real dimension. The spatter stains on the bottom portion of the door show dark red drip marks approximately eight inches in length with three distinct trails. By Sutton's own analysis, these marks indicate fluid hitting the surface of the door and dripping straight down, indicating that Xana suffered a significant injury while facing or running straight toward the door. It seems difficult to imagine how this could have occurred if the door to Xana's room was not closed as she approached it. Sutton wrote:

> Drip stains were noted on the bedroom floor below the door. These drip stains do not appear to have been altered or diluted. Subsequent testing of these drip stains on the floor indicates the blood of Xana Kernodle. The location of these drip stains near the opening edge of the bedroom door represents the furthermost location of undiluted blood from Xana Kernodle. Once Xana Kernodle was actively bleeding, there is no physical evidence that she was ever outside of this location.

Except that diluted blood spatter on the white folding table was matched via DNA to her. This seems to present big problems for Sutton or anyone else trying to argue that blood found in common areas of the second floor came from injuries inflicted in the bedroom.

But before mapping out other obvious anomalies and further questioning Sutton's report, it becomes necessary to add two new disclosures. The first involves a Ring-style security camera located approximately fifty feet west of the house at 1112 King Road. At 4:17 a.m., the camera recorded audio of what most analysts believe to be a woman screaming or yelling, interrupted by what appears to be a loud thud.

The second disclosure involves a photo.

Though not publicly disclosed at the time of this writing, Bill Thompson's massive file contains a Snapchat photograph taken at 2:27 a.m. Sunday. The photograph depicts Dylan Mortensen reclining on the brown couch in the corner of the living room where she, Bethany, and Lakelynn McComas were said to be watching *The Vampire Diaries* on TV.

What stands out is not the fact that, upon closer examination, Dylan's right eye is slightly open, suggesting she was not asleep at all. The real significance of the photograph is that it shows the white folding table in the background, including ten red Solo cups neatly arranged in beer pong formation. Most important, it shows the precise alignment of the table as it stood approximately ninety minutes before the crimes.

Had investigators found this photo and used the console or plank lines on the floor to measure proximity, they would have discovered that the table was not where Nunes found it when he arrived. Analyzing the sound of the Ring cam thud, police might have speculated that it was the table flipping over that stood out in the middle of Xana's screams. Together, the two new clues might have presented detectives the best evidence yet that whatever happened in the living room that night may not have been what witnesses told them.

There is more. On November 16, 2022, just three days after the crimes, Bethany Funke was interviewed at her attorney's office in Reno, Nevada, by MPD sergeant Blaker and Matthew When (Blaker's spelling) of the Nevada State Police. Though we will revisit this interview in depth later, one disclosure warrants mention. According to Blaker's report (Supplemental 90):

> Bethany told me prior to hearing the firecrackers she thought she heard Murphy bark. She also heard what she thought was the beer pong table moving and cups falling. The beer pong table was located in the living room which is above Bethany's bedroom. Bethany stated she was not sure what the sequence of events were for sure, but she knows she heard Murphy bark, the beer pong table, and then the firecrackers first before she called Dylan to see if she had heard the same thing.

The possibility that Xana knocked over the table while fleeing for her life is not hard to imagine. It is perfectly plausible that Bethany was awakened by the violent struggle directly above her bed, and that she mistook the flip of the table for the loud report of a firecracker, followed by "the beer pong table moving and cups falling."

What does not seem plausible to me is the possibility that Dylan heard none of this while standing in her room, less than eight feet away. Even stranger, during three formal interviews comprising four hours of conversation, no one ever asked her a single question about the table, an account of what she told Bethany, or how she heard Xana and her assailant in the bathroom but not the struggle leading up to it.

To this day, anomalies involving the common areas of the second floor have escaped scrutiny. Blood spatter diluted with unknown substances, the inexplicable trajectories, Ethan's DNA in the stairwell leading down to the first floor, and blood that appears to be hidden beneath a White Claw box all beg explanation. But most perplexing is how the beer pong table stood unmoved in the middle of this chaos and how one witness heard it moving while the other did not.

The problem is not that someone knocked over the table; it's that they may have had the time and the inclination to pick it back up. The butterfly wings are roaring.

CHAPTER 5

Starry Nights, 22 MO 1810, Modus Operandi

Dr. Brent E. Turvey is a forensic scientist who was hired by Anne Taylor's law office to analyze Brady materials obtained from Latah County prosecuting attorney Bill Thompson, pursuant to Idaho case CR01-24-31665. Dr. Turvey has broad experience as an expert witness in all manner of criminology, from wound analysis and scene reconstruction to profiling. He is the author of nineteen books, including *Crime Reconstruction* (2006), *Forensic Victimology* (2009), *Forensic Fraud* (2013), and *Forensic Investigations* (2017). According to Turvey's résumé, he serves as director of the Forensic Criminology Institute, is a board member of the International Association of Forensic Criminologists, and maintains an office in Mexico, working "UN model protocol for femicide investigations" throughout Latin America.

If this description sounds a bit formal, it is because Dr. Turvey is a bit formal too. The business of crime scene analysis is a humorless pursuit that leaves little room for error, especially in a death penalty investigation involving four counts of murder. Due to the volume and complexity of evidence in cases like this, attorneys on both sides hire experts to help juries weigh guilt based on the same set of facts. Criminologists like Turvey and Paulette Sutton provide the means by which they do it.

"Crime Scene Analysis is the process of examining and interpreting the specific features of a crime, related crime scenes and relevant contextual information," Turvey wrote in the introduction to his January 29, 2025, report to Taylor. He had full access to the files.

> It requires consideration of the complete forensic investigation, to include context, forensic victimology, and the subsequent examination of available physical and behavioral evidence (e.g. crime reconstruction and Modus Operandi). It can also be used to infer motive.

Though limited in some regards by a nondisclosure agreement, Dr. Turvey agreed to discuss his work during a September 26, 2025, interview with me. The first questions focused on findings.

"What brought me to the case was the scabbard," he said. "They were concerned, because from the perspective of the attorneys, they hired me to address the question of what role the scabbard played in the commission of the crime."

A scabbard is a sheath for a bladed weapon.

No specific number has been disclosed, but records indicate Anne Taylor hired several criminologists to make sense of evidence gathered by police. Only geneticist attorney Bicka

Barlow has been publicly identified, and that is because she sat with Kohberger at the change of plea hearing. Barlow is a widely respected expert in DNA analysis, a role that makes sense considering evidence found on the KA-BAR sheath was a cornerstone of Bill Thompson's case.

"Just looking at it, it's wrong," Turvey stated, pulling no punches. "The scabbard is placed wrong, it's too clean, it's upside down, it's underneath the body, hanging out off the side of the bed. Just looking at that one set of pictures, related to the scabbard, I said, 'Okay, we need a top-to-bottom reconstruction and crime scene analysis, because this is wrong.'"

One must remember that DNA linking Kohberger to the murders is inextricably tied to the sheath. The job of the defense is to poke holes in the prosecution's representation of where it was found, who found it, and how it was handled on its way to the lab. If the chain of custody for the sheath is found to be a problem, the DNA found upon it must be considered a problem also. Lawyers call it "fruit of the poisonous tree."

"The scabbard, itself, is wrong for this case, wrong for the crimes," Turvey explained. "And then once we expand out from there, the next question becomes the logistics of how the crimes were committed. The idea that one person could do all of this in such a narrow time frame is difficult to make sense of. Then, also, the fact that police found nothing on him, no indication that he carried any evidence from the scene when he left."

Turvey is right; evidence presented by Bill Thompson at Kohberger's change of plea hearing suggests plot gaps that are massive in scope. The most important might be his assertion that a lone offender entered the house at four o'clock in the morning, killed four college students in less than five minutes, left a witness unharmed, and escaped without a trace. Yes, there is the matter of DNA, but Turvey has a great deal to say about its origin, and therefore its validity. In short, he does not buy it.

"The victims are soaked in blood; the floors are soaked in blood in the bedroom. There's nothing on him at all."

He was talking about Kohberger, and the fact that during extensive multiagency searches of his Pullman, Washington, apartment, his Hyundai Elantra, and his parents' home in Pennsylvania, not a scintilla of forensic evidence was found.

"So, because those things are true, you start small and then use your information to expand with questions and try to figure out how that blood moves around the scene or fails to move around the scene and how one person couldn't have done it in as short of a time. Then you start realizing that all the evidence points to more people, or at least two people, and multiple causes of death, that multiple weapons were used, and it just sort of builds out. You start asking questions and the logistics make it impossible for the narrative to hold."

Many of the follow-up questions seem obvious.

How does one reconcile Talbott's December 6 reports with the handwritten inventory he filled out on November 13? If police found the knife sheath in the bed under Mogen's thigh, why did Talbott state in his November 13 inventory that it was found on the floor? Why does the sheath not seem to appear in Nunes's body camera footage as Warner looks down, shining his flashlight from less than two feet away? When Nunes goes back to look for himself, why does he not seem to notice?

"Because it wasn't there," Turvey believes. "Detective Talbott wrote, during his search, that he found the sheath on the floor. Perhaps we should believe him."

If this is true, how important is all this within the larger investigation?

"Huge," Turvey said with a nod. "Because the first people at the scene—the first documentation at the scene—does not indicate its position. It isn't even mentioned by first responders, and that is a huge deal. If you walk into the room, and you walk around the corner of the bed, you're gonna see it."

Perhaps Nunes and Warner saw the sheath, but they did not mention it in their reports.

"Her leg [Mogen's] is outside the bed with her foot on the floor, and the knife scabbard is underneath her thigh, and it's sticking straight out," Turvey argued. "If you are seeing her, you are seeing the scabbard." So, Turvey believes this could mean "either that it wasn't there when they first looked, or they are lying about it not being there."

Paulette Sutton does not directly address this issue in her report. Bill Thompson does not mention it in his change of plea statement of facts. To date, no one from either side has discussed apparent discrepancies in how, when, or where the KA-BAR sheath was found.

"Is it possible for them to miss it in a case where you're looking at a bunch of blood and a bunch of bodies?" Turvey said with a shrug. "Yes, but these officers are not idiots. These people are from Idaho; they know what a knife scabbard looks like. They are not new to the game."

A review of all known reports shows no mention of the sheath prior to Talbott's search warrant discovery.

"And then Talbott says he found it on the floor. That's the most difficult part, because it's . . . not on the floor, according to photos." Turvey believes that this is a mistake that is repeated throughout the file. "That it's found on the floor. Once he says it, other people start saying it, and what's funny about that is that you can tell who looked at the crime scene photographs and who didn't."

Loop feedback is common to both police investigations and what Ed Lorenz theorized about chaos. Once information is introduced at a crime scene, it tends to be repeated over and over until everyone considers it truth.

"This statement is now in the ether," Turvey said. "There are people out there repeating it in documentaries; there are people repeating it on the internet, different discussion boards. People think that is where the scabbard was found, and so for me, this is an obvious problem. The placement of the scabbard is a problem."

Photographs released to the public show the tip of the KA-BAR sheath lodged beneath Mogen's outstretched leg, where the leg is hanging off the edge of the bed. She is wearing black sweatpants that provide clear contrast to the brown leather sheath, as do the bloodstained off-white sheets and a light-beige comforter.

"You have a knife sheath placed upside down underneath the thigh and it has got just a teeny little bit of blood on it, but the bed sheet underneath it is spattered with blood, with little dots all over the place like a starry night. And the sheath doesn't have hardly any on it? When it slides on top of those bloodstains, those blood spatters, it doesn't disturb them? It means they were dry." So, Turvey believes somebody, after the blood had dried, slid this knife sheath under her thigh.

I think it's a valid point. The porous nature of leather suggests that contact with liquid on the sheets would have produced transfer smears.

"But it didn't smear. It didn't. So, if it didn't smear and it didn't transfer from the sheets to the knife sheath as it was being shoved under the thigh, that means the blood on the sheets was dry. And if that is true, that means either the offender was there after the blood dried—that's one possibility—or law enforcement found it as Talbott said, on the floor, and shoved it under the thigh to make it look like it was dropped contemporaneous with the crimes."

Again, if the KA-BAR sheath was found on the bed, as Talbott's photos suggest, and not on the floor as Talbott recorded, how did it end up lodged beneath Mogen's thigh without any transference? How did liquid blood from these horrific murders soak the bed, the sheets, the comforter, and the victims' clothing but not transfer to the sheath?

"Either way," Turvey said, "somebody deliberately placed it there. It doesn't matter who, at this point; somebody deliberately placed it there. And then you add what appears to be a fabricated chain of custody and it becomes a piece of evidence that is, essentially—in any other courthouse in America—inadmissible."

"An apparent fabricated chain of custody?" I asked. No allegations of this kind have been made among dozens of *in limine* motions by the defense. "What chain of custody?"

At this point Turvey produced a photograph never before disclosed to the public. It depicts a brown paper bag that has been folded flat and sealed with red-and-white tape labeled "EVIDENCE". The bag itself is hand-dated 11-16-2022 and is signed by someone who, though difficult to read, appears to be Shannon Amident.

There are three white stickers affixed to the bag. The first, at the top, says "Chain of Custody" and shows transfer on 12/16/22 from a person named Kandy Florio to C. McKenna. On the line directly beneath that, the form documents same-day transfer from C. McKenna to a person only identified by the initials TDO. That is just a guess, however, because the penmanship is abysmal.

Beneath the label marked "Chain of Custody" is a second sticker titled IDAHO STATE POLICE. Beneath that it says PLACE BAR CODE HERE, though the barcode is actually placed at the bottom of the bag. That barcode sticker is labeled M2022–4841, Lab Item #1, "BIO Suspected Bio Stain (Swbs/Misc Itms) KBAR SHEATH WITH USMC LOGO."

After that the label is marked MOSCOW POLICE DEPARTMENT, Agency Case # 22-MO9903.

Returning to the label above, someone has handwritten case number "D22–30," followed by "Description: KNIFE SHEATH," "Offense Date: 11/13/22," "Subject: UNK."

Most important, according to Turvey, the chain of custody portion of the form shows the following:

FROM	TO	DATE
Scene	Det. Talbott	11/13/22
Det. Talbott	MPD Det. Payne	11/14/22
Det. Payne	MPD Evidence	11/14/22
Evidence	CPL Willerfonn	11/16/22
CPL Willerfonn	CPL Turrentine	11/16/22
CPL Turrentine	ISP F.S.	11/16/22

"So?" I shrugged. "It's a bag with a chain of custody form attached."

"So, I'm gonna do a little exercise," Turvey answered. "How many people, according to this chain of custody, have handled this item of evidence? How many different names?"

I counted them. "Six on the forms, plus the name on the bag. That's seven."

"Seven, yes: Amident, Florio, McKenna, Talbott, Payne, Willerfonn, and Turrentine."

It is not unusual to find seven names on one piece of evidence, but it is odd to find two separate chain of custody forms. It is even stranger to have an evidence storage vessel, in this case a brown paper bag, marked with a name that does not appear on either of the two chain of custody forms. It seems to be a real problem that the date on the bag reads 11.16.2022, three days after the evidence was supposedly bagged.

"First we need to know that this is actually from this case," Turvey said, laying the foundation of his argument. "Moscow Police Department, there it is—this is the knife sheath, collected on November 13, 2022."

I immediately asked Turvey about the fact that in Detective Talbott's December 6 reports, he stated that the sheath was seized by C. McKenna, not Kandy Florio or Shannon Amident. I held off mentioning that Talbott documented the direct involvement of ISP detectives Jake Schwecke, Gideon Roberts, Hugh Powell, and Darren Gilbertson; ISP forensic scientists Jennie Ayers, Kerry Hogan, Tara Martinez, and Wyatt Barie; MPD evidence technician Tim Smalldridge; and ISP trooper Kristen Noah. At no time did Detective Talbott or anyone else at the MPD or ISP ever mention anyone named Florio or Amident.

"What matters is that we have one handwriting up here—from Florio to McKenna—and then McKenna gives it to somebody else, which is just initials that aren't even legible," Turvey said. "But that's just the first label. Let's go down to the actual chain of custody, and we know it's the actual chain of custody because it fucking says 'Chain of Custody' on it, right there."

Turvey is a forensic scientist, but he is passionate too. This is a death penalty prosecution of four horrible murders. The stakes could not be higher.

"So, now, we've got six people on here, let's say seven with Amident on the bag. But how many forms of handwriting on this actual chain of custody form? The one in the middle that says, 'Chain of Custody'?"

"One. All the names, dates, and other information appear to be written by the same person."

"Exactly." Turvey nodded. "So, I want you to understand—this is a problem. It is a significant problem for the prosecution."

He took time to let the gravity of this statement sink in.

"No matter what else happened," Turvey opined, "they would be Giglio'd."

He was referring to a 1972 Supreme Court case known as *Giglio v. United States*, which expanded Brady mandates regarding disclosure of exculpatory material to the defense. It requires that prosecutors disclose all information that could impeach the credibility of any witnesses, including police officers.

"*Giglio* says that anything having to do with someone's character or reliability, or integrity, is fair game," Turvey explained. "If you withhold that from the other side, if you lie about their background and don't disclose that up front, that's a Brady violation."

Meaning the defense could request and the judge could grant exclusion of all evidence tainted by any proven violation.

"Specifically, there's a concept in law enforcement called the Giglio list. This is a list of all officers who cannot testify because they are known to have given false evidence and testimony."

According to Turvey, this might include everyone on the possibly falsified KA-BAR chain of custody form. If any potential falsification was proven, it would render them unable to testify. It might have included Payne, Talbott, and McKenna. Regardless of intent or any wrongdoing, and there have certainly been no charges here, the defense could've presented this in court. Possible exclusion of these three witnesses alone would have significantly damaged the prosecution's case at trial. The state cannot present evidence without testimony from the officers who seized it.

"Seriously, I don't think most people realize what a fundamental problem this could have been. I'm on the stand sometimes, and even the prosecutor will say, 'Well, I don't know what a chain of custody, or whatever words you're making up, is. Is this something you've come up with in the books you've written or is this a concept?' And I say, 'Uh, pick up the piece of evidence that you put forward, counselor, turn it over on the back, and it says chain of custody.' The concept has been around since long before Brent Turvey was born. I didn't just make it up. You should know it, too, because it is on every item of evidence you are holding."

He's right, of course. Chain of custody is taught in police academies precisely because the provenance and handling of evidence is critically important within the rules of criminal procedure.

If the prosecution cannot demonstrate who handled each exhibit, where those exhibits were kept, and when they were handled, it is impossible to prove they were not corrupted. Chain of custody is particularly important in the matter of the KA-BAR sheath, because DNA found on the thumb snap was heralded as the most compelling evidence in this case. If the sheath were found to be corrupted or its lineage in any way uncertain, the DNA could have been deemed corrupt as well. Fruit of the poisonous tree.

"And prosecutors seem to have no problem leaving out this information, or they just haven't read it," Turvey claimed, referring specifically to the Kohberger case. "Most people ignore chain of custody these days, but remember the O. J. Simpson case? The blood found on the gate and the glove found behind the house? Johnnie Cochran's challenges included chain of custody irregularities that pale by comparison to these. That was massive. It is huge here too."

Then why was it never mentioned in the Kohberger prosecution? Why did Anne Taylor seem to not take this seriously?

"I think she took it seriously, but this all happened within the last weeks before the trial," Turvey explained. "We did not discover it until the very end. Once we did, I decided, because of the way this stuff works, that we needed to actually do chain of custody inquiries on every piece of evidence. But it was too late."

Kohberger changed his plea less than one week after Turvey discovered the issue.

Turvey believes that this chain of custody was fabricated "because when the Idaho State Police got the knife sheath, they went back to the Moscow Police Department and said, 'There's no chain of custody with this. We need the chain of custody.'"

To underscore the importance of this previously undisclosed potential bombshell, we need to restate that not only did ISP lead detective Jeff Talbott file evidence retention reports three weeks after the crime, he also apparently never filed a chain of custody at all.

Detective Talbott and his team picked up the KA-BAR sheath in Mogen's room, placed it in a brown paper bag, and sealed the bag with clear plastic tape labeled "EVIDENCE." He apparently did not document the time, place, or even the file number of the case anywhere on the bag. And how do we know this?

"Because we have a photo of the bag. And we have an email from the ISP crime lab to Detective Talbott saying they cannot process the contents of the bag without a chain of custody documenting its path. Remember, this is the knife scabbard, the foundation of the case against Kohberger, and we have an email from the state police lab to the guy who seized it saying it has no chain of custody attached."

Is this not just an administrative oversight, one might ask? At the end of the day, what impact would it have had on the case?

"Let's make this very clear," Turvey continued. He believes that this is not an issue of possible mishandling of a work product; "it is much more serious. And this isn't covered by any nondisclosure agreement between me and Anne Taylor, so we can talk about this all day long; this has nothing to do with my work on the case. The question came up because the defense investigators were looking at this, and I see this chain of custody thing and say, 'What do you think about this chain of custody thing?' And they said, 'Holy shit, this is massive; we didn't catch it the first time.' So, I said, 'What we're going to do is over the next week, we're going to check the chain of custody for every single piece of evidence.' Four days later, the case got shut down."

Dr. Turvey has testified as an expert witness in countless high-profile prosecutions throughout the United States and in several foreign countries. His integrity as a forensic scientist has never been besmirched. This case bothers him.

"Chain of custody isn't just about who touched it; it's about when and where it was collected. That's the first thing. Then, who has handled it, and then in the process of handling it, what tests were performed that may have altered or even damaged and destroyed the evidence. Because in testing DNA evidence, they will sometimes cut a clipping out or they will do a swab, or they'll do something that destroys an area of the evidence."

Here, he made an important distinction: When evidence of a crime is destroyed in testing, the only actual proof lies in paperwork. Without a credible provenance attached to the DNA sample itself, the defense would have had a field day challenging its worth. In a death penalty case where guilt has to be based on proof beyond a reasonable doubt, it seems plausible that jurors would have leaned toward suspicion.

"That's what chain of custody is for; it's to understand the changes and processes and dynamics the piece of evidence has gone through before it gets to trial."

When asked why the chain of custody form on the KA-BAR knife was not addressed until three weeks before the trial, just days before Kohberger changed his plea, Turvey blamed it on the sheer volume of the prosecution's disclosure. Bill Thompson's office sent tens of thousands of documents to Anne Taylor—hundreds of thousands of data points, everything from victim toxicology reports to registration records of every car parked legally on the U of I campus.

"Nobody even knows about this," he lamented. "Just the defense team and me."

Until now, of course.

"It's interesting that they initially approached me just to look at the scabbard. They were so paranoid, they wouldn't even tell me what case it was, wouldn't tell me what I was looking at, and then, of course, we discovered that the single most important piece of evidence should have been excluded. Without a chain of custody, the sheath was no good."

But there were other potential problems too.

"Once you start to analyze these core questions with posing and the placement of the scabbard and the movement of the killer through the house, you start to figure out that blood transfer doesn't match up either—not with the narrative that is being given, that it's him [Kohberger] by himself running around at night, killing four people but not killing two others, including a face-to-face witness, leaving blood trails that mysteriously get diluted."

All of which Turvey says he disclosed not only to Taylor but to Thompson's team as well, because disclosure in a case like this goes both ways.

"So, my report goes to the prosecution, and they come back saying, 'We have our own expert,' and she actually agrees with some of what I said. Not the most important parts, of course, like blood pattern analysis and timeline. They said, 'Her theory is that the killer was running around the house naked.' They said they believed the killer took off his clothes and cleaned up and then got dressed afterwards . . . that's what prevented bloody transfer outside the house."

Wait. The prosecution believed Kohberger committed the crimes naked?

"Yes." Turvey nodded. "Paulette Sutton concluded that Kohberger must have been running around the house committing these murders naked. And once that was in her report, the prosecution had to go with it."

To prove his assertions, Turvey provided copies of Sutton's analysis and walked me through each of the conclusions. Some of Sutton's theories seem so implausible, we will have to revisit them, in detail, later.

"The problem is that Kohberger would have had to wash up somewhere, but the bathrooms on the second and third floors showed no evidence of that. They looked undisturbed. The first-floor bathroom, however, was completely clean. There were no towels, no laundry, no toothbrushes, makeup, not even any toilet paper. Nothing. It was pristine, empty, it was missing everything.

"Again," he interjected, "the state alleged that Bryan Kohberger was running around the house naked? It was thirty degrees outside, but he somehow stripped off his clothes before entering with deliberate intent to commit what prosecutors concluded were 'non-sexually motivated crimes'? Or he came in wearing clothes, but then he somehow snuck down to the first floor where he cleaned up in the bathroom, got dressed, and ran back upstairs, where Dylan Mortensen saw him dressed in black, wearing a balaclava. But he did not kill her. Are they serious?"

According to statements made by the prosecution, the killer supposedly did all of this without leaving a drop of blood on the floors of any common areas in the house. Why, one might ask, would being naked somehow reduce the likelihood of transferring blood?

"That's Paulette Sutton," Turvey said with a shrug. "It's all in her reports."

To be clear, there are three.

"The first one details her findings," Turvey explained. "Then we have the next part, which is her rebuttal where she directly responds to my report, point by point. Her response to me is 'I agree with Turvey,' but she ignores a bunch of stuff she can't seem to explain. She ignores things she has no answer for but has to address, like the lack of bloody transfer. That's when she says he's running around naked in the crime scene."

Before we return to a full examination of Paulette Sutton's findings, it seems prudent to address underlying context. If it was the KA-BAR sheath that first brought Dr. Turvey into the case, it would be the bodies of Kaylee Goncalves and Maddie Mogen that lured him deeper. Whichever way one leans at this point in the investigation, Turvey's crime scene analysis presents doubt in linear, well-reasoned fashion. As we will see, his approach to the chaos of the Idaho murders might have made Ed Lorenz proud.

On January 22, 2025, Brent E. Turvey, PhD, provided Anne Taylor Law with a twenty-four-page document titled "Crime Scene Analysis." This was Turvey's forensic assessment of physical and behavioral evidence gathered during the investigation of murders at 1122 King Road on November 13, 2022. Although Turvey would not discuss detailed contents of this document, it was obtained independently by the author. A portion is here transcribed verbatim. It should be noted that this is Turvey's opinion and does not represent something proven in a court of law; it represents exactly what he told the defense team.

IV. MODUS OPERANDI

Modus Operandi (MO) is a Latin term that means method of operating. It refers to the manner in which a crime has been committed. A criminal's Modus Operandi is comprised of choices and behaviors that are intended to assist in the completion and concealment of a crime. Black's Law Dictionary (Black, 1990, p. 1004) translates the phrase modus operandi as "method of operation of doing things," and states that it is "used by police and criminal investigators to describe the particular method of a criminal's activity." Specifically, Modus Operandi is comprised of individual and heuristic choices and behaviors that are intended to assist in the completion of a crime (see generally Atchereley, 1913; Turvey, 2022; Weston and Wells, 1974).

The physical and behavioral evidence in this crime evidence the following elements related to Modus Operandi:

A. **Planning and Precaution:** The elements of Planning and Precaution demonstrated in the Modus Operandi of this crime are low skill with respect to planning and execution and high skill with respect to precaution.
    1. **Planning:** Whatever planning may have taken place with respect to this crime, it resulted in an excessive number of victims with an excess of bloody transfer

and bloody clothing on the part of the suspects. This took additional time to both effect and clean up before they could leave.

2. **Precautionary Acts:** The precautionary acts in this case include the execution of living witnesses, the clean-up of bloody hands, feet/foot-wear and clothing before leaving; and the disposal of said clothing along with the weapons used. Direct evidence on this clean-up can be found in at least some of the dilute blood transfer which was located in different areas of the home. Indirect evidence includes the absence of bloody transfer from feet and hands, despite the movement of suspects within the home, the necessary opening of doors, and the absence of bloody footwear patterns at the scene in general. All of this would have required an extensive amount of time at the scene to clean, perhaps hours, which is inconsistent with the State's theory that these crimes were committed within a time interval of less than 15–20 minutes, subsequent to 4 am.

B. **Number of Suspects:** At least two suspects were involved in this attack. This is indicated by the fact that multiple weapons were used against Kaylee, that multiple types of lethal force were used against Kaylee; and that Ethan and Xana appear to have been attacked at the same time. This is inconsistent with the State's theory that these crimes were committed solely by one individual.

C. **Posing:** As mentioned prior, posing is evident in the present case. This is based on the following facts and evidence: This refers to intentionally arranging the scene for effect. In the present case, the bodies of Kaylee and Madison were posed together after the lethal attacks suffered by both, and then they were covered together with a comforter.

D. **Staging:** Crime Scene Staging refers to an attempt to confuse or misdirect a law enforcement investigation by altering, fabricating, or planting evidence in relation to a crime scene (Chisum & Turvey, 2012). In the present case, a Ka-Bar Knife Sheath was discovered in the crime scene by law enforcement. Evidence of staging with respect to this item of evidence is as follows:
    1. The sheath was found precariously placed just slightly under the body of Madison Mogen and partially covered by the comforter that was placed atop the midsection of her body by the suspects. It could not have fallen accidentally into this location.
    2. The sheath was new and unused, as indicated by the absence of damage or wear to the leather.
    3. The sheath was face down and had received only a few areas of minute blood spatter (impact or aspirated) while resting atop a sheet with significant impact spatter all around. The inconsistency of blood spatter dispersion and density indicate transfers occurring at different times, under different conditions, with different levels of intensity.
    4. The sheath was placed at the location without receiving bloody transfer from the hands or fingers of the suspect that did it. This means it was done after the attacks/posing, but also after the suspect had washed their hands, subsequent to clean-up efforts at the scene.

E. **Primary Target:** The Primary Target in this case was Kaylee Goncalves. She was specifically targeted by the suspects, and the rest of the victims in the home were collateral. This is based on the following facts and evidence:
   1. Kaylee's room was the least convenient and most risky to access in the home, yet she and Madison were attacked first.
   2. The attack suffered by Kaylee was the most extensive, involving the most injuries, and was therefore the most time consuming.
   3. Kaylee was stabbed repeatedly in the face until she was unrecognizable. No other victim suffered this amount of close up facial attention or damage.
   4. Kaylee suffered multiple types of lethal force (stabbing, blunt force trauma, and asphyxiation). All other victims suffered only one form of lethal force. This level of unnecessary close interaction and brutality are characteristic of primary targets in cases motivated by anger and rage.

F. **Motive:** The physical and behavioral evidence in this case evidence an Anger-Retaliation motivation. As explained in Turvey (2022), this is "evidenced by crime scene behaviors that involve a great deal of rage, either toward a specific person, group, or institution, or a symbol of either." It is also evidenced by what may be referred to as overkill—injury beyond that needed to cause death, involving the repeated infliction of injury subsequent to the application of lethal force. In combination with multiple types of lethal force against one victim and not the others, this motive is all but confirmed.

In a search warrant affidavit filed February 22, 2023, Detective Jeff Talbott stated that he had "been a trained and qualified peace office [sic] for eighteen years." At the time of the filing, he was employed by the Idaho State Police, and as stated previously, was designated the agency's lead investigator in charge of the search. In his sworn affidavit, under a heading that read "Item Number Eight," Talbott stated, "On 11/16/22 evidence identified as 22M-1810 was transported by ISP to Idaho State Police Forensic Lab in Meridian, Idaho for forensic testing. This evidence was returned to MPD on 12/16/22 (see Exhibit M for evidence list.)"

According to laboratory documents disclosed by Bill Thompson's office, Exhibit M, otherwise known as 22 MO 1810, is the KA-BAR knife sheath seized from Mogen's room. This is the evidence Turvey believes to be corrupted.

Dr. Turvey wrote in his report to Anne Taylor:

> As with any forensic examination, Crime Scene Analysis requires an assessment and consideration of the nature and quality of any underlying forensic investigation and examinations. This is a crucial step in any scientific process, necessary to reliably establish that due diligence by government agencies has resulted in a showing of Evidence Integrity, and an absence of negligence.

Remember, an affidavit is a sworn statement provided to the court, in this case by an eighteen-year veteran of the Idaho State Police.

> This scientific requirement also accommodates the legal reality that every victim, and defendant, has the right to access justice. This includes a competent investigation into the essential elements and evidence associated with the criminal charges brought by the state, by competent investigators and examiners.

If Turvey's forensic analysis of the crime scene is correct, evidence gathered by Detective Jeff Talbott may be tainted. Under rules of criminal procedure in almost every local, state, and federal jurisdiction, the remedy to the accused in a matter of tainted evidence would be exclusion.

"If this had gone to trial," Turvey opined, "it seems almost inconceivable that Judge Hippler would have allowed it. The KA-BAR scabbard and the DNA evidence supposedly found on it would never have been introduced."

Why in the world, one might ask, would Anne Taylor choose not to challenge the single most important piece of evidence against her client?

"I asked her that myself," Turvey responded. "I asked her twice—once the week before Kohberger changed his plea and once about two weeks later. I recorded my Zoom call with her, and I asked her all the hard questions."

"You recorded your call with Kohberger's attorney?"

"Yes, I did," Turvey said. "I asked her how it was possible that she allowed her client to plead guilty in light of such damning contradiction. You can watch it. But before you do, you have to look at the rest of what I discovered while analyzing this case. After twenty-seven years in this business, I barely believe it myself."

PART 2

THE AUGUST EFFECT

10.09.2023

Dear Amandayzz,

In the abstract sense, and via intuitive capacities, the August effect can be analogized to the gravitation of Hearts promise unto the green pastures ahead . . .

Always in your Heart,

Bernnzz

Bryan C. Kohberger

Letter to his sister

Latah County Jail

CHAPTER 6

The Vampire Diaries, BORG, Black Balaclava

Whatever happened inside 1122 King Road at four o'clock Sunday morning, only one survivor is known to have come face-to-face with the killer. According to widely scrutinized reports, Dylan Mortensen, a nineteen-year-old U of I sophomore, was standing in the doorway to her second-floor bedroom when a masked intruder, later determined by police to be Bryan Kohberger, passed within inches. In hopes of gathering additional information, law enforcement interviewed Mortensen at her residence in Boise four days after the crimes. Although the interview was recorded, and we will excerpt transcripts later, police saw fit to file Supplemental 0003, paraphrasing statements.

In the interest of clarity, it makes the best sense to read this report verbatim.

1. On November 17, 2022, at approximately 12:05 p.m., myself, Idaho State Police Detective Victoria M. Gooch,

and Moscow Police Department Sergeant Dustin Blaker interviewed Dylan Mortensen at her residence [redacted by author]. The interview occurred with Ms. Mortensen's attorney present via computer (audio/video), Robin McPherson, an attorney in Moscow, Latah County, Idaho with the law firm, Sullivan Law Offices.

2. The interview was also audio recorded by me and Sgt. Blaker. The thumb drive of this interview was assigned Tag #220004172 (01) in the Tiburon Case Management System on November 20, 2022. The audio file of the interview had been downloaded onto the thumb drive on November 18, 2022, and the thumb drive was maintained in my sole care and custody until entered into evidence on November 20, 2022.
3. Ms. Mortensen stated the following:
4. She is a sophomore at the University of Idaho studying pre-Physical Therapy. She has been a University of Idaho student for both years (freshman and this year).
5. She had been residing at the residence where this incident occurred since August 2022.
6. Her friend Bethany and she moved into the residence and the other female roommates she knew through their sorority (Pi Phi), Maddie and Xana prior to this year, and had also met Kaylee before, but Kaylee belonged to another sorority. She explained Kay was a senior in school.
7. She described Xana as being a year older than herself.
8. She also described two additional friends, Emily Alandt and Josie, but they were not residents in the house. Dylan explained Emily Alandt introduced her to Xana last year. Both Ms. Alandt and Josie reside in the "Whites"

apartments (an apartment complex on campus that houses sorority members).

9. She described the layout of their residence, and where each of the roommates resided (paraphrased based on Dylan's description of their residence, "when you walk in, there is a door, there is downstairs with a bathroom and Bethany's bedroom; when you walk into the door, there is a hallway with her bedroom and the kitchen and the sliding door, and upstairs is Kaylee's room and a bathroom and Maddie's room; Xana is on the same floor as her bedroom").
10. Initially, she was asked to describe what the girls did on the 12th of November, but she described there was a ball on Friday night, November 11, 2022, a Pi Phi Sorority ball, which she briefly attended. She explained she started drinking at 4:30 p.m. on the 11th.
11. She described the individuals at the ball, including her roommates as well as Ethan and his triplet brother Hunter, Emily, Josie, and her boyfriend Linden, Jenna, Claire, Hayden, and Gideon. Yessi, Lisa, Matt, and Aaron, and their dates who were FIJI fraternity members, Maddie Thornton, Lake (Lakelynn) and Lake's date, Hayden.
12. Kaylee Goncalves was Dylan's date for the ball.
13. Dylan described how she got home on Friday night by using an Uber from the Pi Phi ball to their residence. She explained she and her roommates normally have Eric as their Uber driver, but not on the night of the 11th. She does not remember the name of the Uber driver on Friday night. This was around 8:30 p.m. She explained she and the roommates trust Eric.

14. She advised the party initially transitioned to the Whites apartments, but she got bored and wanted to go home. It was she, Maddie, and Xana, and Ethan regarding the roommates who attended the ball.
15. Eventually a group from the Pi Phi event transitioned to Dylan and the other roommate's house, and there was a party that continued there until the early morning hours of November 12th (Saturday). She requested to look at her cell phone during this point in the interview to verify the timeline. She was advised she could use her cell phone to provide times during the interview.
16. She advised the other individuals that came to the house on Friday night were Jenna, initially she said it was Hayden but corrected herself to say it was not Hayden but Zach (Jenna's twin brother) who came to the house, and Yessi as well as herself. They were consuming large amounts of alcohol and playing music. She went to bed a little after 12:10 a.m. and then added she went to bed sometime between 12:10 a.m. and 12:30 a.m. that morning (November 12th).
17. Eventually she advised Maddie Mogen came home and eventually Kaylee (Goncalves), but she was not certain about where Kaylee was when she went to bed.
18. She then explained on Saturday morning (November 12th) at approximately 12:15 p.m. (she then corrected the time to 11:44 a.m.), the roommates went together to get coffee and the store to get more alcohol. They still had champagne from the previous weekend, which she explained was U of I parent's weekend.
19. She explained the plans for that Saturday night included

a Sigma Chi fraternity party on campus. Dylan explained Kaylee was not going to this function because she was a senior and typically seniors do not attend the fraternity functions on campus because they are old enough to go to the local clubs. Dylan explained she was going to the Sigma Chi party. Dylan further explained at one point Maddie was at this function but left the function to go to the club with Kaylee.

20. They were all at the house together at 5:00 p.m. on Saturday November 12th. Dylan stated Kaylee decided to go and take a nap, and she (Dylan), Maddie, Xana, Bethany, and she were on the couch watching a movie.
21. Dylan explained they were all together Saturday afternoon at the house, and they all decided to take naps, and each of the girls set their alarms for 8:00 p.m. Dylan believes Ethan may have come over to the house at this time, but she was not certain if this is the time Ethan came over, or if he showed up at a different time.
22. Dylan explained she had an assignment due in her psychology 215 course, so she posted the assignment at approximately 10:12 p.m. She believes she then left the house at approximately 10:30 p.m. (Saturday night).
23. When Dylan left the house, Kaylee was still there with one of her friends, however, Dylan does not know the friend's name. She described the friend was female and was nice.
24. After leaving the house, she saw Maddie between their residence and the Whites Apartments, and Maddie was holding a box of White Claw while she was walking toward their house. She advised she talked to Maddie, and then

Dylan continued to the Sigma Chi function. She believed Maddie was going back to their residence to get ready to go to the club with Kaylee. (Sgt. Blaker asked Dylan to give more details about the route she took when she encountered Maddie, and she provided those details in this interview).

25. She explained when she got to the Sigma Chi function, she wanted to meet up with Xana and Bethany, and she called Xana on her cell phone to find out which apartment they were in, and she was told they were in Apartment #4. Others who were at Apartment #4 at this time were Ethan, and his triplet brother, Hunter, Xana, Yessi, Gideon (Claire's friend). Dylan explained she and Gideon were going in and out of the front of the fraternity lodge together for part of the night. Dylan explained there were not a lot of people at this function.
26. She further explained after, she met up with Gideon, and the two of them then went to Peter's apartment.
27. She was with Ethan (Chapin) and Xana during part of the night, and Dylan explained Ethan had been trying to get in contact with his sister (one of the triplets), Maizie, because she had been upset about something and he was worried about her, but Dylan did not know what the issue was. She remembered Maizie told her brother she had not been answering her cell phone because she had been sleeping.
28. She described Ethan as being very protective of his sister as well as protective with all of the roommates.
29. The group of them then went to visit Aly, who she had previously met through Xana, and Kenzie, was also there, including she, Yessi and Gideon. Jenna, Claire, and Lake

were also there, as well as Ava and Zach (Jenna's twin brother).

30. When asked how much alcohol she had consumed, she explained she had been playing "Rage Cage," which she described was a drinking game, and when she awakened from her nap, she consumed three White Claws (with an alcohol content of 5%). She denied there was any drug use, and stated Xana and Ethan used Adderall. She advised neither Maddie or Kaylee did drugs. She explained she nor Bethany "never touched that stuff."
31. [REDACTED]
32. [REDACTED]
33. She advised it was only she and Lake that went back to the residence, using the Sobro. She did not believe anyone else was home.
34. When the two of them got home, which she believed was sometime between 1:15 a.m. and 1:30 a.m. (November 13th), she was intoxicated and because of that, she does not remember what time it actually was, but she believed it was between the two times mentioned.
35. She further advised she made popcorn in the kitchen, and she and Lakelynn watched "Vampire Diaries" together.
36. Approximately 20 minutes later Bethany (Funke) returned home. The three of them laid down and continued to watch Vampire Diaries. She believes Lake may have walked home, and then she advised she does not know what time Bethany and Lakelynn went to bed. She had already gone to bed and does not know when Lake may have left or when Bethany went to bed.

37. Approximately 2:00 or 2:30 a.m., she awakened because Maddie and Kaylee arrived home with Grub Truck food, and they had Mac and Cheese, which Dylan explained they normally got. All four of them were together, which included Dylan, Bethany, Maddie and Kaylee. Dylan advised they were taking selfie videos. All the girls talked about getting Grub Truck food. She did not believe Xana and Ethan were home because their bedroom door was open and she did not see them, and she discussed whether she may have been mistaken about this fact, and then she said she was certain she saw their door was open and they were not home.
38. She then went to bed, which she advised was after texting Eric the Uber driver.
39. Dylan looked at her phone to determine what time she had texted Eric the Uber driver and said her phone said 3:10 a.m., but after further discussion, Dylan admitted she was somewhat confused about whether she was using Moscow time or Boise time, and Dylan explained her timeline may be off by an hour because of the issue (specifically during this interview referencing Boise time instead of providing the time it would have been in Moscow when these events were occurring on the 13th of November).
40. She explained she uses Snap Chat as well as her cell phone to communicate with her friends. She advised if there is a lack of texted communications on her cell phone it was because she had transitioned to using the Snap Chat app for her communication method. She advised her log in information with Snap Chat is [redacted] and her password

is either [redacted]. She denied knowing her roommate's passwords to their cell phones.

41. While they were together, they talked about ordering Grub Truck and she then texted Eric, the Uber driver, at approximately 3:10 a.m. She explained she texted Eric, "Are you driving by chance?"
42. At approximately 3:13 a.m., Eric texted her back. She then went to bed. She does not believe Eric ever came to their house because she never responded to his text about the fact that he was still driving.
43. She advised Eric the Uber driver is in his 30s, is married and has one child. She advised all of the girls knew him and liked him.
44. Dylan advised she is not certain if she stayed awake to watch more Vampire Diaries episodes, or if she went to sleep. She was not certain if she locked her bedroom door, and she was not certain if she locked the sliding door, because she was the one who usually did, but she also volunteered in her statement that she believed that Moscow was a safe place, so the sliding door was not always locked.
45. She does not remember if anyone locked the sliding door before she went to bed. She was the first to go to bed ahead of the other roommates.
46. She explained that she previously has had a lot of dreams where she had been kidnapped in her dreams, and she further explained these types of dreams started in high school, and she knew they were dreams, and she would let those things happen in her dreams because she realized they were dreams. She advised she does not suffer from

anxiety and denied prior life trauma, other than divorced parents.

47. Dylan explained she was awakened to a noise sometime between 4:00 and 4:20 a.m.
48. She was asked to explain the amount of alcohol she had consumed before going to bed, and she again explained while she was playing Rage Cage, which included the White Claws, part of Lake's Borg, and maybe two or three more drinks (White Claws) at Aly's house. She denied drinking after she left Aly's house. She advised she had been consuming the alcohol until approximately 1:15 to 1:30 a.m. on Sunday morning. She denied drinking anymore alcohol after she and Lake got back to her residence.
49. At 4:22 a.m. (she confirmed this information by looking at the texted communication on a cell phone) she texted Kaylee asking her "what's going on?" She advised her phone said 5:22 a.m., which she advised would have been 4:22 a.m. Moscow time.
50. She advised around 4:00 a.m. or 4:20 a.m., she heard Kaylee singing and playing music. She heard who she believed was Kaylee walking up the stairs, and Dylan advised she heard Kaylee say, "someone's here," and she sounded frantic. Dylan described Kaylee's tone as somewhere between talking and yelling it. She believed it was Kaylee who was walking up the stairs with Murphy.
51. She said she heard who she believed to be Kaylee running down the stairs. She advised Murphy was barking at this time.
52. [REDACTED]

53. She does not believe Murphy is normally a barker.
54. She further advised she believes it was Kaylee who was running down the stairs after she heard her say "someone is here". She further explained she does not know if she actually heard this, or whether she was drunk and did not actually hear any of this. She heard the footsteps of who she believed to be Kaylee. She explained all the girls wear Doc Martens and that is when she believed she was hearing Kaylee coming down the stairs wearing her Doc Martens because of the sound of the footsteps coming down the stairs.
55. Dylan called Bethany at 4:19 a.m. Then Xana at 4:20 a.m. Kaylee at 4:20 a.m., and then Bethany again at 4:20 a.m. Dylan advised Bethany told her about seeing fireworks. She texted Bethany a last time at 4:27 a.m., before she went to Bethany's room.
56. Dylan then explained when she first opened the door, and she said she did not see anyone.
57. The second time when she opened the door, she heard who she believed to be Kaylee crying, and Dylan believed Kaylee was in the second floor bathroom. She then heard a male voice, which she stated she had never heard before say "It's okay, I'm going to help you". Dylan believed the unidentified male was in the bathroom and with the person who was crying. She believes it was Kaylee who was the one that was crying. Dylan stated that now she has gathered additional information, she now believes it was probably Xana who was crying. At the moment of hearing the crying, she stated she believed it was Kaylee who was crying. She advised she knows the male's voice was not Ethan's voice.

58. She described the last episode of Vampire Diaries, and she remembered it was two males rescuing a female. She explained it was not violent. She advised the male figure in the last episode was wearing all black, but Dylan explained that was normal for the series.
59. She is not certain whether she heard Murphy barking during the first time she opened the door, but she advised it was possible he was barking but Murphy was moving away from the house. She described Murphy was a puppy, and Dylan had just met him in August. She could not describe Murphy as being skittish.
60. She advised she opened and closed her door a total of three times, and the fourth time is when she left her bedroom to go downstairs to Bethany's bedroom.
61. Dylan advised she continued to call and text her roommates but received no answers. She provided the time she called and texted her roommates and the time span she advised would have been between 4:20 a.m. to 4:27 a.m. She advised she never thought about an intruder, and in her mind, she stated she was not processing what was occurring as threatening.
62. She advised she believed the male was directing his conversation at who she believed was Kaylee. She advised she did not believe the male was directing that statement to her.
63. In discussing why the offender did not harm her, it was discussed that it was possible the male knew her and wanted to protect her, and she said she understood that was possible, but she denied knowing who the suspect was.
64. Dylan further explained she Snap Chatted Ethan but

received no answer from Ethan. Dylan thought Ethan was still either at Sigma Kai or was at home, she was not certain.

65. The third time Dylan opened her door she said her vision was blurry, or fuzzy, but she advised she saw a figure of someone that was dressed in all black, and they were masked, and he was holding an item of what she initially perceived was a vacuum, but she said that it did not make sense to her. She described the suspect as not being muscular but being skinny and toned, like a basketball player. She further described him as being taller than her 5'10" frame by at least 3", so he would have been 6' in height. She advised he had to have heard her call Kaylee and Xana, and she thought he would have had to have heard her calling for them and she was confused as to why he did not come to her room.
66. She described the item the suspect was holding, which she advised was like a cylinder, and she remembered a "cop" talking about a bow, so she was trying to ascertain if what she saw was in fact shaped like a bow. Dylan further stated she thought that maybe it was a firefighter because of what Bethany told her about seeing a firecracker. She advised he would have been approximately 3' away from her and she believed she saw him walking out the back, sliding glass door. He had looked at her before walking out the back door. She was not certain if he could see her whole body or just her head.
67. At 4:22 a.m., then Dylan corrected her time and stated at 4:23 a.m., she advised she texted Bethany, and they conversed about someone wearing all black, and Bethany said

something to the effect of "What the fuck, why is Xana wearing all black." Dylan explained she was not certain if she had been dreaming this or if it was real.

68. Dylan explained she saw the suspect holding something she believed to be a cylinder shaped and also shaped like a triangle at the bottom of the cylinder shape. She advised the suspect was approximately 3' away from her and he looked at her but was walking out the sliding door when she saw him. She said she saw his eyebrows.
69. At approximately 4:23 a.m., she texted Bethany to tell her she saw a masked suspect in the house.
70. Bethany responded at approximately 4:25 a.m., telling her to come to her (Bethany's) bedroom and that "it's better than being alone." Dylan then left her bedroom after opening her door the fourth time and ran to Bethany's bedroom downstairs.
71. Dylan advised when she left her bedroom she looked down the hallway to Xana's bedroom and could see Xana lying on her back in her underwear, but she thought at the time Xana was passed out. Dylan stated she never went into Xana's bedroom, and she could only see Xana from the hallway as she was running to get to Bethany's bedroom. She advised she was too scared to go into Xana's room, and she knew Bethany was awake, and she knew to go there because she was scared. She saw Xana was wearing her underwear, and she explained Xana was comfortable enough with the roommates that she would wear her underwear around them, so this was not unusual.
72. When asked about the lighting conditions inside the

residence, she advised that possibly Xana's light was on, or the party lights were on and that is how she was able to see Xana because otherwise she would not have been able to see her lying on the floor without any lights being on. She was not certain if the bathroom lights were on, but she was not certain what lights were on if any. She advised Xana did not say anything. Dylan stated she did not think anything was wrong. She later offered she may have been able to see Xana lying on the floor because they also had a Scentsy light and it could have been she was able to see Xana from the Scentsy light.

73. She explained she was trying to determine what was real from everything that she had been talking about with Sergeant Blaker and myself. She advised she knew the time with Bethany, Kaylee, and Maddie were real because she has the video of them together. She was not certain how Lake (Lakelynn) got home that day.
74. She further explained she has been trying to piece together things because some things do not make sense to her.
75. She stated that she is being truthful, but some of what she has been discussing, she is not certain is factual. She has been working through it to try to remember what happened.
76. Dylan was asked if the first female who was crying was saying anything, and she advised no, the female was only crying, and the male was the only one talking.
77. She described the item the suspect was holding was cylinder-shaped and was also triangular shaped. She could not remember if the lights were on or off when she

encountered the male suspect. She advised she does not know if this is even something she saw, or it was something she dreamed.

78. She advised the last time she saw Xana was at Aly's house at approximately 11:04 p.m. (Dylan confirmed this by checking her cell phone). Xana had been holding a White Claw. She was with Kennedy at Aly's at 12:49 a.m.
79. She further advised Xana and Ethan did not stay at Ethan's house with any frequency. Because of Ethan's grades, he could not reside at the fraternity. He had his own apartment, but she does not know where his apartment is because she had never been there.
80. She knows Kaylee and Maddie were home when she went to bed, and Bethany, and from when she saw Xana lying on the floor, but she was not certain about whether Ethan was home.
81. She advised she left Kennedy and Aly's house at approximately 12:49 a.m. to return home.
82. Dylan stated she is certain at 3:11 a.m. (which through discussion might have been 2:11 a.m. Moscow time) Bethany, Kaylee, Maddie, and she were all in the house. She was not certain about Xana and Ethan, because she does not know when they came home.
83. She denied perceiving a threat, even after encountering the male in the hallway. She said there were people coming in and out of the house all the time. She denied remembering what his face looked like and said she could see that his head and mouth were covered, but she could see his eyebrows, and further advised she was not certain she could

see his nose. When asked if she knew what a balaclava was, and she said no, so I asked Sgt. Blaker to show Dylan a picture of a balaclava from his cell phone, and upon looking at a picture of a balaclava, she said it "could have been, that could have been it." She does not remember seeing his mouth or nose, but she could see his eyebrows.

84. When asked if any of her roommates told her about prior incidents involving anything that occurred with them, and she advised Kaylee had told them (Dylan and the other roommates) about an incident a month prior when she was outside with Murphy about a subject who had been watching her. This subject was in the apartments above the girls' residence.
85. Dylan further explained that two to three weeks ago, while at Winco, Kaylee told her about a male subject who followed her from the Winco store all the way to Kaylee's car. Even when Kaylee went to leave the subject was standing by Kaylee's car.
86. Also, two or three weeks ago, all of the roommates went to Starbucks together and when they got home, their front door was wide-open, and they do not believe it had been open when they left. She explained there were prior issues with the front door, so she said it was possible the door opened because there had been a snow storm, and she explained possibly the wind caused the door to open. Also, when she got home the washer was going, which she described was not unusual, but this also concerned her. She explained because of this these things they went to get Ethan's golf clubs to protect themselves when they searched the house.

87. Dylan explained weeks prior to the 13th, Kaylee told the roommates she heard a woman scream, but no one else heard it.
88. Dylan was asked if she was telling either Sergeant Blaker or I anything to prevent us from solving this and she advised no, that she understood my question, and she advised that she knew she did not sleep through the whole incident because she has texted communications and other things that she knows would have required her to be awake. She advised she knows what she heard, especially about hearing who she believed was Kaylee crying and the male voice telling her he was there for her. She stated again she does not know how much of what she had been telling us was not factual because she is still processing the events.
89. When asked why she believed she was spared after the male suspect saw her, she said she does not know why, and she does not believe anyone ever tried to open her door during the time he was in the house, and he could easily have done so, and why he would have passed by her room multiple times. She volunteered that to come through the sliding glass door the person would have had to have scaled a tall wall. She advised the suspect would have known her room would have been occupied because he appeared to have known the layout of the house. She also said it could have been someone who was in the house last year when other girls were living there in the house.
90. She advised there was no one she knows who would have wanted to hurt the girls, and the girls were loved by

everyone. She said she had never heard even rumors which were negative about any of the victims.

91. When asked about Kaylee's ex-boyfriend Jack, Dylan advised the breakup was mutual and they have their dog Murphy in common, and Jack comes to their residence and plays with Murphy, and he and Kaylee continued to be friends. When asked if they "co-parented" Murphy, she said yes. Kaylee told her the relationship with Jack had run its course. Dylan thought Jack had handled the break-up well because every time he came to their house there did not seem to be an issue.
92. [REDACTED]
93. Dylan advised that recently Kaylee started talking to Mason Barstow, but Jack seemed okay with that.
94. Dylan offered her DNA. (Sergeant Blaker secured a swab from Dylan at the conclusion of the interview). She advised there might be difficult to locate the offender's DNA because they had conducted a deep clean of their residence leading up to the parent's weekend. When asked about when the deep clean of the residence occurred, it would have been before the weekend of the crimes.
95. She was advised there was evidence left in the residence, and she sighed and said she was glad to hear that there was evidence found at the scene.
96. [REDACTED]
97. When asked if she would be able to provide a description to a police composite artist, she said she would not be able to describe enough of the suspect to be helpful. She further

advised the only thing she remembered about his face was that his eyebrows were bushy.

98. She advised she was confused about why the offender would have taken the patio door out of the residence because of the drop off from the patio.
99. She advised she remembered that cars do come by their residence a lot, and she said there was a black truck driving past Bethany's window, and she further said she was not absolutely certain it was a black truck, but there was a vehicle that went by their residence and she could see the tail lights but she did not remember if the headlights were on, but what drew her attention to it was the red lights on the back of the truck, and when asked if she meant the brake lights she said yes.
100. When asked what occurred after she went to Bethany's bedroom, she said they eventually fell asleep, and when she awakened she was lying next to Bethany in Bethany's bed.
101. She advised a friend of theirs, Sophia, and Sophia's mother are planning a memorial event and that has helped her emotionally. She advised Bethany is crying a lot over this, but she has not been crying.
102. [REDACTED]
103. When she awakened that morning, Bethany was next to her in bed. They were both too scared to leave Bethany's room to even go to the bathroom.
104. She advised at approximately 11:23 a.m., Dylan then corrected the time to 10:23 a.m. (Moscow time). Dylan said she texted Maddie asking her if she was up.
105. At 11:29 a.m. (Moscow time), Dylan texted Kaylee, "are

you up." She could tell her Snap Chats were not being read when she was texting them through Snap Chat.

106. Dylan advised she called Emily Alandt, one of her closest friends, about what happened that night with the masked man.

107. Dylan then explained when she reached out to Emily (Alandt) in the text message, which Emily told her was at 10:50 a.m., but she thinks Emily was mistaken, Emily told her she would send her boyfriend Hunter (Johnson) to their house because of their concerns about what had occurred during that night. When Hunter got to the house, which she described was before noon, she is not certain if he came in through the unlocked door or had to use the code to the front door to get into the residence, and when he got into the house, he asked about the location of a knife, and she directed him to the knife.

108. She advised she initially went upstairs from Bethany's bedroom with Hunter, and she advised when she saw Xana, she realized Xana had not moved since she saw her earlier. She was still thinking Xana was still passed out from being drunk. Hunter then sent Dylan downstairs. She advised Emily and Josie came over after Hunter came to the house, because she had asked them to come to the house. She advised Hunter then came downstairs, and she could tell by his facial expression he had seen something, and he told them to call 911. Bethany was the one to call 911, and Dylan at one point said she was on the phone with Police Dispatch, and the dispatcher was asking her about a defibrillator. They told Dispatch there were people

unconscious. Dylan denied seeing Xana or any of the other victims' bodies.

109. She advised they stayed in the house when the police arrived, and they (the police) were putting the tape up when they realized there had been a crime, and when they saw the ambulance arrive and leave, Hunter told them they would not leave unless there was no reason to stay. She then advised the Vandal Alert came out and that is when they realized their friends were actually gone.
110. She advised they all realized there had actually been a murder committed in their residence.
111. She said Kaylee had a balcony and she remembered looking at the pictures in the news, and Kaylee's curtains were all messed up. She thought the distance of the balcony to the ground may have been too much and brought too much attention if that is how the suspect made entry into the house through Kaylee's bedroom.
112. When asked if she checked the house for anyone else when she initially came home for the night (with Lakelynn), and she was asked if she had to unlock the front door, and she advised she believes she had to unlock the front door to get into their residence. She advised when she first got home she remembered the sliding door was closed, but she did not know if it was locked. She advised when she first got home she went to Kaylee's bedroom to let Murphy out of Kaylee's room, and Kaylee's lights were on, and no one else was in Kaylee's bedroom. Murphy came back into the house after going outside.
113. Sergeant Blaker asked Dylan about the login and username

for the router of the Wi-Fi at the residence, and Dylan advised Kaylee was responsible for that bill. She further explained she nor Bethany were responsible for the Wi-Fi bill because they had just moved into the residence in August.

114. Robin McPherson had some follow up questions for Dylan outside of the interview and as a result the audio recording was turned off at 2:11 p.m. the same date.

Dylan Mortensen was interviewed four times between Bethany Funke's 911 call on November 13, 2022, and Bryan Kohberger's change of plea hearing on July 2, 2025. This substantial body of first-person information does not include the grand jury testimony she provided in May 2023. All but the two initial accounts were recorded in the presence of her lawyer, but only her statements to the grand jury were made under oath.

In more than four hours of seemingly disparate accounts, Dylan Mortensen never verified or even corroborated details of what she claimed to have witnessed that fateful Sunday morning. Police never asked her about what seemed to be glaring inconsistencies, never sought a deeper understanding of still undisclosed evidence, including a blood-covered jacket, a bracelet found on the floor of the spare downstairs bedroom, and shoes matching a tread pattern found in blood near her room. To this day, police have not once indicated in files, internal communications, peripheral interviews, or court filings that they doubted any part of her story. They have never considered her a person of interest. She has never been implicated in or charged with the crimes.

Only two people know what happened inside 1122 King Road between four o'clock that Sunday morning, when the murders occurred, and Funke's call to 911. It is important, it seems to me, that these stories add up.

CHAPTER 7

Rage Kill, Lurid Dreams, Detective Gooch

If justice is the realm of lawyers and courts, it seems reasonable to offer a bit of a primer on how the legal system works. Much of what the public knew about the case prior to the change of plea hearing came from court filings, so maybe that's the best place to start. Anne Taylor's office filed dozens of motions covering everything from supplemental disclosure to change of venue, exclusion of evidence, even prohibition of certain language, including the phrase "bushy eyebrows," and all mentions of "psychopath." Each of these petitions included a healthy dose of Latin, endless citations, and at least a few obscure references to case law that takes years of study to understand by lawyers who cost staggering amounts to hire.

In lieu of law school, perhaps we can go over a few basic terms and phrases that seem to pop up over and over. One of the first might be *voir dire*, which refers not just to the fair and impartial selection of jurors but also to an assumption that when someone raises their right hand and swears to tell the truth, they mean it. This is important because, according to the United States Constitution, all Americans are considered innocent until proven guilty by a jury of their peers. No court will ever impanel a jury in this case, so *voir dire* will apply only to us as we weigh the facts in a truthful and objective manner. It is no small responsibility.

Next, we have to consider that all Americans—including those accused of being monsters—enjoy certain protections under the Constitution. After more than 250 years of ups and downs, the Supreme Court has ironed out a great number of disagreements, turning Fourth, Fifth, Sixth, Eighth, and Fourteenth Amendment challenges into a body of case law that most consider the envy of the world. The standard for guilt is proof beyond a reasonable doubt, and though most would call that a noble measure, no measure is perfect. Fairness and impartiality should be the objective of every investigation.

Which brings us back to the matter at hand, a death penalty prosecution where the defendant changed his plea to guilty after two and a half years of denial. Those who have followed Kohberger's prevarications seem split between acceptance of Bill Thompson's courtroom summary and outrage after the guilty plea disclosures by police that seem to foster doubt. Yes, the families have gained some measure of closure knowing the person behind their unspeakable loss has a name, but a name, here, feels insufficient.

So, then, if we want to believe that justice is blind, we need to understand that it is also tedious, complicated, and prone to error. As we have seen with the knife sheath, experts cannot agree on what should be obvious facts, such as where evidence was found, let alone who handled it on its way to the lab. Maybe this is a perfect example of why America's Founding Fathers built rules and protections into their model of jurisprudence. Procedures that may seem cumbersome in a three-month trial protect us from the days when hysteria-driven vigilantes incited otherwise normal citizens toward lynchings. No matter where one stands, the objective has to be truth, and truth has to be objective. If we believe in the system, we have to honor its rules.

Toward that end, it seems appropriate to introduce a few more terms from our glossary of legal jargon. The *accused*, of course, would be Bryan Kohberger, who through *due process* was also determined to be the *guilty*. He was *indicted* by a *grand jury* at the direction of a *prosecutor* based on *admissible evidence* that was both *material* and *circumstantial*. Pursuant to a *search warrant* executed on various homes and properties, Kohberger was *arrested*, read a *Miranda warning*, confronted with *probable cause*, assigned a *public defender*, and held without *bond* until he changed his *plea* to guilty and was *sentenced* to life in *prison* without the possibility of *parole*. Throughout this process, a *judge* ruled on a broad spectrum of *motions*, navigating investigative vehicles that ranged from *subpoenas* and *affidavits,* sworn out by *affiants,* to *writs* of *habeas corpus* seeking *extradition* within *rules of criminal procedure.* Throughout this process, attorneys hired *expert witnesses* who submitted analyses of everything from blood spatter and autopsy and toxicology reports to *witness statements*, surveillance logs, social media postings, Google search histories, and *chain of custody* forms.

Though most of these terms are common knowledge to the average American, some are not. The word *stipulate*, for example, requires a bit of clarification.

Anyone who has witnessed a trial knows full well that lawyers seldom agree on anything. In fact, it boggles the mind how they argue over minutiae for days before suddenly standing up and admitting to the judge that they accept one or more things as given. In these rare instances, lawyers are said to *stipulate,* introducing a novel concept and a lesser-known term of art.

In this case, both sides have *stipulated* that Kaylee Goncalves, Madison Mogen, Ethan Chapin, and Xana Kernodle were viciously murdered November 13, 2022, in a three-story house at 1122 King Road, Moscow, Idaho. We can all now stipulate that on July 2, 2025, Bryan C. Kohberger pled guilty to those crimes and shortly thereafter was sentenced by Judge Hippler to life in prison without the possibility of parole. Those who have followed the case can stipulate that the Latah County Prosecuting Attorney's office believes Kohberger left DNA on a KA-BAR knife sheath at the scene, used a 2017 Hyundai Elantra to make his escape, and posed for a thumbs-up selfie at approximately 9:47 a.m., while dressed in a hoodie. We can stipulate that, for a time, Anne Taylor disagreed.

Based on what we know so far, we can stipulate that criminologist Paulette Sutton believed certain things about the crime scene that criminologist Brent Turvey did not. We can stipulate that Sutton thought bloodstains in common areas of the second floor may have been diluted with saliva from wounds inflicted upon Xana's nose and mouth. Turvey found this absurd. We can stipulate that Officer Nunes's initial report differs from what his body camera shows, because Ethan did not kill himself and Hunter did not show Nunes the steak knife or say that he placed it on the table. We can stipulate that no one, including Detective Talbott, seems to have noticed the KA-BAR sheath in Maddie's bed until three weeks after the crimes when a December 6 ISP report claimed they did. We can agree that in four statements to police, Dylan Mortensen seemed to offer different information of what happened in the eight hours between the crimes and the call to 911.

In other words, few parties in this case agree on anything. So much for *stipulation*.

Next on our list of legal jargon is *in limine*, a Latin term meaning "at the threshold." In this case, the threshold is a two-and-a-half-year lead-up to a trial that never was. According to rules of criminal procedure in all fifty states, a *motion in limine* may be submitted by either party asking a judge to rule on the admissibility of certain evidence before it is presented to a jury. Examples might include the criminal history of a defendant, offers of settlement, unsuccessful plea deals—things of that nature. The goal, of course, is to prevent unfairly prejudicial information from becoming guilt by insinuation. That only seems fair until you consider that when the penalty is death, attorneys will argue the most picayune assertions, desperate to make their case. It's up to the judge to sort things fairly.

That is precisely what Judge Hippler did for thirty months, spending a good deal of time between January 2023 and July 2025 ruling on a string of petitions. Looking back, I can see how silly some of them seem, including Motion in Limine 4, in which Anne Taylor's office sought to prohibit the state from referring to Kohberger as a psychopath at trial. While this game of sticks and stones may seem petty, defense attorneys get quite serious about the manner in which their clients are described, especially those with spectrum disorders who tend to stare blankly at the wall. Kohberger's appearance has been the subject of widespread speculation, but the prosecution agreed not to take advantage, promising that "based on present circumstances," they would refrain from offering courtroom diagnoses.

Other motions addressed exhibits that could have significantly impacted the case. Motion in Limine 6, for example, was submitted by Bicka Barlow of Anne Taylor's office in hopes of prohibiting an ISP laboratory expert named Rylene Nowlin from referencing "touch" DNA. This motion specifically targeted assertions that Kohberger's DNA had been found on the KA-BAR sheath. Unlike Motion 4, it speaks to the heart of the case.

"Both the term 'touch' or 'contact' DNA or any opinion regarding how DNA ends up on an item, is misleading," Barlow wrote in a document filed February 24, 2025. "In that it assumes facts that must be proven, would be confusing to the jury and waste substantial time in debunking the testimony of an expert that is outside the purview of the field expertise and qualifications."

Barlow's objection was filed long before Dr. Turvey discovered the apparent chain of custody issues that well might have led to exclusion of the sheath and DNA found upon it.

"Furthermore, the opinions of this expert have not been disclosed to Mr. Kohberger," Barlow wrote. "As set forth below, the how and when DNA arrives on an object cannot be scientifically determined and is not the proper subject of expert testimony. The use of this language confuses and misleads the finder of fact and is barred by the Rules 402, 403, as well as due process in that the evidence is overly prejudicial."

For those wondering how it might be unfairly prejudicial to suggest a person could transfer DNA to a sheath by touching it, there are other questions too. Why is the defense entitled to know a laboratory expert's opinion prior to them taking the stand? What makes one person an expert when other experts refute them? What the hell are Rules 402 and 403, and why would a juror care?

The answers lie within the body of Barlow's eleven-page motion. In what otherwise might look like a grad-school dissertation, she uses case law, citations, and various forms of logic to attack the foundation of the prosecution's case.

"Current DNA technology cannot conclusively answer the question of when DNA was deposited on an item or by what mechanism (i.e. direct or indirect transfer)," she wrote, quoting the state's own report.

> It is possible the DNA detected on M2022–4843 Item 1.1 resulted from secondary transfer; however, based on Nowlin's training and experience it is her opinion given the quantity of DNA detected on M2022–4843 Item 1.1 (0.168 ng/ul) and given the DNA profile obtained is single source, it is more likely the result of a direct transfer.

For whatever reason, Barlow mentions the FBI's Combined DNA Index System (CODIS) but not the fact that DNA swabbed from the sheath failed to meet their minimum requirements for what is known as Y-STR submission. By a lot. She did, however, make a point to cite numerous academic journals, including one that claimed it is impossible to determine from quantity alone how Kohberger's DNA might have ended up on a sheath.

"G. Meakin, A. Jamieson, DNA transfer: Review and implications for casework, Forensic Sci. Int. Gentet.97 (2013) 434–443," she wrote, demonstrating the range of knowledge a geneticist lawyer might possess.

> The authors introduced the concept of trace DNA defined "DNA that cannot yet be attributed to an identifiable body fluid." (Id. at 435). The authors rejected the term "touch DNA" as misleading as "such a term infers that the DNA recovered from a surface got there via that surface being touched, but this is usually not known." (Id.).

Interesting. But, if motions like this demonstrate how far Kohberger's team would go to limit what the jury could see, others seem almost absurd.

Motion in Limine 7, for example, mentions placement in the Fourth Judicial District of the State of Idaho in and for the County of Ada, and cites the title, RE: Witness Identification by Bushy Eyebrows.

"COMES NOW, Bryan C. Kohberger," wrote Elisa G. Massoth of Anne Taylor's office. "By and through his attorneys of record and pursuant to the Idaho Rules of Evidence, moves this Honorable Court for an *Order in Limine* excluding any evidence referencing 'bushy eyebrows.' More specifically, the Defense asserts that Rules 403, 601, and 602 of the Idaho Rules of Evidence bar witness D.M. (hereinafter 'D.M.') from using the words 'bushy eyebrows' or identifying Mr. Kohberger in that manner."

Why, among all the issues introduced to this point in the story, would it seem necessary to focus on the mere mention of bushy eyebrows as prejudicial to Kohberger's case? Massoth summarizes things so we don't have to:

> On November 13, 2022, D.M. was inside the house when the murders occurred and saw a figure dressed in black . . . when she peeked out of her bedroom door around 4:00 a.m. Shortly after seeing the intruder, she went downstairs to B.F.'s room. The two girls fell asleep. Roughly 8 hours later, a 911 call was made from B.F.'s phone at 11:56 a.m. More than 8 hours after seeing the intruder, D.M. was interviewed by law enforcement at the scene and at the police department.

This much we know. What we did not previously know is that on February 24, 2024, the date of this filing, Taylor's defense team was grasping at straws.

"When describing the intruder to Officer Nunes at the scene," Massoth wrote in reference to Mortensen, "she described the height, build and clothing of the intruder. Her description did not mention eyebrows."

This is important, because initial reports are usually the most accurate, and Nunes's body camera recorded every word. What seems harder to understand is why Taylor thought a terrified nineteen-year-old coed would immediately mention eyebrows as the foundation of her story.

> Later, when she was interviewed at the police department, Detective Mowery inquired about facial features and asked D.M. if she knew what color the intruder's eyes were. She did not know the color of the intruder's eyes or eyebrows. "Everything was kind of blurry . . . like I don't fully remember it." During the Mowery interview, D.M. again mentioned that she was "in and out of it" because she was so tired.

This makes better sense in a legal argument, because D.M. is obviously Dylan Mortensen and her statements did appear to change over time, to the point where she eventually claimed she did not know what was real and what was imagined. Witness credibility should always be a point of contention, and Taylor's team wasted no time attacking Dylan's. Taylor wrote:

> On November 17, 2022, four days later, D.M. was interviewed by Detective Gooch and indicated that she was really asleep and probably very drunk when she woke up around 4:00 a.m. on November 13, 2022. Throughout the interview D.M. expressed uncertainty about what she heard and saw and did not know if it was real or if it was a dream or if her mind was playing with her.

Now comes, an attorney might say, the grist for fascination. While the prosecution tried to make sense of Kohberger's state of mind that fateful morning, the defense went after Dylan's.

> Law enforcement took pictures of D.M.'s room on November 13, 2022, and November 19, 2022, On the walls in her room were many pictures of eyes with prominent eyebrows. Many of which she had drawn. Some of the eyebrows are heavy, voluminous, puffy, or perhaps subjectively bushy. According to detective Lake, he found "artwork of human figures with an emphasis upon the eyes and eyebrows were pinned to corkboards."

Clearly, Massoth was trying to insinuate doubt, but understatement fails the objective. Photographs clipped from magazines and posted on Mortensen's wall feature prominently bushy eyebrows on seven different faces. Among colored-pencil drawings made and tacked to the board, five depict women with similar features. Though not mentioned in Massoth's motion, a corkboard in the second-floor bathroom shows more of the same.

Apparently, eyes were a thing at 1122, but Massoth's assertions were just the foundation for a broader legal assault.

Underscoring the legal research, critical thinking, and countless hours of analysis that go into every defense, she continued:

> When the Manson-Biggers balancing test is applied to the facts of this case, there is no reliable witness identification. As explained in detail above, D.M.'s opportunity to view was seconds at most, her attention was influenced by alcohol and sleepiness and the only identifying attributes are height in relation to her own, a skinny athletic build and a "bushy eyebrow." These general descriptors could fit millions of individuals.

Indeed. In fact, it seems hard to believe that had the case gone to trial, Bill Thompson would have reached this low to make his case. Kohberger had a considerable number of identifying features that distinguished him from other potential suspects. His height and weight would not necessarily have singled him out, but his nose might have. If Mortensen saw only one eyebrow, it was likely because his head was turned, meaning he appeared in profile. Even without Judge Hippler's ruling, it seems plausible that Anne Taylor could have refuted Mortensen's identification based on his profile alone. Massoth wrote of Mortensen:

> Her uncertainty is repeated in each interview, and at least 8 hours passed before she interviewed the first time. Six weeks passed before she was interviewed by law enforcement the final time, and six months passed when she testified before the grand jury. Balancing the Manson-Biggers factors, there is no reliability of the physical characteristics that D.M. has reported. There is great risk that at trial in front of a jury, her testimony will be viewed as a clear identification of Mr. Kohberger. This would be a false identification and would prejudice the proceedings in a way that must be avoided.

When a ghoul commits murder, we want to believe in the dedication and the credibility of the people we hire to find him. We want to trust that cops will be at least as competent as our heroes on TV. We want to have faith in lawyers for both sides as they fairly present facts in front of judges who keep an eye on rules and decorum until juries sort it all out. We want to hope that if we were ever accused of a crime, justice would be done in a manner we could accept.

Whatever one thinks about the validity of Bryan C. Kohberger's motions in limine or the impartiality of Idaho's criminal justice system, one thing remains certain: With the exception of a change in venue, Anne Taylor's efforts were for naught.

In each and every instance, Judge Hippler ruled against her.

On November 19, 2022, ISP detective Brady Walker telephonically contacted Lakelynn Ashlee McComas in the presence of ISP detective Andy Hodl. His report documenting McComas's recollection of events leading up to the crimes at 1122 King Road was filed the same date. It is here transcribed verbatim:

> McComas started at the University of Idaho (U of I) the year before and met Madison MOGEN and Xana KERNODLE through her sorority (PI BETA PHI). She grew close with KERNODLE. She met Kaylee GONCALVES around the middle of August (2022). She met Dylan MORTENSEN and Bethany FUNKE through her sorority the year before and their relationship grew closer after the start of the school year August 2022.
>
> McComas visited 1122 King Road at least once every weekend and described it as a "party house". She would usually arrive at the house before other guests. The parties consisted of playing games and drinking. McComas described the parties as people mingling with each other and playing beer pong and being more relaxed than rowdy or rambunctious. There were only a few occasions where McComas would go there to simply watch a movie or do something other than party. The parties occurred about once a week on Friday or Saturday. And were normally attended by twenty to thirty people.
>
> The parties were normally attended by the same twenty or thirty people. If a person showed up randomly to the party without being invited they would not be allowed to stay. McComas had not been there when that had happened. She knew of a house close by where KERNODLE had lived the year before where athletes would show up at a party if they heard about it. However, they were not welcome and were asked

to leave. McComas later texted me a picture of a map of the neighborhood and circled the residence where KERNODLE lived previously. The address for the house she pointed out was 1118 King Road.

McComas said MORTENSEN was dating a male named Quinn, who lived in Boise, and thought they had dated for a couple of years. She had not met Quinn and did not believe he had visited Moscow. MORTENSEN would usually visit Quinn during school breaks. The only complaint MORTENSEN had about Quinn was how much he played video games. McComas did not believe MORTENSEN had a relationship with another male during this time.

FUNKE did not have a boyfriend at the time.

Ethan CHAPIN stayed with KERNODLE almost every night. McComas did not see CHAPIN and KERNODLE on Saturday night (November 12th) but had seen them on Friday (November 11th) and described their relationship as good. She described CHAPIN as good. She described CHAPIN as helpful to the other girls and said he seemed to fit in the house without any issues.

McComas had met MOGEN's boyfriend a couple of times and had last seen him at homecoming at the beginning of October. She didn't know MOGEN that well and they did not have deep personal discussions.

McComas had not met GONCALVES's boyfriend. When McComas was at the house GONCALVES was usually gone or upstairs in her room.

On the night of November 12th McComas was at another house party with some other friends. McComas later sent me a picture of the location of the other house party which was at 427 Taylor Ave. MORTENSEN listed the attendees of that party as Kennedy Fitzgerald (female), Hayden Edwards (male), Jenna McClure, Claire Cirillo and eventually MORTENSEN. There were potentially other attendees but she did not know everyone so she could not remember. All attendees were students. At this time McComas thought CHAPIN and KERNODLE were still at the Sigma Chi party.

When McComas left 427 Taylor Ave. she and MORTENSEN got a ride from a sober freshman in a fraternity to 1122 King Road. She could not remember the make of the car.

McComas could not remember exact times that she left the party and went to 1122 King Road. She had taken videos and photographs that night and said the timestamp from the last video at 427 Taylor Ave. was at 11:54 PM. The timestamp from the first video at 1122 King Rd. was 12:43 AM.

When McComas arrived with MORTENSEN at 1122 King Rd. she went straight to the bathroom on the main floor. They entered through the front door with the keypad lock. Several other people have the front door code and the sliding door on the main level had not been locked when she was there. She believed FUNKE got home after she and MORTENSEN but knew they all arrived around the same time. She was not aware of anybody else being home and stayed on the main floor the entire time she was there.

After McComas went to the bathroom they went to the kitchen where MORTENSEN had made popcorn. McComas sat on the floor and played with MURPH, GONCALVES' dog. She thought that MORTENSEN had let MURPH out. After the popcorn was made they went to the living room and started watching Vampire Diaries. They didn't have much conversation while watching the movie. McComas took several selfies and videos. After leaving McComas walked back to her sorority house Pi Beta Phi at 517 Idaho Ave. The time stamp on the last photograph she took over King Road was 1:33 AM and the first stamp from media at her sorority was 2:19 AM. She estimated it took about 15 minutes for her to walk home.

While McComas was at 1122 King Road she was only aware of MORTENSEN and FUNKE being present and did not see or know of anyone else being at the house. She left through the front door and did not see any one of note while walking home. After leaving 1122 King Road, she did not hear from FUNKE or MORTENSEN until after receiving the vandal alert the next day.

McComas could not think of anyone who would be capable or involved in this incident. She also could not remember any instance of one of the victims mentioning a stalker or anything of that nature.

McComas sent me several screenshots of social media contacts and contact cards for some of the people she mentioned. She also sent pictures and videos she took that night at 427 Taylor Ave. and 1122 King Road as well as the previously mentioned app screenshots. The audio recording of the interview, as well as the photographs sent, were saved with this report Supplement 62 and will be submitted to evidence at the Moscow Police Department.

Though statements by McComas and others helped police build victimologies and timelines, they added up to little more than a circumstantial composite of the case. At the end of the day, a judge and his jury want evidence, and no matter what the lawyers argue, the best evidence is forensic. Returning to the crime scene, we quickly see that therein lies the problem. Paulette Sutton and Dr. Turvey agreed on almost nothing about what the evidence shows.

Back to my interview with Anne Taylor's criminologist.

"Immediately," Turvey said, when asked how soon, after examining the KA-BAR sheath, he moved on to broader doubts. "Immediately."

Broader doubts included the manner in which Kaylee and Maddie had been killed. The wounds were disproportionate, they were oddly symmetrical, and he believes they could not have been caused by one knife. Turvey felt certain that the bodies had been posed.

"Once you look at the knife, and you just sort of back out, you can see one of the victim's heads was all bloody, and her pillow was all bloody, but the two did not match as police found them. Kaylee's head had been moved after all the blood soaking ended, meaning after she was dead, and then one body was moved on top of the other . . . Kaylee on top of Maddie's right arm as if they were cuddling. And then the sheet, of course, had been drawn over them."

"What about liquid blood on the comforter?" I asked.

How is it possible that police would have found liquid blood, pooled in a porous surface, eight hours after the crime? Is that normal?

"I wouldn't say there is anything normal about a crime scene like this," he responded with a shrug. "But Kaylee suffered significant injuries that led to a tremendous loss of blood, so it's not that uncommon. It depends on the material the comforter was made up of, the type of fabric the blood pooled in. The medium of the barrier itself matters. Cotton acts differently than polyester. But on top of that, what's the temperature in the house? What's the humidity? All these things come into play."

Which presents the perfect opportunity to pause and talk about environmental factors, which the police seem to have overlooked. Things like illumination, precipitation, and ambient temperature certainly come into play when considering the crime scene as a whole. The kitchen door was supposedly left open for eight hours with snow on the ground, for example, creating questions about what was tracked in or out. Darkness would have been an issue for anyone sneaking around through the bushes.

According to online sources and a weather report in Bill Thompson's file, it was twenty-eight degrees Fahrenheit at 4:00 a.m. in Moscow the morning of the murders. Skies were overcast with light fog, winds five miles per hour out of the south, with nautical visibility of six miles and humidity of 89 percent. The moon was waning gibbous, with 82.5 percent relative illumination. Cloud cover would have made the early morning sky feel dark, cold, and wet; foreboding. As Ring cam footage from 1112 King Road so clearly shows, the killer would have found conditions just about perfect for getting in and out undetected.

And before dismissing weather as superfluous to forensic investigation, remember what Dr. Turvey said about the coagulation process of blood. The temperature and humidity inside that house played a factor in how quickly Kaylee's blood dried on the comforter. Just because police may have skipped over important clues does not mean we have to.

According to Officer Nunes's body camera, witness statements, and published reports, the sliding glass door on the second floor of 1122 was found wide open. The only thermostat for the entire house was attached to a wall in the kitchen, approximately twelve feet away. At least one crime scene photograph taken by the Idaho State Police shows the thermostat set at sixty-nine degrees. Common sense dictates that under those circumstances, the heating system, which worked normally, would have read cold air from outside, pumping heat for eight hours straight.

If the main door was open downstairs on the first floor, as witness Justin Nadeau claimed, the effect would have been even more pronounced. The heat would have been running nonstop, making the third floor, where police found Maddie and Kaylee, unbearably hot. That appears not to have been the case, because neither Nunes nor Warner mentioned anything about the temperature of the house, either on camera or in their reports. Neither does Detective Talbott or anyone else who entered to process the scene.

"Let's stick with the bodies and what they tell us about the crimes," Turvey suggested, admitting that high temperatures would have made pooled blood dry much faster. "At least for now. It's natural for all these questions to come rushing in with a case where it's all so complex, but we will come back to that later."

Dr. Turvey is not easily distracted. He thinks linearly, as one might expect of a scientist with three decades of experience making sense out of chaos. He likes to look macroscopically at the mechanism and context of a crime, before zeroing in. He calls it "course graining."

"This all starts in the third-floor bedroom with Kaylee and Maddie, so we start there too," he explained. "Based on timeline and logic, this has to be the first place a crime occurred. They are attacked and stabbed to death right next to each other. That much is obvious. But the idea that one woman is violently attacked and killed while the other is sleeping, that she doesn't wake up and do anything, doesn't fight back, doesn't even respond? That's nonsense. These two women are right on top of each other in a small bed and it's obvious that neither of them ever left the bed. Kaylee was asphyxiated to the point where blood vessels burst in her eyes and lips, then she was severely beaten, before being stabbed and cut dozens of times. Maddie never woke up? We are supposed to believe one killer smothered and beat and hacked at Kaylee while somehow dealing with Maddie too? There has to be a second person involved," he opined.

Turvey cited ISP reports to bolster his conclusions, which he considers fact-based and obvious. He said he followed the evidence as it was presented, building chronology as he tracked what he believes were the killers through the house.

"So, once they get out of that room, they go down the stairs to the second floor, and where do they end up, where do they arrive? In the kitchen. What happens when they get there?"

As Nunes's body cam shows, the killer or killers would have turned left moving out of Mogen's bedroom, taking four or five steps before turning left again and walking down the fold-back stairs. It is plausible to think the killer would have stopped at Dylan's room when he got down to the second floor, especially if she heard him and got up to open her door, as she has stated. Based on Bill Thompson's narrative, this is not what happened.

"In the kitchen, you have Xana eating her food and she's in there on TikTok, and that's when she sees who it is," Turvey surmised. "And she runs down the hallway, and the killers are covered in blood. They have blood on their hands, they've got blood on their clothes, they've got blood on their faces, they have their knives and whatever other weapons they were carrying, which we don't even know because there were no weapons recovered at the scene. But she sees them, sees the weapon, and she runs down the hallway toward Ethan to wake him up and get help. The offender is able, I think, is able to get close enough to injure her, which is why we have her blood in the living room, on the walls and some of the horizontal surfaces."

As previously documented, Xana's blood was found on the side edge of the folding white table. According to Sutton, at least, the state believed she was injured while fleeing to her room.

"That's either the offender tracking her blood back out after the murder in her bedroom or leaving it as he first attacked her. Either way, she gets further attacked in her bedroom, and she gets taken apart. This is a battle, a battle where she fights so fucking hard, and there's blood everywhere. She's stabbed and she's got defensive wounds and all kinds of injuries . . . Ethan was in bed. He never gets out of bed.

"So, either he never wakes up, which is almost impossible based on what is going on . . . things crashing, Xana screaming . . . either he doesn't wake up, or the other offender gets in there, holds him down and stabs him a few times, and he's done. To me, it's not a reasonable inference to suggest that he slept through the violent, destructive, screaming murder of his girlfriend. That's just not reasonable. It all happens right next to his body."

Turvey seems right. None of this makes sense, until one addresses other important considerations. The women on the third floor both suffered what a behavioral analyst might identify as "rage kill" injuries, "signature" wounds. Both women had their throats slit from ear to ear, postmortem. Twice. Each of them had nearly identical gashes on one of their shoulders.

"This is very interesting," Turvey said with a nod. "It tells us a great deal about the killers. You are seeing actions play out from more than one offender."

Before dismissing this as yet another expert opinion, we should stipulate that among Turvey's twenty-two bound publications is a 753-page text titled *Criminal Profiling: An Introduction to Behavioral Evidence Analysis*. He is not only a court-certified professor with a PhD in behavioral analysis; he literally wrote the book on this topic.

"Which lines up with the corkboard representation of several attractive women and their necklines and their shoulders," Turvey said, referring to images on Dylan's bedroom wall. "These appear oddly similar to specific patterns of injury documented in autopsy reports. It is difficult to overlook similarities between these images in the bedroom and specific wounds on the victims."

According to Turvey, self-similar indicators like this are found throughout the house. He specifically noted things like the deliberate posing of Mogen's and Goncalves's bodies, and the infliction of signature wounds postmortem. He pointed to the fact that Xana's partially naked body was left spread-eagle in the doorway to her room, while Ethan's was covered up with blankets, after the killing had ended.

"Why does this matter?" he asked. "Because people will tell you who they are pretty quickly, and you should believe them. All these strange things you see at the crime scene were acted out by the killers. You're seeing a behavioral portrait of the people who did this."

What about Ethan? Why would a killer inflict gruesome wounds only to cover him up?

"Because they're trying to hide it, the fact that he was butchered on the bed," Turvey opined. "Remember, the original call to 911 was that a roommate had passed out, right?"

Turvey believes a possibility is that this may have been done to create the illusion that there was nothing visibly wrong, to stage the scene. "The killers are trying to hide Ethan's injuries, so if you were looking down the hall, you might come to the same conclusion."

Was he referring to the two surviving witnesses? Was his opinion that Funke and Mortensen could have known more than they told police? Turvey is solely expressing his opinion here—neither Funke nor Mortensen has ever been implicated in wrongdoing. He believes they may have been trying to cover.

"Yes, to say, 'Hey, I just looked down the hall, and this is what I saw, and this is what I thought.' The problem is, even if you looked down the hall, you could see the blood is everywhere. It's just a nightmare. And then, the 911 call becomes just utter nonsense. A roommate is passed out from drinking and wouldn't wake up? That's literally what Funke told 911. It's on tape. How else do you explain that call? That Xana is passed out on the floor of her room and won't wake up? She's covered in blood. Lying in blood. There's blood all over the room. And this girl has enough information about her roommate to tell 911 she is passed out and unresponsive, yet she doesn't see all those gruesome wounds?"

Turvey was no longer trying to come up with theories; he had already formed his own opinions. In his mind, this had moved past the point of accusations. He was hired by the defense to poke holes in Bill Thompson's case, and that is exactly what he did. He filed his report as a statement of expert opinion, based on forensic evidence and documented behaviors.

"But let's not get ahead of ourselves," he cautioned. Before moving further on to the survivors, he wanted to address the house itself.

"How does the offender get in? That's the first problem. They've got to have a code to the front door or a key or something, because nothing is broken, nothing is disturbed. Not only that, but this house had been redesigned from top to bottom, meaning the floor plan would not have been widely known to people who had been there during previous semesters."

And why go straight up to the third floor, ignoring Dylan's room on the second?

"Because they had a target, an objective," Turvey asserted. "The people responsible for these crimes had to have had knowledge of the house. Getting up to the third floor is not that hard, but then you have to look through the rooms as you go, passing Kaylee's room until you get to Maddie's."

What about Xana? Ethan? They were killed far from that scene, downstairs and at the other end of the house.

"Exactly. Why? Because once they're done, the killers come down to the second floor and see Xana and realize, 'Oh my God!

These people know who we are and they recognize us and they're witnesses, so we've got to kill her too. Then Ethan, who never gets out of bed while she's fighting for her life on the floor? The only way that works is that there is more than one killer. And the only plausible reason is that they are witnesses."

Then there is the issue of what appears to be a cleanup of the whole second floor.

"There's no doubt about that," Turvey said. "The killers cleaned up the common areas of the second floor, which means they had to have the ability, the motivation, and the time. All that blood diluted with an unknown substance? The substance was water, or a cleanser of some kind; they washed off the walls, the floors, the table—everywhere except where the actual killing occurred. They cleaned up the first-floor bathroom, which we haven't even gotten to yet. And we're meant to believe two survivors waited eight hours before calling police, while all of this is going on? Never heard a thing? How is that possible?"

It's a compelling question. How did all of this happen in less than four minutes, as the prosecution alleged?

"It didn't," Turvey said. "It did not happen in four minutes. The prosecution's narrative makes no sense whatsoever. You see that in Sutton's rebuttal to my report. They have no reasonable explanation for holes in their own data."

And here is the point in any conversation about the Idaho murders where things start to go south. All the normal questions about who, what, when, where, and why start to break down and meld into one overwhelming question: How?

How did Bryan C. Kohberger break into the house at 1122 King Road sometime after four o'clock in the morning, find his way upstairs, ignoring Dylan's room along the way, and silently butcher two women eight feet above her bed? How did he kill Ethan, a six-foot-four, 228-pound former high school football player, while his girlfriend fought for her life on the floor beside him? How did Kohberger clean all the blood off the living room walls, the floors, the beer pong table, and the knee-wall ledge, only to inadvertently place a White Claw box atop a couple stains he missed? How did he transfer Ethan Chapin's undiluted blood to the top of the stairwell? Who sterilized the first-floor bathroom, why did they do it, and how is it possible that police did not seem to care? How did Bryan Kohberger escape, drive to his apartment, and ultimately make it all the way back to Pennsylvania without transferring a single cell of DNA from any of the victims?

"I actually know the answer to that," Dr. Turvey said, nodding confidently. "In fact, I tried to explain it all to Anne Taylor." He claims she wouldn't listen.

Listen to what? Didn't she hire him to poke holes in the prosecution's case?

"Yes, and I believe we have done that ably," he said. "But none of what I or the rest of the team found seemed to matter. Four days after presenting our findings about the knife sheath and the blood spatter analysis and overwhelming contradictions at the scene, her client decided to change his plea . . . take the deal. It shocked me, to be honest. I heard about it on the news, just like everyone else."

Wait. If a PhD in criminology presented compelling evidence to Kohberger's lawyers proving the case against him was so problematic, why would Anne Taylor let her client possibly ignore it? What would be the rationale in allowing a client to accept life in prison without the possibility of parole?

"We'll get there," Turvey assured me. "We will. Trust me, we will."

He'd been thinking about this for months. It haunted him.

"Before we do, we have to look at what the two witnesses tell us. Forget about Dylan for the time being. We need to focus on her roommate."

CHAPTER 8

Baby Daddy, High Noons, Firework

Bethany G. Funke was a nineteen-year-old U of I sophomore at the time of the murders. A native of Reno, Nevada, she had just moved to 1122 King Road in August 2022, pursuing a bachelor of arts degree with a major in public health. Like so many of her peers, she was a member of the Greek community, having pledged Pi Beta Phi sorority, where Maddie Mogen was her "big." By all accounts Bethany enjoyed a rich social life that included close relations with the other women in the house and friends in neighboring apartments. She regularly attended on-campus functions, including house parties like those thrown at 1122. She slept by herself in a bedroom on the first floor of the house, had exclusive use of a bathroom, did not own a car.

Beyond that, what we know about Bethany Funke's movements on November 13 comes directly from what she told police. Officer Mitch Nunes recorded her initial statement on his body camera outside the house, around noon Sunday, but she was interviewed again, an hour later, at the Moscow PD. According to Latah County Prosecuting Attorney's office Supplemental 89, Funke told Officer Dustin Blaker about her movements Saturday night, what she witnessed Sunday morning, and why it took eight hours to call 911. Blaker's interview establishes Funke's first real account of what she witnessed. It was the last time she spoke to police without a lawyer.

After logging personal information such as height, weight, and date of birth, Blaker wrote:

> On November 13, 2022, at around 1347 hours, I interviewed Bethany Funke at the Moscow Police Department in regards to the death of 4 of her roommates. Bethany is a resident of 1122 King Road. Funke was home sleeping in her room, located in the basement floor of her residence when the crimes occurred.

Just the facts is a great approach to any investigation, but Blaker's report seems to be missing a couple big ones. Like dates. Without context, it shifts timeline, moving from the house to events that are not otherwise defined. We can surmise that he was referring to Saturday night.

> Bethany went to the Sigma Chi party at around 2030 hours with Ethan Chapin and Xana Kernodle. They hung out in an apartment for a while together and then Bethany went up to the main part of the fraternity to hang out at the party. Maddie and Kaylee went to the Corner Club together, not sure when they left. Bethany did not see Ethan or Xana at the party and left to go to Kennedy Fitzgerald's residence at 427 Taylor Ave. Bethany

> walked home around 1ish and when she got back to 1122 King Road Dylan and Lakelyn McComas were at the residence and they all watched a movie together.

None of this differs substantively from what Funke told Nunes on camera, but cops tend to rely on interpretations of statements more than the statements themselves, and all too often those interpretations become fact. What Funke said and what Blaker heard seem to differ significantly. Prosecutor Thompson's narrative is based almost entirely on what his investigators wrote down.

Blaker continued:

> Maddie and Kaylee got to the house at approximately 0145 or 0200 hours. Lakelynn left the house, and Dylan went to bed.

This appears to be a bit of a misunderstanding. Bethany actually claimed she was uncertain about specifics due to her inebriated state at the time. She remembered walking home by herself but did not know exactly when Lakelynn left or where Dylan was when Maddie and Kaylee returned. Bethany said she'd had a lot to drink, running down a list of alcoholic beverages that included mimosas, a twelve-pack of High Noon seltzers, and unknown cocktails used in games of Rage Cage. She said it affected both recall and her ability to fully interpret events, which makes sense because she weighed only 118 pounds.

> Bethany hung out with Maddie and Kaylee for a while in Kaylee's room. Bethany and Maddie took Murphy (Kaylee's dog) out to go to the bathroom between 0230 and 0300 hours.

> Bethany did not stay outside for very long as it was cold. Maddie then went to bed and watched a TV show to help her sleep (Baby Daddy).

Blaker mistakenly reported that "Maddie" went to bed and watched *Baby Daddy* to help her sleep. It seems clear he was actually talking about Funke.

> At around 0400 or 0420 hours, Bethany heard what she thought was a firework and saw a spark on the ground from under her door. Bethany then heard Murphy barking. Dylan called Bethany and stated she had seen someone in the house, and Bethany told her she could come down to her room and sleep with her.

These generalized statements appear much more specific in transcripts. Bethany actually remembered considerable detail about the loud noise Blaker referred to as "a firework," and she provided time stamps based on call, text, and Snapchat notifications on her phone.

> Dylan went to Bethany's room and went to bed. They woke up at around 1100 hours and talked to other friends who came over, and they checked on Xana and Ethan and found them deceased. Bethany originally called 911 and stated her friend was passed out and would not wake up.

Despite the extraordinary number of questions this paragraph might inspire, Blaker, a sergeant, seems to have not asked for details or clarifications. Instead, he asked about and then reported on an incident, earlier in the semester, when Kaylee said she saw an unknown male near their house. In the following sentence, without any logical follow-up, he stated that Kaylee had broken up with her longtime boyfriend, Jack Ducoeur, approximately three months prior to the crime because she was moving to Texas.

"Bethany could not provide me with anything else at that time," Blaker wrote, adding that he swore "under penalty of perjury pursuant to the law of the State of Idaho that the foregoing is true and correct."

While it might make sense to compare statements made here with what Funke told Nunes on camera, it's not that easy. If we really want to get to the bottom of what she witnessed that night, we need to examine statements she made three days later, and seven hundred miles away, in the presence of her lawyer. As luck would have it, there are two different but equally interesting versions of this conversation. In one file, we read a report summarizing what the Idaho State Police report says about the two hours of conversation. In the other, we hear Funke speaking plainly in her own words, with every pause, stutter, and inflection recorded.

We start with the former.

On December 28, 2022, Idaho State Police detective Dustin Blaker filed Supplemental 90 with the Latah County Prosecuting Attorney's office, summarizing a third interview of Bethany Funke. The interview was also recorded, copied to a DVD, and "booked into property," according to Blaker. A summary of the report of Funke's interview is here transcribed verbatim:

On November 16, 2022, around 1155 hours, I met with Bethany Funke at her attorney's office at 327 California Avenue, Reno, Nevada. Present during the interview, besides me and Bethany, were her attorney Tom Viloria, and Matthew When with the Nevada State Police Investigative Division. This was a follow up interview with Bethany related to the homicide in Moscow, Idaho.

I asked Bethany who had the front door code. Bethany told me the following people had the door code.

- Bethany Funke
- Dylan Mortensen
- Maddie Mogen
- Kaylee Goncalves
- Xana Kernodle
- Ethan Chapin
- Jenna McClure
- Claire Cirillo
- Lakelynn McComas
- Hunter Johnson
- Emily Alandt
- Josie Lauteren

I asked Bethany about Murphy's routine. Murphy was Kaylee's dog she had purchased when she was still dating Jack Ducoeur. Bethany stated Kaylee would primarily take Murphy out, but Maddie would also help. Bethany stated they never just left the door open because he would run away, so they would have to use a leash when they took him out. Bethany stated Murphy would not bark that often and was very friendly. Bethany stated Murphy would primarily sleep in Kaylee's room and if Kaylee was not home he would be left in the room.

I asked Bethany if any of the girls who lived in the house had jobs. Bethany told me Maddie and Xana both worked at Mad Greek on Main Street. Bethany told me Kaylee worked for an online company and worked from home. Bethany did not know who the company was. Bethany told me Maddie also worked for an online company, but it was not the same company. Bethany said the company Maddie worked for was out of Boise, and during the summer she had worked for them in their office in Boise.

I asked Bethany about the drug use in the house and who used. Bethany told me Ethan and Xana both took Adderall when they drank alcohol. Bethany told me she saw Ethan and Xana both use Adderall the night before the murders. Bethany told me she saw Ethan take a pill and she saw Xana crush up a pill and snort it by using a rolled-up bill in her room. Bethany also said she thought Kaylee also used Adderall but was not sure.

I asked Bethany if she has had any issues from any of the other people who live around them. Bethany stated besides the 3 to 4 noise complaints they had, there were no other issues.

Bethany told me Kaylee would look up who the registered sex offenders were who lived in the area. Bethany stated Kaylee had found a registered sex offender who lived close to them in the Blue apartments on Queen. Kaylee stated he was older, in his 30s to 40s. Bethany stated Kaylee was looking at the sex offender registry within the week or so before the murders.

Bethany stated Kaylee was into crime shows. Bethany stated there was nothing that happened to prompt her to look up the sex offender registry.

I asked Bethany about the two other incidents where Kaylee had mentioned some weird things had happened. She told me about an incident at WinCo where a male had followed her around the store, watched her check out, and then followed her to her vehicle. Xana was waiting in the vehicle. Bethany stated Kaylee said the male was African American and in his late 20s. Bethany felt it happened sometime before Halloween, so mid to late October. Bethany stated Kaylee purchased a case of White Claws for Xana.

Bethany and her roommates had found the door open on November 4th at around 10:57, and they entered the house and grabbed golf clubs out of the west 1st floor bedroom. Bethany and the other roommates walked around the house with the golf clubs to check the house. Kaylee was not home for this incident as she had gone home for the weekend. Wind was blowing and the screws on the hinges were loose, and Xana's dad fixed it before he left that weekend.

Kaylee told everyone about an incident where she saw a male watching her when she had taken Murphy out back to go to the bathroom. Bethany could remember when this happened, but she could not provide an actual day. Bethany stated she had been at a chapter meeting at the time Kaylee called them, asking them if they were going to be home soon.

The following is a timeline of events of November 12, 2022, to November 13, 2022.

Bethany stated she was the last one in the house to wake

up, and when she got up, Ethan was in the house in the living room with Kaylee. Dylan, Maddie and Xana were all gone. Bethany felt she got up some time between 10:00 and 11:00 in the morning. Bethany stated she checked her Find My Friends app and saw they were at Taco Bell at the time. Once Dylan, Maddie, and Xana got back, they started getting ready for the day. Kaylee, Dylan, Maddie, and Bethany were in Kaylee's room, and they were getting ready for a party at 621 Taylor Street (The Whites). The house belonged to Bianca, Saylor and Kayla. The apartment is located on the second floor, on the far east side of the apartment building. Bethany stated this was between 11:00 to 12:00 in the afternoon. Bethany stated Kaylee left for The Whites before the rest of the group. Bethany stated she left at around 2:00 p.m. with Maddie, Dylan, Xana, Ethan, Hunter Johnson, Josie, Linden, Kai, Aly Benson and Sky Speck.

Bethany stated she started drinking at around 1130 or 1200 when still at 1122 King Road. She stated she was drinking Mimosas and High Noons throughout the night. Bethany also stated she also played a drinking game called Rage Cage later in the night. Bethany felt she drank a 12 pack of High Noons during the night, two Mimosas in a standard wine glass. Bethany was unsure of what she had been drinking when she played Rage Cage.

Bethany stated she was at the Whites up until around 1548 hours when she left with Xana. Maddie, Kaylee, and Dylan stayed at The Whites. Ethan had left before her and Xana. Bethany and Xana went to Aly Benson's place somewhere on Taylor. Bethany and Xana left there at around 1651 and went back to 1122 King Road. Bethany, Xana, Maddie, Kaylee, and

Dylan were all at the house and made food. Ethan was not at the house during this time. At around 1800 hours, Bethany, Xana, Maddie, Kaylee, and Dylan all went to take a nap, and they all set alarms for 2000 hours. Bethany got up at 2000 hours.

Once they all woke up, they got ready to go to the Sigma Chi's for a house party. Maddie and Bethany left first to go to Peter's apartment at Sigma Chi at around 2100 hours. Kaylee stayed home and was not going to go to the party at Sigma Chi. Ethan and Xana came over to the party after Bethany and Maddie. Dylan did not come with the rest and walked over at a later time. Maddie was not there for very long, and she went back to the house to go to the club with Kaylee. Bethany felt Maddie left some time after 2109 hours.

Bethany stated she walked home at around 0100 hours, and Dylan and Lakelynn McComas were the only ones at the house. Bethany, Dylan and Lakelynn were watching Vampire Diaries for a while and at around 0122 hours Lakelynn left. Dylan went to her room after Lakelynn left. At around 0200 hours Kaylee and Maddie came home. Maddie, Kaylee, Dylan, and Bethany went up to Kaylee's bedroom once they got home. Kaylee was getting ready for bed as they were hanging out in her room. Bethany, Maddie, and Dylan went downstairs, and Maddie and Bethany took Murphy outside to let him go to the bathroom. Bethany only stayed outside for a short time, and she then went back into the house and put something away in her cupboard and grabbed a bag of chips. Bethany went downstairs to go to bed.

Bethany stated nothing was unusual about Maddie and Bethany's [sic] demeanor when they got home. Bethany stated they both appeared to be happy. Bethany said Maddie was highly intoxicated and she had not seen her at that level of intoxication for a very long time.

Bethany said when she went to bed she was using her iPad to watch a TV show off of Hulu. Bethany said she was watching Baby Daddy. Bethany could not remember what episode she was watching or how long she was watching. As she was watching the show Maddie came downstairs and asked her if she had Murphy with her because she could not find him. Bethany told her no. Bethany said her door was locked and she normally locks her door when she goes to bed. Bethany told me she eventually turned off the show and her iPad and went to sleep.

Bethany said she woke up after falling asleep to hearing what she felt was a firecracker go off, and she thought she saw a sparkler going off through the crack under her door. Bethany stated she did not know what happened. Either Bethany called Dylan or Dylan called Bethany and Dylan stated she thought she had just seen someone dressed in all black in the house. Bethany said Xana had been wearing all black. Dylan responded by saying she thought he had a ski mask on. Bethany said she didn't really know what to say to what Dylan said. Bethany admitted both her and Dylan get scared easy. Bethany even thought maybe one of Ethan's frat brothers could have been playing a joke. Bethany told Dylan to come down to her room and Dylan ran down to her room.

Bethany tried calling Kaylee, Maddie, Xana, and Ethan's phones and nobody answered. Bethany said it was normal for Kaylee, Maddie, Xana, and Ethan not to answer if they were sleeping if she called late at night. Bethany looked at her phone, and it showed Bethany called Dylan at 0419 and at 0420 Dylan called Bethany back. During the call Bethany asked Dylan if she heard a firecracker and Dylan said she did. Bethany could not recall if it was during this call where Dylan was talking about seeing someone in black walking in the house.

Once Bethany and Dylan were in Bethany's room together they continued to talk about what they heard and saw. Bethany told me Dylan said the male in black was walking out the back door and they had made eye contact with each other. Bethany said Dylan said the male was white with a big nose and that he was possibly holding a small vacuum type object.

Bethany and Dylan did not call 911 at the time because Bethany thought Dylan was imagining what she was talking about. Bethany stated both her and Dylan were both still drunk and they were very groggy.

Bethany told me prior to hearing the firecracker she thought she heard Murphy bark. She also heard what she thought was the beer pong table moving and cups falling. The beer pong table was located in the living room which is above Bethany's bedroom. Bethany stated she was not sure what the sequence of events were for sure, but she knows she heard Murphy bark, the beer pong table, and then the firecracker first before she called Dylan to see if she had heard the same thing.

Bethany told me she tried calling Xana and Maddie at 0421 and then tried calling Ethan at 0422. Bethany stated she tried calling Maddie, Kaylee, and Xana several more times once Dylan got into her room.

Bethany told me when she went to bed she remembers most of the lights being left on inside the house.

Bethany told me after trying to contact the other roommates she fell back to sleep and then woke up at around 0730 and tried calling her dad about her tooth. Bethany called her dad again at 0800 but there was no answer, her house at 0801 with no answer, and then called her mom at 0802 and she answered and asked to talk with her dad. Her dad called back at 0809 and she talked to him and eventually took Advil for her tooth. Bethany then fell back to sleep. Bethany woke up at around 1100 hours and noticed no one else in the house was up. Bethany stated she knew this because Xana's Snapchat location was not on, and it should have been. Bethany and Dylan got scared because they should have been up. Bethany then called her friend Jenna and told her she and Dylan were scared and asked if she would come over and get them. Dylan then called Emily and asked her to come over. Dylan and Bethany knew Emily was with Hunter so they knew he would come over with her.

Hunter arrived at the house and came through the front door. Hunter went up the stairs first and when she and Dylan went up the stairs Hunter turned around and told Dylan and Bethany to get out of the house and to call for help. Bethany stated she could see Xana on the floor of her bedroom. Bethany said Xana was wearing underwear and a sweatshirt. Bethany stated the door was partially open but stated the door should normally be closed. Bethany called 911 and was trying to talk to the dispatcher but was having a hard time talking. Bethany had to give the phone to her friend Josie so she could talk to the dispatch.

I asked Bethany if she has ever seen Xana on the floor like she did that morning. Bethany told me she has never seen this

> but has heard Xana would pass out on the floor in the past when she is highly intoxicated. Bethany told me Hunter went back into the house. Bethany could not remember if Josie and Emily went into the house. Bethany told me she believed Hunter grabbed a knife from the kitchen when he went back into the house.
>
> Bethany stated the police arrived as she was still on the phone and disconnected with dispatch. Bethany did not provide any further information related to this incident.

It would be easy to imagine that among Bethany Funke's four statements to police, her November 16 recollections would be the most accurate. The Reno interview was conducted seven hundred miles from the crime scene, in the safety of a nonconfrontational setting, with assurances that she was nothing more than a witness. At that point in the investigation, events would still have been fresh in her mind, and she likely had the benefit of several nights' sleep. She would have received emotional support from friends and family, far from the press conferences and media frenzy descending on Moscow. She would have had the luxury of trying to make sense of things with friends like Hunter Johnson, Emily Alandt, and Linden Beck, refreshing her memory about what led up to and then followed the crimes. She would have spent a second night with Dylan, sharing a motel room once their house was sealed off by police. It did not hurt that she had an attorney who sat with her through every question.

Not only had a madman crept into her own house in the middle of the night to butcher four of her friends but he had also left her unharmed before escaping without a trace. Police had no suspect at that point, no motive, no leads, no real sense of what had happened. The community was scared, the campus had closed for Thanksgiving, the entire country was starting to respond with questions and dismay.

"From December 3, 2022, through January 23, 2023, I, Idaho State Police (ISP) Detective (Det.) Joe Lake had been communicating with surviving victim Bethany Funke's attorney Thomas Viloria, for Victimology Investigation needs about the quadruple murder on November 13, 2022, at 1122 King Road, Moscow, Latah County, Idaho," Detective Lake wrote.

His report of investigation, titled Supplemental 152, was filed February 23, 2023, approximately four months after the crimes. This was almost seven weeks after authorities held a press conference announcing the indictment and arrest of a Washington State PhD student in criminology.

> On December 20, 2022, national news outlets released arrest information and an image of suspect Bryan C. Kohberger. Also on December 30, 2022, Viloria sent Latah County Prosecuting Attorney (LCPA) Bill Thompson an email stating, "So glad an arrest was made. Bethany does not recognize the on-line photo of the person arrested and has never heard of him."

There is no way to tell if Detective Lake's two-month lag in contacting Funke suggests obfuscation, or if one more interview would have proven helpful. Bethany said she never saw or came into contact with the murderer, so it is understandable that she was not asked to view a photo spread of suspects. Lake did not explain, however, why a victimology team would have no further questions about the masked intruder Dylan saw leaving the house at 4:20 a.m., carrying a vacuum. The two women had spent eight hours locked in a room together, after all; perhaps they had discussed details that might help tie Kohberger to the victims.

If we go simply by Lake's report, he seemingly had no interest in Bethany's possible connections to Washington State, the town of Pullman, or any of Kohberger's known associates. He did not ask about a pool party where it was alleged that Kohberger might have interacted with one of the victims. Lake did not indicate why he accepted a two-sentence email from Funke's attorney without requesting face-to-face comment. He simply wrote:

> No additional information was required of Funke from the Victimology Team.

In the end, there's no way to know if a sit-down with Bethany might have helped answer unresolved questions. Once Blaker and When finished their interview on November 16, Bethany Funke appeared to never again meet with or be questioned by investigators until called to a grand jury. Her testimony there has been sealed and lies outside the reach of this author.

Regardless, what we do know, at this point, is that information Bethany Funke provided November 16 to Blaker and When was far more extensive than previously reported. We know that Funke's interview was recorded, burned to DVD, and entered into evidence. We know that during more than two hours of conversation, she offered critically important details that appear not to have been adequately probed, understood, or even mentioned by police. Fortunately, we now have the recordings and transcripts. It is time to look back on what detectives might have missed.

•

"So, just real quick, just so I can say on this recording who is all here," Blaker says in his opening statement. He sounds casual for a homicide detective; this is clearly not an interrogation. "So, myself, Sergeant Blaker with the Moscow Police Department and then I have . . ."

"Sergeant Matthew When."

"With the Nevada . . ."

"Uh, it's technically now the Nevada State Police Investigation Division," When clarifies. "Commonly and affectionately referred to as NDI, so . . ."

"Then Bethany Funke?"

•

He pronounces it "funky," but Bethany corrects him.

•

"Foonka."

"Foonka, sorry about that."

"That's okay."

"Here, with me, is her attorney Tom Veelora?"

"Viloria," the lawyer says. "Yeah, we're at 327, uh California Avenue, Reno, and the transcriber at the time is approximately 11:55."

•

This interview begins so casually, it sounds like a coffee shop chat.

•

"So, there's a lot of different types of questions I'm going to be asking today," Blaker says. "I'm not here just to go back through another timeline again."

"Mm-hmm," Bethany agrees.

"Based on our investigation, we now have some other things that we kinda want to get some information on? And we're hoping that is something you can provide to us. Okay? So, I'm actually gonna start with those questions first, and then at the end we're gonna go back over your timeline a little bit better, okay?"

"Uh-huh," Bethany says. Then Detective Blaker launches into more than ninety minutes of what I view as largely inane softballs about everything except the murders.

•

He asks about the day-to-day routines of the house. He establishes that Bethany moved in at the beginning of the school year, that Ethan often stayed with Xana but lived alone near a 76 gas station at the other end of town. He asks about Eric the Uber driver, boyfriends and love interests, and then several people by name, including Jack Showalter, Ethan Runge, Connor Chesnut, Cole Barenberg, and Christian Gonsales, "whose name just came up."

At the thirty-two-minute mark, Blaker establishes that Maddie and Xana worked at the Mad Greek. Forty-four minutes into the interview, he asks about neighborhood sex offenders. After almost two hours, the questioning finally turns to events leading up to the murders.

Baby Daddy, High Noons, Firework

•

"Do you have any idea," Deyective When interjects at the 1:43 mark on the tape, "thinking a little bit more, based on what you know is in your house, what that firecracker could have been, that firecracker sound and the sparkler could have been?"

•

As a Nevada State Police detective with no specific jurisdiction, he has acted as a silent observer throughout most of the interview, but he's finally had enough. Details about what Bethany heard and saw that morning remain a mystery to this day, and like everyone else, When wants answers. Once he gets involved, the inquiry turns logical, incisive, and pertinent.

•

"I really have no idea," Bethany tells him. "I have no idea where it came from or, like, what it could have been."

"Well, in addition, you told him you heard the pong table slide on the floor like someone had bumped into it."

"Mm-hmm," Bethany agrees. "Or the cups fall or something."

"You heard what?"

"Either cups fall off of it, or like the table move to the side."

"Is that right over your room?" Blaker asks.

"Yeah."

"Do you remember what position the beer pong table was in before you went to bed?"

"Either it was just like that . . . like straight," Bethany explains.

•

It sounds like she's demonstrating with her hands.

•

"Coming from . . . ?" When asks.

"Uh, the kitchen," Bethany says. "It's like right in front of it."

"So, not off to the side a little bit?" When asks. "A little bit like that?"

"Uh-uh, not unless someone moved it to get past it or something."

"Was it normally in that same position?"

"Yeah."

"So, if I were to walk from your kitchen and Dylan's area of the house, there's the step up."

"Uh-huh."

"And I walk into the living room area, it's gonna be literally right in front of me? So kinda centered in the door?"

"Pretty much? Or like a little to the side of the door? So, some people can get through, but . . ."

"To the right or to the left?"

"The right."

"So, it would be pushed to the right?"

"It would be pushed to the left, like toward the wall."

"Okay, so where that little nightstand is?"

•

Blaker is referring to the brass console, but he's probing a wider issue. If the killer was chasing Xana from the kitchen to her bedroom, attacking her with a knife as the forensics prove, how did two wildly animated adults navigate the six-inch step and a six-foot table? How did the deadly attack rage through the living room, violently transferring blood from Maddie, Kaylee, and Xana to the walls without disturbing a lightweight plastic table blocking the only imaginable path? It's an obvious question no one else had asked.

•

"Yeah."

"Okay," Blaker says. "'Cause it wasn't straight when they found it. It was kinda crooked a little bit, so what you're saying makes sense to me now."

•

This does not appear to be correct. The table was aligned in Nunes's body cam video. Blaker must have seen it during Talbott's search when the table was moved slightly so detectives could move past it.

•

"Mm-hmm . . ."

"So . . ." When jumps in. "I'm not familiar with the house. So, your room is on the bottom floor. So, is there a set of steps? A half set of steps?"

"There's a full set of steps."

"So, like twelve steps? Ish?"

"Fourteen," Blaker tells him.

"Yeah, something like that, I don't know."

"And when you get to the bottom of the steps, where is your room? If I was walking . . . ?"

"Um, there's one room straight across, but no one lives in there. There's a bathroom right next to it and if you go down the little hallway, that's my room."

"So, like for something to be like reflecting underneath your door, you'd have to have something basically down in that hallway," Blaker clarifies.

"Yeah, that's what it would seem like to me, the [unintelligible] or something, I couldn't tell what it was."

•

At that point, the questioning veers off on tangents about where visitors might have placed their beer cans and about unresolved stains on the floor. Bethany is asked about lighting but doesn't remember details. She answers a few questions about her walk home, stating that she saw no unusual cars, that she walked in through the front door. It was cold and foggy.

•

"She just told me she thought it was a mini vacuum," Bethany responds when asked what Dylan told her about the intruder and the object he was carrying. "She said it was like something wrapped around or something? And then a mini vacuum?"

"So, something wrapped around his waist?"

"I don't know," she says. "Yeah."

When asked about what first alarmed her, prompting calls to friends, then 911, Bethany seems uncertain. She says she did not go upstairs to check on her housemates but did in fact call their phones.

"We were kinda freaking out because we were like, they would have been up by now. And then I called my friend Jenna and told her we were like scared and didn't know what was happening, and so she offered to come get us. And then we called Emily 'cause we knew that Hunter was with her, and he would come over and like help look around the house."

•

No one asks why she suddenly felt scared, so long after Dylan showed up in her room.

•

"The only last question I have," Blaker says just before ending the interview. "Are you still communicating with Kaylee, er, um, Dylan?"

"Yeah, a little."

"Do you know why she's very hesitant to talk to me right now?"

"Mm-mmm," Bethany responds. Meaning no.

•

Blaker does not ask Bethany why she arrived with a lawyer of her own, though she had never been mentioned as a person of interest. And though we will return to details of this interview later, one other thing bears mention. When asked about electronic devices the roommates might have used in the house, Bethany said Dylan owned and used an Alexa. She kept it in her room, next to her bed.

Those who think police might have seized on this as a potentially valuable lead would be mistaken. Neither Blaker nor anyone else has ever expressed any interest in the device or speculated that due to its location, it might have recorded the whole thing.

Based on recordings and reports, it appears that police never asked Dylan about the Alexa or where she kept it. A review of body camera footage, photographs, search warrant inventories, and dozens of interviews discloses no evidence of the device.

If there was an Alexa in Dylan's room at the time of the crimes, no record of it or the data it captured has been found.

CHAPTER 9

Mad Greek, Tree House, Interview Jazz

Of all the reference tools available to a major case detective, timeline might be the most underrated. While lab reports, profiles, and forensic analyses receive overwhelming attention, a timeline forms the backbone of the investigation, helping police build a living, breathing history of events. In most instances, it is a formal document that evolves organically as police set leads and document their findings. In complex, multiyear investigations, it serves as a central clearinghouse of information as the body of evidence grows.

The matter of *State of Idaho v. Bryan C. Kohberger* is no exception. By the time Bill Thompson was ready to go to trial, police had turned Officer Nunes's initial report into a 108-page spreadsheet composed of well over a thousand individual cells. Each entry listed date, time, the nature of the event, and the source from which the information was derived. It proved invaluable, not just to police, but to Thompson's team of prosecutors as they lined up their arguments, exhibits, witnesses, and presentations. Almost as important, it now provides websleuths and authors a road map of where authorities got things right and where they may have gone so badly wrong.

Though comprehensive in scope, not everything in the MPD report makes sense. The very first entry, for example, states that Bryan Kohberger replaced the battery in his Hyundai Elantra in July 2020, more than two years before the crimes. The next shows him replacing his brake pads, two days later, at a place called Colonial Auto, near his parents' home in Pennsylvania. Those wondering what this might have to do with four murders two years later in Idaho will note that it wasn't until December 9 of that year that he even submitted an application to Washington State University. If police were looking for early signs of premeditation, that seems like a bit of a stretch.

There is no question, however, that investigators took great interest in the months and years leading up to Kohberger's matriculation west. They recorded his purchase of an Amazon gift card on March 20, 2022, for example, and that someone used it one day later to order a KA-BAR knife and sheath that was delivered to his parents' home in Albrightsville. They do not explain why they assumed this is the same knife sheath found, in pristine condition, 2,560 miles away, partially lodged under Maddie Mogen's thigh. It was not until a week after the KA-BAR purchase that Kohberger even received an admission certificate from Washington State University. Only then did he receive a funding package through the spring of 2023, securing enrollment as a PhD student in criminology.

Beyond these examples, Bill Thompson's timeline is painstakingly thorough. Police focused on Kohberger's day-to-day life, everything from coffee purchases at Starbucks to shopping sprees at Marshalls, Ross Dress for Less, Crimson & Gray (a WSU school store), Dick's Sporting Goods, Macy's, and Big 5. They recorded the purchase of a toilet brush, nitrile gloves, and a Swiffer WetJet at Walmart, haircuts at Powers Barbershop, an "SW Plastic M" he bought at Target. They recorded where and when he watched TV, the exact time he photographed a bulletin board at WSU, dates he explored "the Palouse" and Wawawai County Park, the very moment AT&T activated the plan for his new cell phone.

But the timeline was not just focused on the suspected killer. They documented other aspects of the crimes like search warrant applications, laboratory submissions, surveillance activities, witness interviews, and selfie and social media posts of people who had nothing to do with the crimes, right alongside specific references to matters of interagency cooperation. Their timeline built a two-year prologue to the murders, followed by hundreds of entries immediately surrounding the crimes, then hundreds more documenting the fourteen months leading up to what was supposed to be the trial. It references family members, Greek affiliations, lovers and friends, persons of interest, relevant tips, and other consequential events. It catalogs work histories, text chains, biometric collection regimens, personal interactions between the victims, and a broad array of associates. It is as varied as it is comprehensive.

Which, of course, makes perfect sense. It would have been challenging for Bill Thompson's office to maintain focus in such a highly sensationalized case, especially as voracious media built their own narrative. It was not enough for prosecutors to lay out forensic evidence based on laboratory analysis and expert opinion; they needed to understand the larger universe of factors coming into play that horrible night, a meticulous inventory of events leading up to the crimes. They needed to document the lives of the victims, the movements of any possible suspects, a sense that there might have been some rhyme or reason to what appeared to be senseless crimes. Once Kohberger was indicted, they needed to build a portrait of the murderer himself—matching his life as a former police cadet and PhD student in criminology with four vicious murders. That would not be easy; this was by no means an open-and-shut case.

Oddly enough, the timeline was just as valuable to the defense. Anne Taylor's office used it to map potential police missteps and poke holes in their investigation. We know, for example, that Bicka Barlow, her genealogy expert, felt confident that DNA found on the knife sheath was shaky at best. Even after Judge Hippler ruled against important motions, the defense still had laboratory reports that appeared to show the FBI committed significant violations of their own protocols in arriving at conclusions. According to reports, the sample taken from the sheath snap seems barely 20 percent of the CODIS minimum for Y-STR submission, and FBI HQ deliberately made the decision to access databases that had always been off-limits to the police. During a highly contentious legal process called a Franks hearing, Anne Taylor's team revealed that a private Texas laboratory had been hired and then fired by police due to genetic analysis that did not match Thompson's narrative. Video surveillance of Kohberger's white Elantra was shaky at best; defense experts were ready to testify that cell tower analysis was riddled with bad math and technology claims that would have been countered at trial.

Thompson disagreed, of course, telling anyone who would listen that the evidence was overwhelming. But trial prep is at least partially theater, and confidence is just part of the show. No matter how strong their case, experienced lawyers know that juries are a fickle beast. No matter what an expert like Paulette Sutton claimed about blood spatter, jurors want to look across the courtroom and decide for themselves whether the man in the dock could have done what he is accused of. They want to know where he grew up, where he went to school, how he spends his time, why he shows no emotion at all when presented with gruesome details about unspeakable crimes.

Jurors would want to know why a person who looks as creepy as Bryan Kohberger would have lived twenty-seven years at home with his parents before driving cross-country to pursue a PhD studying serial killers. They would wonder what made them feel so uneasy in his presence, ask themselves who in their right mind would turn off their phone in the middle of the night while driving around looking up at stars. They would want to know why this particular man chose that particular morning to sneak into a strange house and butcher four kids he had never even met.

While proof beyond a reasonable doubt usually comes down to hard evidence, the real challenge for the prosecutors is to answer these questions by building a larger picture of what the forensics fail to show. Though we will return to Kohberger in following chapters, it is essential to look at the timeline as a map of how the State of Idaho built its case.

There is no need to summarize; they have done that for us.

In November 2023, investigators with the Moscow Police Department and the Idaho State Police produced a formal timeline for the Latah County Prosecuting Attorney's office. Presented in spreadsheet format, this document provides detailed and insightful glimpses into the crimes themselves, as well as all the people involved. Anyone trying to make sense of information disclosed to the defense would do well to start with an understanding of how police lined things up. Transcribed here is their timeline.

Date	Time	Description of Event	Source
11/11/2022		Formal ball at Pi Phi Sorority–Kaylee was Dylan's date to the ball. Xana and Ethan attended too. They return home around 8:30 p.m. by Uber. They had a party at 1122 King after the Ball until early 11/12	Mortensen Interview 11/17/22
11/12/2022	1100–1200	Bethany wakes up. Only Ethan at the house. Other roommates at Taco Bell return shortly	Bethany Funke Interview 11/16/22
11/12/2022	1100	Chesnut wakes up at his Fraternity in his room–Per Chesnut	O'Neil Supp Report 11/21/22
11/12/2022	1200–1300	Hunter at 1122 King "pregaming" for football game	Mowery #42
11/12/2022	1221	Madison takes a Lyft unknown locations. 20 minute ride	Lyft Receipt

Date	Time	Description of Event	Source
11/12/2022	1254	Dylan sends Madison, Kaylee, and Josie an Instagram Message	Mortensen cell pg 3055–3056
11/12/2022	1430–1500	Kaylee and roommates arrive at Kayla Nguyen's apartment 621 Taylor Street "bucks for all of what I owe you."	Rosinsky Supp 19
11/12/2022	1400	Bethany leaves with Maddie, Dylan, Xana, Ethan, Hunter Johnson, Josie, Lynden, Kai, Aly Benson and Sky Speck to 621 Taylor Street Apartment. Kaylee had previously left before them (Nguyen says they left at 1700–1800Hrs - Rosinsky Supp19) (Hunter says they left at 1430–Mowery 42)	Bethany Funke– Interview 11/16
11/12/2022	1430	Showalter and Chesnut at party at the Whites - Per Showalter Chesnut says this occurs from 1300–1400 Per Chesnut in O'Neil Supp Report	Supp Report 37
11/12/2022	1430–1500	Kaylee and all her roommates arrive at Kayla Nguyen's house. They take a picture there. (Kayla lists this as 11/13 in Rosinsky's report but must be typo)	Rosinsky's report
11/12/2022	1512	Dylan sends Josie an Instagram Message	Mortensen Phone report pg 3075

(continued)

Date	Time	Description of Event	Source
11/12/2022	1548	Bethany and Xana leave the party at the Whites. Ethan had left before them. Everyone else was still there. Bethany and Xana go to Aly Benson's house on Taylor Ave	Bethany Interview 11/16
11/12/2022	1616	Showalter at his apartment to stretch his back and ibuprofen. Chesnut at the Whites still. Mention of going to get food	Text messages between Chesnut and Showalter.
11/12/2022	1651	Bethany and Xana leave Aly Benson's and return to King Rd. Bethany, Xana, Maddie, Kaylee, and Dylan made food.	Bethany Interview 11/16
11/12/2022	1650	Maddie sends an Instagram Message to Dylan, Kaylee, Xana, Bethany	Mortensen Phone report pg 3077
11/12/2022	1700–1730	Chesnut passes out in his room and Showalter returns home - Per Chesnut. (This is inconsistent with the timestamp on Tallman's phone, indicating Showalter is requesting a ride from Delt at 1930)	O'Neil Supp Report
11/12/2022	1703	"Erika" sends Ethan a message saying "ur getting cheated on"	Work Product
11/12/2022	1732	Xana texts Ethan saying she is taking a nap until 8	Ethan phone timeline page 73

Date	Time	Description of Event	Source
11/12/2022	1736	Dylan receives a phone call from Bethany. Call length 00:00:12	Mortensen Phone report pg 3079
11/12/2022	1744	Dylan calls and has a 00:03:51 phone call. Number returns to a Natalie Dayton per TLO	Mortensen phone report pg 3080
11/12/2022	1800–2000	Bethany, Maddie, Xana, Dylan all napped at King House. (Dylan says from 1700–2000)	Mortensen Int 11/17/22
11/12/2022	1919	Explorer leaves the King house	Ford Explorer logs pg 2453
11/12/2022	1926	Explorer arrives at Kappa Alpha Theta house Per Maizie - Formal event at "Hunga Dunga" Ethan, Maizie, Hunter Chapin, Regan Stancil, Darius Meyers, Hannah Beihn, Jack Katavick and Riley Black attended together and rode in their car.	Ford Explorer logs pg 3228 Per Maizie Chapin Vargas Supp #69
11/12/2022	1959	Explorer leaves Kappa Alpha Theta	Ford Explorer Logs pg 3228
11/12/2022	2004	Dylan calls Maddie who doesn't answer. She responds with a message "Can I call you later?" Dylan says "Yes we J called u to wake up and come down"	Dylan cell records 3084

(continued)

Date	Time	Description of Event	Source
11/12/2022	2006	Ethan, Maizie, Hunter Chapin, Regan Stancil, Darius Meyers, Hannah Beihn, Jack Katavick and Riley Black arrive at Hunga Dunga	Per Maizie Chapin–
11/12/2022	2007	Ethan tells Xana he is going to her house to change	Ethan cell page 87
11/12/2022	2040	Kaylee texts Eric and asks if he is working tonight	Gower Interview Blaker
11/12/2022	2057	Kaylee posts picture on Instagram, sends to Xana	Xana Cell Phone Pg 2952
11/12/2022	2057	Kaylee sends Dylan an Instagram Message	Dylan cell pg 3088
11/12/2022	2058	Dylan sends Kaylee an instant message and says "can u send me those photos pllsss"	Dylan Phone Records Pg 3088
11/12/2022	2059	Maddie calls Xana	Xana Cell Pg 2952
11/12/2022	2100	Maddie and Bethany Leave King house to go to Peter's apartment at Sigma Chi. Ethan and Xana came over after Bethany and Maddie. Kaylee was not going to the Sigma Chi party. Dylan walked to the party alone later.	Bethany Interview 11/16
11/12/2022	2102	Ethan, Maizie, Hunter Chapin, Regan Stancil, Darius Meyers, Hannah Beihn, Jack Katavick and Riley Black leave Hunga Dunga	Per Maizie Chapin– Vargas Supp #69

Date	Time	Description of Event	Source
11/12/2022	2106	Ethan, Maizie, Hunter Chapin, Regan Stancil, Darius Meyers, Hannah Beihn, Jack Katavick and Riley Black arrive at Kappa Alpha Theta	Ford Explorer Logs pg 2530, 3240
11/12/2022	2109	Maddie leaves Sigma Chi party to meet Kaylee and go to the Club.	Bethany Interview 11/16
11/12/22	2108–2110	Dylan takes 12 photos	Dylan cell pg 3082
11/12/22	2118	Dylan calls Maddie 00:00:14	Dylan Phone Records Pg 3093
11/12/2022	2121	Explorer (believed to be driven by Ethan) leaves Kappa Alpha Theta. Maizie does not go with the rest of the group. She remains at Kappa Alpha Theta	Ford Explorer Logs pg 2530 Maizie Chapin interview by Vargas Supp #69
11/12/2022	2124	Explorer (believed to be driven by Ethan) stops at Sigma Chi	Ford Explorer Logs pg 3274
11/12/2022	2125	Explorer (believed to be driven by Ethan) leaves Sigma Chi	Ford Explorer Logs pg 3276
11/12/2022	2127	Explorer (believed to be driven by Ethan) arrives at 1122 King	Ford Explorer Logs pg 2482, 2537

(continued)

Date	Time	Description of Event	Source
11/12/2022	2131	Dylan calls Xana 00:00:18	Xana Cell Pg 2953
11/12/2022	2139	Ethan receives Notification - Cougar Den - Dylan, Maddie, and Bethany enter new chats. Bethany adds Ethan to the Group	Work Product
11/12/2022	2126	Ethan sends Hunter Johnson a Snap Message - Drinking w Xana and Bethany. Come Hang With	Ethan Snap Messages
11/12/2022	2230–2300	Josephine Tourville sees Maddie and Kaylee at the Corner Club	Pesina Supp #11
11/12/2022	2200–2215	Maddie and Kaylee arrive at Corner Club in a Prius type vehicle with another unidentified female. (Dylan says Kaylee was at the house with a female friend (Riley Moreland) at 2230 when she left - Gooch Supp 0003) They were driven by Eric Gower.	Blaker Supp #108 Gower Text Messages–5930–5933
11/12/2022	2200	Bethany's friend Yesi arrives at Sigma Chi party and hangs out with her.	Bethany Interview 11/16
11/12/2022	2208	Bethany calls Claire - no answer	Bethany cell pg 54
11/12/2022	2230	Chesnut wakes up and plays games in his room the rest of the night–Per Chesnut	O'Neil Report 11/21/22

Date	Time	Description of Event	Source
11/12/2022	2230	Dylan arrives at Sigma Chi apt 4–Ethan, Hunter, Xana, Yessi, Gideon were there. Dylan and Gideon were in and out of the lodge before going to Peter's apartment.	Mortensen Interview–Gooch 11/17/22
11/12/2022	2230–2245	Bethany and Yesi go to the main house for Sigma Chi Fraternity.	Bethany Interview 11/16
11/12/2022	2234	Kohberger in store purchase at Walmart in Pullman; Bounty Napkins, Toilet Paper, Grocery	Receipt in Evidence
11/12/2022	2244	Kohberger in store purchase at Safeway in Pullman; Grocery Items	Receipt from Apartment
11/12/2022	2314	Bethany sends Maddie a snapchat. Unknown contents	Photo 132
11/12/2022	2321	Maddie and Cole Barenberg take a photo together at Corner Club–sent with a text to Leo Romero	Hoxie Supp 0002
11/12/2022	2404	Dylan sees Xana for the last time at Aly's. Xana is holding a White Claw	Mortensen Int 11/17/22
11/12/2022	2421	Ethan receives a Text from Hunter J - "Are you guys still at sig chi"	Ethan's cell phone timeline page 104
11/12/2022	2440	Maddie facetime with Ruby Simpson for 40 seconds while at the Corner Bar with friend Ayden	Beckner Supp 14

(continued)

Date	Time	Description of Event	Source
11/12/2022	2443	Ethan texts "yup" when responding to Hunter J asking if he is still at Sigma Chi	Ethan Cell phone timeline page 105
11/13/2022	0003	Bethany takes photos unk location at a party of a girl	Bethany cell pg 214
11/13/2022	0004	Dylan takes a photo IMG_4971	Dylan cell Pg 3098
11/13/2022	0016	Xana calls Ethan - unanswered Ethan misses a call from "Lil Noodle" Xana	Ethan cell pg 108
11/13/2022	0017	Bethany sees Ethan and Xana in Peter's apartment before leaving. Bethany and Yesi walk to Aly's house on Taylor where Aly, Jenna, Hayden, Kennedy, and Yesi were the only people at the house.	Bethany Interview 11/16
11/13/2022	0020	text from Xana to "Pistol Pete" "you good?"	Xana Cell Pg 2956
11/13/2022	0022	Kaylee pays bar tab at Corner Club with her credit card. She paid for 9 well vodka and 2 add juice	Lanier Supp #13
11/13/2022	0031	Bethany calls Jenna McClure on Facetime and has a 00:22 call	Bethany cell pg 54
11/13/2022	0031	White / light colored sedan e/b on Lauder passing Ridge Rd.	1125 Ridge Rd video
11/13/2022	0043	Ethan receives notification from "Erika" ur getting cheated on	Work Product

Date	Time	Description of Event	Source
11/13/2022	0056	White / light colored sedan w/b on Lauder passing Ridge Rd.	1125 Ridge Rd video
11/13/2022	0100	Chesnut goes to sleep alone in his room–Per Chesnut	O'Neil Report 11/21/22
11/13/2022	0100	Cole Barenberg walks home from Corner Club.	Hoxie Supp 0002
11/13/2022	0115–0130	Dylan calls a SoBro for a ride for her and Lake because Lake is very intoxicated. They go back to 1122 King- and watch Vampire Diary	Mortensen Int 11/17/22
11/13/2022	0100	Bethany walks home from Aly's house on Taylor. (Time confirmed by Jenna McClure) When she gets there only Dylan and Lakelynn McComas were at the house. They watched Vampire Diaries	Bethany Interview 11/16
11/13/2022	0100	Kaylee engages in conversation with John "Jack" Showalter	Lanier Supp #13 Corner Club Video
11/13/2022	0114	Maddie joins conversation with Kaylee and Showalter at Corner Club	Corner Club Video
11/13/2022	0116	Xana calls Ethan–not answered	Xana Cell pg 2954
11/13/2022	0122	Lakelynn McComas leaves the house. Dylan goes to her room.	Bethany Int 11/16

(continued)

Date	Time	Description of Event	Source
11/13/2022	0122	Kaylee sends a picture of her and Maddie at the Corner Club and says "Maddie just called me a buck tooth bitch" to Dylan, Bethany, Xana, Ethan	Snapchat Message
11/13/2022	0137	Showalter, Kaylee, Maddie leave Corner Club across the parking lot in the westerly direction.	Lanier Supp #13 Corner Club video
11/13/2022	0138	Picture taken from Xana's phone	Xana cell phone records 2957
11/13/2022	0142	Kaylee purchases Mac of the Week from Wondering Kitchen. Showalter is with them as seen in video	Receipt for purchase
11/13/2022	0145	Kaylee texts Gower and asks if he can pick her and some friends up from Grub Truck	Gower Text Messages 5930–5933
11/13/2022	0149	Peyton Rossi goes to Corner Club to pick up Jack Granger, Jack Ducouer, and Nathan Rios and drop them off at their apartment off of King Road. Peyton went home after dropping them off.	Rosinsky Report–interview with Peyton Rossi
11/13/2022	0149	Eric Gower arrives at Grub truck to pick up Kaylee and Maddie. They were dropped off at 1122 King Rd after the 3–4 min drive.	Blaker Supp #113 Gower Interview AV000090

Date	Time	Description of Event	Source
11/13/2022	0151	Jack Ducoeur leaves Corner Club	Lanier Supp #13 Corner Club Video
11/13/2022	0154	Bethany calls Maddie - no answer	Bethany Phone timeline page 54
11/13/2022	0155	Bethany sends photo with message "Get me some Mac" to Xana, Ethan, Dylan, Kaylee and Maddie.	Ethan Snapchat Messages
11/13/2022	0200	Kaylee and Maddie arrive home. Girls all go upstairs while Kaylee is getting ready for bed. Taking Selfie videos. Maddie and Bethany take Murphy outside. Bethany comes back in after a few minutes, grabs chips and goes down to bed.	Bethany Interview 11/16
11/13/2022	0200	Xana takes a picture with Jaclyn Belliveau. Jaclyn leaves Sigma Chi and Xana and Ethan stay	Beckner Supp 10
11/13/2022	0201	Cooper Atkinson attempts to call Ethan five times on Facetime.	Work Product
11/13/2022	0202	Bethany takes several pictures with Murphy in Kaylee's bed	Bethany cell pg 212
11/13/2022	0210	Dylan sends message to Eric Uber "R u driving tonight by chance" Mortensen tells Gooch this is at 3:10am in 11/17/22 interview	Dylan cell pg 3121

(continued)

Date	Time	Description of Event	Source
11/13/2022	0213	Dylan receives text from Eric Uber "I am" Dylan tells Gooch this is at 3:13am in her 11/17 interview. She says she goes to bed sometime after this but unsure when. Says she is the first of the roommates to go to bed.	Dylan cell pg 3122 Mortensen Interview
11/13/2022	0215	Door Dash Jack N the Box ordered by Xana	Xana Cell pg 2958
11/13/2022	0216	White / light colored sedan turning left from w/b Lauder to Ridge Rd.	1125 Ridge Rd video
11/13/2022	0216	Calling for Murphy and whistling can be heard on 1112 King recording	1112 King Video
11/13/2022	0217	Barking can be heard on 1112 King recording	1112 King Video
11/13/2022	0222	Light colored sedan w/b on Lauder passing Ridge Rd.	1125 Ridge Rd video
11/13/2022	0226	Jack D. Calls Kaylee they talk for 17:04 minutes	Jack's Cell Data
11/13/2022	0243	Kaylee Calls Jack - Not answered	Jack's Cell Data
11/13/2022	0244	Kaylee Calls Jack - Not answered	Jack's Cell Data
11/13/2022	0244	Kaylee Facetime Calls Jack - Not answered	Jack's Cell Data
11/13/2022	0247	Kaylee Calls Jack - Not answered	Jack's Cell Data

Date	Time	Description of Event	Source
11/13/2022	0247	Kaylee Facetime Calls Jack - Not answered	Jack's Cell Data
11/13/2022	0250	Maddie Calls Jack D. - Not answered	Jack's Cell Data
11/13/2022	0251	Maddie Calls Jack D. - Not answered	Jack's Cell Data
11/13/2022	0251	Maddie Calls Jack D. - Not answered	Jack's Cell Data
11/13/2022	0252	Maddie calls Xana–no answer	Xana Cell pg 2958
11/13/2022	0253	White vehicle traveling SE on Nevada in Pullman WA towards SR 270	Payne Supp #136
11/13/2022	0253	Kaylee Calls Jack - Not answered	Jack's Cell Data
11/13/2022	0253	Kaylee Calls Jack - Not answered	Jack's Cell Data
11/13/2022	0253	Maddie calls Bethany - Not answered	Bethany Cell pg 54
11/13/2022	0231	Bethany active on phone	BF Phone Records
11/13/2022	0325	White Sedan seen traveling WB 787 block of Indian Hills Drive in Moscow Idaho	Vargas Supp Payne Supp #136
11/13/2022	0328	White Sedan seen WB on Styner at Highway 95. Crossing South Main Street from Styner to Lauder Ave	Payne Supp #136

(continued)

Date	Time	Description of Event	Source
11/13/2022	0329	White / light colored sedan w/b on Lauder passing Ridge Rd.	1125 Ridge Rd video
11/13/2022	0351	Dylan creates phone contact for Brittany Fernande	Dylan Phone records pg 3123
11/13/2022	0351	Emily Alandt Venmos Xana $14	BB Card for Emily
11/13/2022	0354	Xana text message to Door Dash - "Are you having trouble finding it?"	Door Dash Records
11/13/2022	0356	Vehicle seen on video from 1112 King Road recording	Mowery #28
11/13/2022	0359	Door Dash Delivery by McMichael	Xana's cell Report
11/13/2022	0400–0420	Dylan hears Kaylee singing and playing music and walking on the stairs. She hears Kaylee say someone is here, sounding frantic.	Mortensen Interview 11/17/22
11/13/2022	0401	White / light colored sedan turns right on Ridge Rd. from e/b Lauder	1125 Ridge Rd video
11/13/2022	0404	White vehicle seen traveling EB King Rd, stopping and turning around in front of 500 Queen #52, then driving back WB on King; attempts to park or turn around in the road, continues to intersection of Queen and King where it completes a 3 point turn, driving EB on Queen Rd.	Payne Supp #136

Date	Time	Description of Event	Source
11/13/2022	0412	Xana still active on TikTok	Xana Cell pg 2965
11/13/2022		Dylan opens her door 1st time–sees no one	Mortensen 11/17/22
11/13/2022		Dylan opens her door 2nd time–thinks she hears Kaylee crying in the bathroom and a male in the bathroom with her say it's okay I'm going to help you. Now thinks it may have been Xana in the bathroom.	Mortensen Int 11/17/22
11/13/2022		Dylan opens her door 3rd time–sees someone dressed in all black, masked holding an item like a vacuum, they were at least 3 in taller than she is. They were approx. 3 feet away from her walking out the back slide door. He looked at her before walking out.	Mortensen Int 11/17/22
11/13/2023	0424	Bethany text to Dylan "so am I"	DM cell pg 3126
11/13/2022	0424	Dylan text to Bethany "My phone is going to die fuck"	DM cell pg 3126
11/13/2022	0424	Bethany text to Dylan "Come to my room" "Run" "Down here"	DM cell pg 3127
11/13/2022	0424	Dylan snapchat call to Ethan 00:12	DM cell pg 3127

(continued)

Date	Time	Description of Event	Source
11/13/2022	0424	Dylan text Bethany "I'm screwd tho"	DM cell pg 3127
11/13/2023	0425	Bethany text Dylan "Ya Ik but its better than being alone"	DM cell pg 3128
11/13/2023	0427	Dylan opens her door a 4th time and before going down to Bethany's room. Dylan sees Xana on the floor in her underwear in her room but doesn't go in.	Mortensen Int 11/17/22
11/13/2023	0427	Dylan calls Kaylee	Dylan cell pg 3128
11/13/2023	0428	Dylan sees a dark colored truck drive by when she gets down to Bethany's room	Mortensen's 2nd Interview.
11/13/2022	0428	Dylan calls Xana	Xana Cell pg 2965
11/13/2022	0430	Bethany calls Madison	Nunes Report
11/13/2022	0431	Bethany calls Kaylee	Nunes Report
11/13/2022	0432	Dylan message to Kaylee "Pls answer"	Dylan pg 3128
11/13/2022	0445	Neighbor Brayden Pollow at 1127 King Rd #3, hears dog stop barking, sounds like someone let him inside	Snyder Report
11/13/2022	0500	Activity Sensor data reports Dylan distance traveled 30.77	Dylan cell pg 3129
11/13/2023	0525	White vehicle traveling NB Johnson Rd. Then N on Bishop Blvd and NW on SR 270	Payne #136 Grand Jury Exhibit 54b

Date	Time	Description of Event	Source
11/13/2023	0527	White vehicle seen NB on Stadium Way at Nevada Street, Stadium Way at Grimes Way, Stadium Drive at Wilson Rd and Stadium Way at Cougar Way.	Payne Supp #136
11/13/2022	0730	Bethany wakes up and tries calling her dad about her tooth. He didn't answer.	Bethany's Interview 11/16
11/13/2022	0800	Activity Sensor data reports Dylan distance traveled 3.52	Dylan cell pg 3129
11/13/2022	0800	Bethany tries calling her dad again, no answer.	Bethany's Interview 11/16
11/13/2022	0801	Bethany tries calling her house no answer	Bethany's Interview 11/16
11/13/2022	0802	Bethany calls her mom and says she needs to talk to her dad	Bethany's Interview 11/16
11/13/2022	0809	Bethany talks to her dad, takes an Advil and falls back to sleep	Bethany's Interview 11/16
11/13/2022	0900	Activity Sensor data reports Dylan distance traveled 3.52	Dylan cell pg 3130
11/13/22	0912	PER LAW ENFORCEMENT– Kohberger's phone pings in the area of S Highway 95 in Moscow, ID. A car matching the description of Kohberger's is seen on surveillance camera from 1311 S. Main St., Moscow, ID	FBI Report

(continued)

Date	Time	Description of Event	Source
11/13/2022	1000–1001	Dylan sends 7 outgoing messages via snapchat and receives 2 incoming. Content of message unknown	Dylan Phone Records pg 3131
11/13/2022	1000	Showalter wakes up to watch NFL	Millar Supp Report
11/13/2022	1003	Dylan accessing indeed site on her phone	Dylan cell pg 3131
11/13/2022	1004–1023	Dylan sends and receives multiple snapchat messages. Content of message unknown	Dylan cell pg 3133–3135
11/13/2022	1008	Justin Nadeau leaves for a walk and the door to the front of the King residence is open (Nadeau recalls this as 0900 but video shows it occurred at 1008)	Morris Supp Report #20 1112 King Road Video
11/13/2022	1023	Dylan texts Maddie "R u up" (DM tells Gooch this message was at 11:23)	Photo 129 of Maddie's Phone
11/13/2022	1029	Dylan texts Kaylee "R u up ??"	Dylan Phone records pg 3138
11/13/2022	1031	Kohberger Selfie in apartment bathroom	BK Phone Image 12175
11/13/2022	10:49	Showalter at Floyd's	Lehman Supp 76
11/13/2022	1049	Bryan at Washington Trust ATM, Pullman, WA Pulls $100 cash	WA Trust Records

Date	Time	Description of Event	Source
11/13/2022	1052	Ethan receives notification that Sean Dremann sent a Chat	Work Product
11/13/2022	1059	Justin Nadeau returns from walking his dog and front door to King residence still open	Morris Supp Report #20 1112 King Video
11/13/2022	1100	Activity Sensor Data reports Dylan total samples count 3.00, distance traveled 120.75, flights climbed 2.00	Dylan Phone Records 3136
11/13/2022	1100	Bethany wakes up	Bethany Int 11/16
11/13/2022	1109	Ethan receives notification that Maizie "lil sis" said "sorry I fell asleep"	Work Product
11/13/2022	1100–1132	Dylan on Instagram and Snapchat sending and receiving messages. Content of message unknown	Dylan cell pg 3136–3139
11/13/2022	1120	Jenna McClure sends a text to Bethany to see if she is awake	Per Jenna. Mowery 42
11/13/2022	1123	Dylan sends a snap to Maddie asking if she is up (DM phone records show this was 1023)	Mortensen Int 11/17/22
11/13/2022	1135	Dylan accesses Yik Yak	Dylan cell pg 3139
11/13/2022	1136	Dylan accesses Tiktok	Dylan Phone
11/13/2022	1137–1138	Dylan sends and receives Snapchat messages. Content of messages unknown	Dylan cell pg 3145

(continued)

Date	Time	Description of Event	Source
11/13/2022	1139–1140	Dylan gets message from her dad "Hey DMM, when can I call you today and just chat. Does 1:00 work? Or is 2:00 better?" Dylan responds "2 works better" Message from Dad "Okay. I'll call you at 2:00. Just 5–10 minutes. Want to catch up.	Dylan cell pg 3145
11/13/2022	1149	Bethany calls Jenna McClure saying that her roommates aren't answering	Cellbrite report pg 53
11/13/2022	1150	Dylan calls Emily Alandt via Snapchat length 01:48	Dylan cell pg 3146
11/13/2022	1150	Dylan receives message from Jenna "bro"	Dylan cell pg 3146
11/13/2022	1150	Dylan Texts Emily about what happened last night and the masked man. (Emily tells Dylan this is at 1050)	Mortensen Int 11/17/22
11/13/2022	1151	Jenna texts Dylan "do u guys need me to come get u"	Dylan cell pg 3147
11/13/2022	1151–1154	Dylan accesses Instagram (com.burbn.instagram)	Dylan cell Pg 3147
11/13/2022	11:56:33	911 Call placed by Bethany Funke	Cellebrite Report pg 53
11/13/2022	11:55	Hunter and Emily on scene	Warner's report

Like so many aspects of this case, a representation of fact does not mean it's the truth. As we have seen and will see moving forward, what police wrote down is only what they observed or believed at the time. Even a 108-page spreadsheet can overlook critically important details while getting others wrong, especially as breaks in the case appear promising, only to fade. Police reported Bryan Kohberger ceasing use of his debit card on November 11, for example, and failed to change that entry after it was proven wrong. They claimed he employed "anti-forensic methods" to clear evidence from his school computer and got that wrong too.

These are small details, of course, barely worth mentioning in such an overwhelming case, but as we will soon discover, it is the details that matter. Just as Lorenz predicted, tiny variations at the beginning can lead to unpredictable consequences at the end. Bill Thompson's investigative timeline does more than outline his narrative; it plots what I believe is its demise.

CHAPTER 10

Halloween, Victimology, Terrible Toothache

Hearsay is one of those legal terms that feels familiar, yet hard to pin down. Law dictionaries define it as secondhand evidence, where one person tries to convey what another person said through the prism of their own understanding. Few people use the word outside a court of law, but looking back on Officer Nunes's body camera footage, we see how important it is to ask the right questions and accurately record the answers.

One of the biggest problems with this case is that police may have ignored or dismissed what witnesses told them. When Dylan Mortensen described the masked man as two inches shorter or taller than herself, for example, Nunes wrote down the latter. When she told him Xana was the person she saw lying unconscious on the floor, he wrote down Kaylee. When Hunter Johnson told him about the steak knife on the table, he seemed to ignore it, only to detail a different conversation in his report. This is not about one officer's possible mistakes; it is about the tendency of the system to accept them. Lorenz's theories on chaos make more and more sense when we look at the role of hearsay as we dig into the file.

The concept of misunderstanding is nothing new, of course, and it is not purely the domain of lawyers and courts. Think about the times you have suffered consequences at home or on the job based simply on what someone thought they heard someone say. Humans, in general, are prone to miscommunication, and cops are no exception. In fact, the American justice system is so vulnerable to opinion, the phrase "he said, she said" has become cliché.

So why bring up more legal jargon in a case that will not go to trial? Because what the public has heard about events inside that house early Sunday morning is based on two and a half years of gag order speculation followed by a slow drip of disclosures based on FOIA requests. It is easy to argue now that even Bill Thompson's narrative during Kohberger's change of plea hearing appears to be rife with possible errors, omissions, and misstatements of fact. News articles, documentaries, and media accounts have sensationalized rumors based on insinuation and leaks. Video-recorded witness statements have been summarized in poorly written supplementals. Laboratory findings are buried in reams of statistics and protocols, shaping science to fit the prosecution's case.

It does not stop there.

Careful analysis of this investigation shows that everything changed once Kohberger became the focus of attention, even though no one else was ever named as a suspect. Hair found in Ethan's hand and on Maddie's bed was mislabeled as "debris" and never tested for DNA. Important evidence, like a broken bracelet and a blood-soaked jacket found in the spare bedroom, was misplaced, mishandled, or never taken at all. Claims by Molly McMichael that the man she saw in the car could not have been Kohberger were dismissed. Statements by Justin Nadeau that the front door was open all morning may have been ignored. Insinuations by WSU students that Bryan Kohberger was creepy in class and at pool parties became prima facie fact. By the time Kohberger pled guilty, it seems to me that pretty much everything in Bill Thompson's file had started to fade gray in a case he claimed to be black-and-white.

It did not help that highly accomplished lawyers faced off every day for years, asking the court to rule on motions in limine, predetermining what jurors would be allowed to hear. Even criminologists like Paulette Sutton and Dr. Brent Turvey disagreed, standing behind well-educated judgments and certified points of view. Anne Taylor's office seems not to have found it odd that the state was going to trial claiming living room bloodstains were diluted with Xana's saliva, or that the assailant ran around the house naked to avoid tracking DNA back to his Elantra. Even the defendant's own admissions of guilt seem inadequate considering the court could have required what is known as "allocution" as a condition of the defendant's plea. Judge Hippler apparently chose not to do so; Kohberger never explained a thing.

Whatever one thinks about hearsay, we have to deal with its role in this case. Once police named their suspect and got him indicted, it was all too easy to go back and shape their narrative based on things people heard. They listened to various AI-generated opinions before narrowing their search of white sedans to one that matched his car. They seem to have ignored what witnesses told them about a yearslong pattern of awkward selfies to publish one Kohberger took the morning of the crimes. They listened to an FBI expert's highly questionable claims about cell tower pings without checking the math. They identified, investigated, swabbed, printed, surveilled, and named more than a dozen serious "possible subjects" based on overheard conversations and rumor, before dropping them all without explanation once they found their man.

Is this all hearsay, as a court would define it? Perhaps not, but none of that mattered once Kohberger was sentenced. Virtually all the evidence in this case could be considered secondhand once Bill Thompson retired and the state moved on to other pressing matters. The case was closed without allocution, meaning the public was left with nothing but what law enforcement selectively released through FOIA requests, outside the regulation of courts. Yes, the public has gained access to the motions in limine, affidavits, and Franks hearing transcripts, but few of those filings sort underlying facts. It feels like small consolation that journalists have won disclosure of hundreds of reports when tens of thousands are held back.

The problem, of course, is motive. We have none.

No matter what Bill Thompson's office has speculated about the relationship between Bryan Kohberger and his victims, it all comes down to gossip. We have uncovered no evidence, secondhand or otherwise, that explains the rage inherent in the extreme violence of the murders, the timing of the intrusion, or the selection of that particular house on that particular day.

After nearly three years of investigation, the prosecution has never disclosed a single statement Bryan Kohberger made about his own involvement in the crimes. Despite all the discussion about coworker complaints, sexual harassment, unfair grading, and Tinder dates feeling uncomfortable in his presence, it appears that no one has ever expressed concerns about him being violent. Not one person has suggested any possible connection between Bryan Kohberger and Kaylee or Maddie, the two most likely targets. No friend, colleague, or associate admits to eavesdropping on an inculpatory comment. Interviews of numerous former cellmates and jailhouse snitches disclose not one single utterance Kohberger made about involvement in the murders; not a slipup, not a brag.

In hundreds of interviews, no one has ever mentioned anything that would presage murder. Nothing resembling hearsay was introduced in court during the change of plea hearing, where it would not have been allowed.

Perhaps that factor alone haunts people most with regard to this case. How would it be possible for the killer to plan and execute these crimes without ever slipping up with a comment? Kaylee Goncalves and Maddie Mogen were certainly targeted for a reason, but no one ever heard Kohberger mention their names? No one ever heard him express opinions about how the killer got into the house or why he walked directly past Dylan's room on his way upstairs? Not a peep about knowledge of the house, late-night trips to Moscow, premeditated intent? If posing of the bodies indicates subtext, where is it? If signature wounds suggest statements by the killer, as behavioralists suggest, what was Kohberger trying to say?

Things only look stranger when one considers overwhelming statistical evidence that murder is a crime of familiarity. According to the FBI's 2019 *Crime in the United States* report, of

13,927 people murdered that year, only 9.9 percent were killed by a stranger. That is one in ten, a striking number; hard to ignore, considering police have never tied Kohberger to 1122 King Road or any of the people inside. What was his motivation for rage? Why did the killer ravage Kaylee far worse than the others? How did he know where to find her?

The answer, oddly enough, brings us back to hearsay.

To augment forensic evidence with a larger understanding of the scene, police have come up with a tool called *victimology.* It is a whole discipline now, taught in academies and accepted as a valid way to gain context. While lab techs focus on forensics, detectives hit the streets, seeking perspectives from friends and family about the victims—things like drug use, romantic interactions, day-to-day routines. Much of what they discover is based on opinion, but none of it will show up in court, so the rules barely matter. It's all about context, painting the larger picture.

Victimology allows investigators to flesh out the facts of their case based on what people think or feel. It's what Turvey referred to as "course graining," a broad-brush look at the totality of circumstances; an overview cops can start with to dig down into as things become clearer. We see the concept plainly here in two brief reports. The first was filed January 9, 2023, a month after Kohberger was arrested.

> On November 16, 2022, I, Idaho State Police (ISP) Detective (Det.) Joe Lake was assigned by ISP Det. Sergeant (Sgt.) Darren Gilbertson to lead the Victimology team for the November 13, 2022, Moscow, Latah County, Idaho quadruple murder investigation.

According to Lake's report (ISP Supplemental 89), police started building character sketches of their victims within days of the crimes. As we will see moving forward, they tried to narrow their search for suspects based on modus operandi and Dylan's physical description of a white male with average height and weight.

Because the first two murders occurred in Maddie's room, they looked to her current boyfriend, Jake Schriger, then to gossip involving a drunken tryst with a Delta Tau Delta member named Connor Chesnut. (Neither Schriger nor Chesnut has ever been implicated or charged.) They tracked Maddie's movements Saturday night to a bar called the Corner Club, where they interviewed patrons and staff and tracked camera footage of a mysterious Grub Truck guy wearing a hoodie. They looked into at least one of Kaylee's former boyfriends, interviewed a man she might have invited home from a bar, identified and eliminated a WinCo stalker. They surveilled a student from Boise who abruptly left campus Sunday morning with an unexplained gash on his hand that he didn't have treated. He drove a white sedan that looked very much like the one they saw on Ring cam video.

Hearsay? Some of it, yes. Acceptable in a victimology? Absolutely.

Moving further afield, police looked at alcohol dependence and drug dealing, social media profiles on dating sites like Tinder, commercial sex platforms like OnlyFans. There was a persistent rumor that one or more of the victims had earned money posing online in a bikini or selling photos of their feet. Bethany Funke was asked about this in the presence of her lawyer and admitted that it might have been a thing at 1122, but she was not involved. As with so many aspects of this investigation, hopeful leads proved fruitless. Persons of interest became possible suspects; possible suspects became the focus of intense scrutiny but, in the end, were all washed out with no credible ties to the crimes. Eventually, the personal lives of victims began to emerge, and the world of 1122 King Road started to make sense, but it took a lot of effort from a who's who of agencies. Joe Lake wrote:

> The Victimology team consisted of me, Federal Bureau of Investigation (FBI) Special Agent (SA) Jonathan Riggs, FBI SA Jared Thompson, FBI Tactical Specialist (TS) Carrie Hadaway, and statewide ISP Detectives and nationwide FBI Agents for out of area interviews.

For those wondering about jurisdiction, murder is not typically a federal crime. The FBI can offer resources under the purview of police cooperation, however, and due to the widespread notoriety of this case, the bureau jumped right in. Senior management ran things from headquarters in DC, but the office of origin was designated the Salt Lake City Division. Agents Thompson and Riggs commuted from an outpost known as the Lewiston Resident Agency. The file number was designated 9A-SU-3683464.

Lake wrote in his report:

> The Victimology team was responsible for understanding relationships, social groups, public lives, and private lives of the victims and survivors, and the connection to a suspect(s). On January 3, 2023, ISP Det. Sgt. Gilbertson assigned me the additional investigative duty of coordinating the priority of investigation tips related to suspect Bryan C. Kohberger

(KOHBERGER). The coordination of tips includes prioritizing interviews of people associated to KOHBERGER.

At first glance, it might seem surprising that law enforcement would focus such broad multiagency attention on the day-to-day interactions of people inside the house. In the broader picture, however, it is easy to see how crimes like this could overwhelm a small community with limited resources. In 2022 Moscow had a population of 26,249. According to statistics maintained by the Idaho State Police, they reported zero homicides in 2021 and zero homicides in 2023. The only homicides in 2022 were those of the four victims in the matter at hand.

We know from previous reports that the MPD reached out almost immediately to other specialized units for support. Within hours, the ISP crime lab had responded with its evidence analysis team. We know the FBI added significant specialization through the Consolidated DNA Index System (CODIS), the Critical Incident Response Group (CIRG), a cross-country surveillance element known as a Special Operations Group (SOG), and the Cellular Analysis Survey Team (CAST). Moscow police were offered but did not accept help from the FBI's National Center for the Analysis of Violent Crime (NCAVC) or "profilers" from its famous Behavioral Analysis Unit (BAU).

"During the period of November 16, 2022, through January 7, 2023," Lake wrote in a second document (Supplemental 101), dated January 10, 2022:

I conducted telephone triage interviews with people associated to the victim and survivors of the quadruple murder in

> Moscow, Latah County, Idaho. The triage telephone interview determined the extent of information the person possessed, and if an in-person interview should be conducted.

Use of the battlefield term *triage* might seem a bit extreme until one considers the pressure law enforcement felt during the early weeks of their investigation. It would not be a stretch to liken the pressure to combat, the workload to trying to sip water from a fire hose. With four dead coeds, a gruesome crime scene, and international attention focused on a community that had never previously felt the need to lock their doors, the pressure must have seemed daunting. Dozens of law enforcement professionals from several agencies had been called into the investigation by the time Officer Lake formed his team; the case file had grown to tens of thousands of pages. Things were running 24/7. As Lake wrote near the beginning of his report:

> On December 7, 2022, I telephoned Kayleigh Tavernier. Kayleigh claimed she knows victim Ethan Chapin and "others" and was present at the Sigma Chi party with her best friend, Kyley Eppenstein. She believed Ethan wasn't acting like himself and keeping to himself. Kayleigh later stated she may have mistaken the identity of the person she believed was Ethan. She provided, via email, a vague video from the party; no evidentiary value was obtained in the video. The provided video is added to evidence data of this report.

If this video exists, I could not find it in Bill Thompson's massive disclosure to the defense. There is no emailed copy of the "vague video from the party." It seems likely that Anne Taylor had not even heard about it, because there is no mention in formal supplemental discovery requests as cataloged in two terabytes of files.

Even more troublesome is the fact that neither Kyley Eppenstein nor anyone else has ever apparently been asked what might have been bothering Ethan. Bill Thompson's files contain documentation of a text sent from "Erika" to Ethan at 5:30 p.m. Friday saying, "ur getting cheated on," but there is no further context. Ethan received a second nearly identical text from "Erika" at 12:43 Sunday morning, but no one seems to have determined what this meant in terms of his relationship with Xana. The fact that Ethan was murdered, naked, in his girlfriend's bed only complicates Joe Lake's mission to figure out why.

And while we are focusing on victimology, it feels prudent to reach beyond Officer Lake's one-paragraph memorial to look deeper into the only male life stolen that morning: Ethan. As Judge Hippler stated at the change of plea hearing, he was a human being who should be remembered as such. Ethan Chapin was a vital, accomplished son and brother, cut down in the prime of his life by a vicious assassin. He deserves more than a brief mention in a mysterious text from someone named "Erika."

According to police files, Ethan James Chapin was twenty years of age at the time of his death, a U of I freshman. He was a six-foot-four, 228-pound native of Conway, Washington, majoring in recreation, sport, and tourism management. He was a member of Sigma Chi, lived by himself in an off-campus apartment, and drove a red Jeep registered to his father. According to friends and a published obituary, "He laughed continuously. He smiled when he woke up and was still smiling when he went to bed. He was kind to all and a friend to all."

Diving deeper, we know that on December 1, 2022, Officer Joe Lake interviewed James Chapin, whom he referred to as "the loving father of his triplets, Ethan, Hunter, and Maizie." In Supplemental 153, filed February 23, 2023, Lake reported that Ethan was a leader who had a great relationship with his girlfriend of almost a year, Xana Kernodle. He was the first delivered of triplets, all of whom attended the U of I.

"E. Chapin was very close to his siblings and Peter Elgorriaga was his closest friend," Lake wrote. At that time, police had started handing out Victim Background Questionnaires to friends, family members, and acquaintances. "J. Chapin is not aware of anyone or any event which could have led to the murder of his son and the other three victims."

Peter Elgorriaga agreed with Ethan's dad that he was Ethan's best friend. In a December 5 interview (ISP Supplemental 157), he told Officer Lake he was a member of the Sigma Chi fraternity, where he lived in apartment 5. He said he had once had a romantic relationship with Xana. Lake wrote:

> Elgorriaga stated Kernodle had a lot of admirers, but she and Chapin were perfect for each other. The night before the murders, Chapin told Elgorriaga it can be difficult to be in a relationship with Kernodle because she draws so much attention.

Lake learned more on December 1, when he interviewed Ethan's fraternal triplet Hunter. He wrote in Supplemental 154:

> Both E. Chapin and Kernodle were well-liked by others and the life of the party. They regularly had parties at 1122 King Road, Moscow, Latah County, Idaho, but it was generally the same twenty, up to seventy people who frequented the parties, and all were associated with the University of Idaho Greek life.

On December 1, Ethan's sister, Maizie, told Detective Dani Vargas that other than Xana, her brother spent most of his time with Elgorriaga, Hunter Johnson, a student named Kyle Frei, and Emily Alandt. Vargas reported:

> Maizie said she met Xana once during sorority rush but had gotten to know her through Ethan, and that the two had been dating for about a year. She said Ethan often spent time at the Mad Greek, where Xana worked, but that the two "never mentioned having weird feelings about anyone" (customers or employees).

Maizie told Vargas her brother did not use drugs but "drank a lot, which was normal for the fraternity life." She said Ethan never got into fights and confided no history of negative interactions with anyone at all, including Xana's housemates at 1122 King Road.

"Maizie said in the evening Ethan went with her to her formal event, which was at Hunga Dunga from 1900 to 2000 hours," Lake wrote, noting that this was a private event hosted by her sorority.

> Maizie said she texted Ethan at approximately 2014 hours telling him she did not want to go with them to Sigma Chi and

> was going to stay at her sorority. Maizie said Ethan texted her several times, trying to convince her to come to Sigma Chi, but she did not go and eventually fell asleep around 2200 hours.

Reaching further into details of Ethan Chapin's life on campus, ISP detective Brady Walker contacted a student named Tim DeWulf on November 18 (Supplemental 53). Walker wrote:

> It was reported to me that DeWulf had text conversations with Ethan Chapin the night of the incident. But DeWulf denied that. DeWulf had been in the same fraternity as Chapin for a year and a half and described Chapin as one of his best friends.

This interview stands out among others because police found it somewhat difficult to pin down the movements of Ethan and his girlfriend late Saturday night into early Sunday morning. Though Chapin spent a good deal of time at the Sigma Chi fraternity house, he was not permitted to live there due to low grades, so no one paid much attention when he left. Adding to the confusion, a police search of Ethan's cell account showed that he had been blocked by a woman named Dylan Sturrock and by another named Lydia Varga. To date, it appears that no one in law enforcement has definitively identified or interviewed either woman, so there is no way to tell if these blocked contacts have anything to do with his mood Saturday night or the "cheating" text from Erika. No one has established where he was last seen or what time he and Xana returned to King Road. It remains a nagging void in the timeline.

According to Walker:

> DeWulf was present with Chapin in the lodge at Sigma Chi, but they didn't have much contact. DeWulf said he did not text or have any other electronic communication with Chapin that night. He did not know when Chapin left the Sigma Chi party.

DeWulf told Walker his friend had been dating Xana for about seven months and that they stayed together "about six nights a week."

> DeWulf said there was a party at 1122 King Road at least once a week and that most were attended by fifty or sixty people. He knew Kernodle well, but not the others, though he said they "all seemed to get along really well."

Detective Walker also interviewed a student named Jaedon Shepherd on November 19, 2022, and documented that information in the same supplemental.

> Shepherd was roommates with Ethan Chapin last year and was currently a roommate of Tim DeWulf. On November 12th, Shepherd attended the Formal party and went to the Sigma Chi party afterwards. He left the Sigma Chi party around 0100 and went to a party at the Whites apartment building accompanied by Trent Gwinn and Tim DeWulf. The apartment unit they went to was referred to as "The Rack." They were at the Whites until around 0500 hours when they returned to their unit at Sigma Chi. They went to bed around 0530. Shepherd had no contact with Chapin since the formal and did not have any contact with Kernodle that day.

Walker tried without success to gather more detail from Gwinn, who said he saw and spoke with Ethan sometime before 0115 Sunday morning at a Sigma Chi "after party," following the formal. On November 30, 2022, Idaho State Police detectives Alderson and Van Leuven started interviewing other fraternity brothers of Ethan's, including chapter president Reed B. Ofsthun, Kyle Frei, John Felin, Drew Carter, Ryan Moffet, Kelvin Cobbley, Conrad Harrison, Matthew Manson, and Wesley Rebeck, "for victimology purposes." According to ISP Supplemental 178, the detectives gained little or nothing of value. Returning to Lake's victimology (Supplemental 101) we see that on December 21, 2022, he telephoned a Delta Gamma member named Kyli Pierson for more information.

> Kyli is a Delta Gamma and friends with victims Ethan Chapin and Xana Kernodle. Kyli knew victim Kaylee Goncalves as a previous neighbor but were never close. She did not have contact or a relationship with victim Madison Mogen or the surviving victims Bethany Funke or Dylan Mortensen. Kyli recalled Ethan always being the "funny guy" in the room and Xana knew and was liked by everyone. Kyli had attended the Sigma party with Sophia Oxarango and ran into both Ethan and Xana. They were both in good spirits. Kyli believed Ethan's best friends were Kai (LNU), Jayden Shepard, and DJ Myers.

LNU, of course, is cop talk for "last name unknown."

> Kyli believed Xana's best friends were Emily Alandt and Josie (LNU). Kyli had never been to the 1122 King Road, Moscow,

ID residence and doesn't know anyone who would want to hurt the victims.

Based on these reports and the rest of Lake's victimology, it seems clear that detectives considered Ethan an unfortunate bystander who was killed merely because he had gone home with Xana. In order to study her and the other women in the house, however, we will have to reach beyond what Lake documented in these two brief reports. Though Ethan's life makes sense within the scope of a few pages, Maddie's and Kaylee's do not. We will return to them shortly.

Of all the people best suited to summarize the lives of Maddie Mogen, Kaylee Goncalves, Xana Kernodle, and Ethan Chapin, Bethany Funke might stand alone. Regardless of how one looks at seeming contradictions in her accounts of that horrible Sunday morning, her recollections of the three women and one man who died there that night hold singular importance. She chose to memorialize her housemates in a victim witness statement at Kohberger's sentencing hearing on July 23, 2025. Her thoughts, as read in court by Emily Alandt, are here transcribed verbatim:

> My name is Bethany Funke, and I was roommates with Maddie, Kaylee, Xana, and Ethan. I not only lost some of my best friends, but I also lost a sister. Never in a million years would I have thought that something like this would have happened to my closest friends. I thought that we were going to wake up

and go upstairs see them and tell them how they had scared us and that they were going to tease us about how we're constantly scaredy cats and make jokes about it as we would go to Taco Bell like always, but sadly, that is not what happened and what turned out to be my worst nightmare when I first woke up that morning; I had no idea what happened.

I woke up around 7:00 with a terrible toothache, so I called my dad, who was a dentist, and asked what I should do. He told me to take Advil, so I did, and I went back to sleep. I was still out of it and still didn't know what happened. If I had known I of course would have called 911 right away. I still carry so much guilt for not knowing what had happened and not calling right away, even though I understand it wouldn't have changed anything, not even if the paramedics had been right outside the door.

I was so frantic that morning and scared to death, not knowing what had happened, and when I made the 911 call, I couldn't even get out the words and from then on, I don't remember a thing. It was like my brain wiped that whole memory. That was the worst day of my life, and I know it always will be. While I was still in shock, trying to process the fact that my friends were truly gone, I had been attacked by the public. I was grieving, numb, and unsure if what had happened was even real and at the same time I was getting flooded with death threats and hateful messages from people who did not know me at all or know the dynamic of our friendship. Social media made it so much worse, and strangers made up stories to entertain themselves. The media harassed not just me but also my family. People showed up at the house, they called my phone, my parents' phones, other family members' phones, and we were chased while I was still trying to survive, emotionally, and grieve the loss of my friends.

I hated and still hate that they are gone, but for some reason, I am still here, and I got to live. I still think about this every day. Why me? Why did I get to live and not them? For the longest time, I could not even look at their families without feeling sick with guilt. I did not know what to say or what to do.

I was terrified that my presence just made their pain worse and I was still here when their kids, their siblings, and their friends, their loved ones should have been here instead. After everything that happened, I was afraid to go into my own backyard or alone in my house. I was scared that the person who did this would come for me next. I was always scared that the media would try to catch me at any moment of any day even when I was just walking around my house. I made my parents close all the blinds during the day so no one could see me even in the slightest chance. I barely left the house, and when I did, I made sure I was never alone.

I slept in my parents' room for almost a year. I made them double lock every door, set an alarm, and still check everywhere in the room just in case someone was hiding, and I still checked my room every night, before, and I double lock it. I have not slept through a single night since this happened. I constantly wake up and panic, terrified someone is breaking in or someone is here to hurt me, or I'm about to lose someone else that I love. The fear never really leaves. For a long time, I could barely get out of bed, but one day I realized I have to live for them. They did not get the chance to keep living, but

I do, and I will not take that for granted, so, now, every day I remind myself to live for them and everything I do, I do it with them in mind. I am still scared to go out in public, but I forced myself to do things because I know that they would want me to keep living my life to the fullest. I am beyond blessed to still be here, and I refuse to take that for granted when they did not get a chance.

Our house was not just a house; it was a home. It was where we laughed till we couldn't breathe, made meals, did crafts, binge-watched reality shows, played games, and spent lazy days on the couch. It was movie nights, wine nights, morning debriefs, pranks, hot chocolate, cookies, and warmth. I would cherish those memories, forever, and I will not let what happened erase how special our home was or how much those memories meant to me.

Now, I would like to share some bits and pieces of who they were, as people, and some of the memories that we shared. One of my favorite memories was Halloween, and we all went to Sigma Chi, but instead of partying, we just sat in an apartment talking and laughing all night long. I do not think I've ever laughed that hard in my life. We did not care about the party; we were just happy to be with each other.

Xana was one in a million. She was the life of the party, but she was also the kindest and funniest person I knew. Everyone loved her because she made everyone feel so loved. She was just someone you always wanted to be around, no matter the circumstance. One of my favorite days with Xana was when she laid on the couch, when we laid on the couch together all day watching movies and snacking and when she, Maddie, and

I would go and get margaritas, chips, and salsa. She would also light up a room with her presence alone.

Kaylee had the most beautiful, radiant smile, and she was so kind, but also one of the funniest people I've ever known. She loved playing little pranks. She always had us laughing so hard that we could not breathe. She was so full of energy and life. I really believe that she could have ruled the world if she wanted to, and she would have been America's sweetheart.

Ethan was the sweetest, most genuine guy. He was always smiling and always making other people smile too. Ethan was the kind of person you wanted around. He was so kind and easy to talk to, and just so fun, and the way he cared for Xana was truly something to admire and really was proof that storybook love and true romances really do exist. It was not only obvious to me, but everyone—Ethan and Xana were absolute soul mates.

Maddie was not only one of my best friends, but she was the older sister I would have always wanted. There was no one I looked up to or admired more than Maddie. She was truly a ray of sunshine, and everyone was drawn to her. She was so kind, loving, funny, fun, and passionate. She had the sweetest soul and wanted nothing but the best for everyone, and to love and show love to everyone. She took me under her wing and always made me feel so safe and included and above all, loved and valued. She never failed to make me laugh or put a smile on my face. Still, to this day, I'm beyond grateful that she chose me to be her sorority "little," and I thank God, every day, that I not only got to know her, but had her as one of my best friends. Honestly, I cannot pinpoint one favorite memory with Maddie, because I have so many, and this would be a very long read if I did. Little memories with her that I cherish is when the two of us made a nice dinner and split some wine, or when we would binge-watch *Jersey Shore* or *Summer House*. When we came up with a whole dance routine on Halloween and danced and sang all night like no one was watching. All the late-night walks home from going out and just little shopping trips, and so much more.

I am beyond blessed that I had the chance to know each and every one of them. They changed my life in ways I would have never put into words. I hope that they are remembered for who they are, not what happened to them, because who they were was so beautiful and they deserve to be remembered in the highest way.

My heart breaks every time I go to text one of them, or how badly I wish I could see and hang out with them. Then I remember I cannot. I will never be able to again, but I still talk to them in my prayers every single night and I always will.

I wish, more than anything, I could hug them one last time, and I wish I could tell them how much I love them. And even though I cannot, I still tell them every night I will keep living for them as long as I am lucky enough to still be here, and they were all truly one of a kind, and they will be in our hearts forever and always.

Oddly enough, Detective Lake's victimology barely even mentions Xana. Based on early reports, we know she was twenty years old the day she died, a U of I marketing major from Avondale, Arizona, who had moved to the small town of Post Falls, Idaho, where she played volleyball and soccer in high school. She was a member of Pi Beta Phi sorority, worked at the Mad Greek restaurant with Maddie Mogen, and had an older sister named Jazzmin who was a student at Washington State University, where Kohberger studied criminology. Xana had a large circle of friends who described her as fun-loving and kind—the type of person who would light up any room. According to an obituary published in the *Bonner County Daily Bee*, Xana loved her dog, Shoeshine, electronic dance music, and "going on trips with her sister and father."

What is less known about Xana is that she overcame significant adversity on her way to finding success at college. Xana's parents were divorced, and her mother had suffered serious legal problems as a result of alleged substance abuse, as reported in the police files. In fact, Cara Kernodle was incarcerated the night her daughter was killed.

"On November 20, 2022, at approximately 2220 hours, Idaho State Police (ISP) Detective Timothy Snell and ISP Sergeant Jess Stennett conducted an interview of Cara D. Kernodle at the Kootenai County Jail," Snell wrote in ISP Supplemental 82.

> I was advised C. Kernodle had been recently arrested by the Kootenai County Sheriff's Office (KCSC) due to having a warrant for her arrest involving drugs. I was advised by KCSO Sergeant Solar Larsen during her arrest, C. Kernodle had made statements regarding the homicide of her daughter Xana Kernodle and her drug involvement somehow being involved.

Though not mentioned in this report, it would later be revealed that Anne Taylor's office had represented Cara Kernodle as a public defender.

> Upon arrival at the jail, C. Kernodle was placed into an interview room with Sergeant Stennett and I. Upon explaining why we were there, C. Kernodle began speaking prior to being able to activate the audio recording device.

Review of the actual audio recording indicates that Cara learned of her daughter's death from the news and had not been notified by police or given any details prior to the November 20 interview. She sounded emotionally distraught at the news and upset that police would provide almost no information about the crimes. When asked about the crimes being somehow related to revenge, she denied it.

Snell summarized their conversation thusly in his report:

> C. Kernodle said she last spoke with X. Kernodle about a month prior to the homicide when she attempted to coordinate having lunch with X. Kernodle. C. Kernodle said X. Kernodle ended up being too busy with classes and was not able to meet.

During their nine-minute conversation, Cara said she was unaware of anyone who would want to hurt her daughter and added that her ex-husband had specifically asked if she had "any involvement with the cartels." He wanted to know if Xana could have been killed as a result of her mother's exposure to "organized crime." Cara has never been implicated in any way in her daughter's death.

Police followed up on this on December 4, when Detective Joe Lake interviewed Jeff Kernodle, handing him a Victim Background Questionnaire while building victimology. This was actually the second time police interacted with Xana's dad. Captain Anthony Dahlinger had first met him at the crime scene Sunday afternoon, shortly after Nunes responded to the 911 call. Kernodle was in town for parents' weekend at WSU with Jazzmin and had stopped by the house when Xana failed to respond to texts. The only things Dahlinger reported learning was that Xana worked at the Mad Greek, had no enemies, and last called her dad Friday at around 9:40 p.m.

Lake wrote in ISP Supplemental 156:

> He telephoned his daughters about three times per week, regularly visited them, and would fly them to his home in Arizona at every opportunity. J. Kernodle helped X. Kernodle financially, he bought her a vehicle and paid insurance.

Lake inquired about reports that the women had come home recently to find the front door to their house wide open. Kernodle, a construction contractor, told Lake the front was "barely hanging on the hinges," so he fixed it using longer screws.

When Lake returned to information germane to victimology, Xana's dad told him that Xana was a state champion gymnast who "wasn't scared of anything." He said Xana and Ethan Chapin had a healthy, sustained relationship, that she was not the type who would "lead anyone on," and that she would "handle advances with class."

On February 14, 2023, Cara Kernodle was interviewed again by ISP detective Michael Van Leuven regarding her interactions with Kootenai County public defender Anne Taylor. Detective Van Leuven noted in his report that Cara was an inmate at the Spokane County Jail at the time. According to public records, this incarceration involved offenses committed after, and completely unrelated to, the murders.

> Kernodle advised she had met with a lawyer she believed to be Anne Taylor on multiple occasions when she was an inmate in the Kootenai County jail. This person was representing her on recent charges involving controlled substances. She advised her last charge was approximately four days after her daughter, Xana A. Kernodle had been murdered.

Van Leuven's report states that he showed Cara a photograph of Anne Taylor, but Cara claimed not to recognize the woman in the photo. This is important, because Taylor left her job as a county attorney due to apparent conflict-of-interest issues with one or more of the victims' parents. He asked her where she had gotten the name Anne Taylor. She said someone had showed her a Reddit thread where it stated her attorney was Anne Taylor. He told her that Anne Taylor was the head public defender for Kootenai County, and her name would be on paperwork because it was her office that was defending her, not necessarily Anne Taylor herself. Kernodle expressed regret in having confused the identity of the public defender she had met with.

So why add Xana's mom to the Lake team's victimology if she was in jail at the time of the murders and had only limited contact with her estranged daughter? We must turn to MPD corporal Brett Payne's November 13 interview of Emily Alandt to gain insight.

•

"What's your relationship to the people in the house?" Payne asks Alandt immediately after the audio portion of the tape kicks in.

"Xana was my best friend," Alandt states. She sounds poised, though distraught, which makes sense considering it's been less than two hours since the discovery of the bodies. She saw Xana lying dead in a dried pool of blood on her bedroom floor.

"Ethan is her boyfriend, who's also one of my best friends. And Maddie Mogen and Kaylee are great friends to all of us, too, because they live with them."

•

Payne asks about sorority affiliation, to which Alandt responds that all the women in the house were members at one point, but that she and Xana were not anymore. Though she did not volunteer details at the time, it was widely known that Emily was Dylan Mortensen's "big" at Phi Beta Pi. Their relationship within the sorority at least partially explains Dylan's call Sunday morning.

•

"What about Ethan?" the detective asks.

"Ethan's in, um, Delta Tau, with his brother, Hunter."

•

The fact that she got that wrong only underscores the problems in building a victimology. Direct witness testimony is notoriously unreliable. Hearsay is just about worthless.

CHAPTER 11

Range Rover, Homecoming, Murphy the Goldendoodle

Kaylee Jade Goncalves was a twenty-one-year-old U of I senior at the time of the murders. Though she paid rent and kept a room at 1122 King Road, she had completed all the coursework necessary to graduate and had moved home to her parents' house in Coeur d'Alene, where she worked remotely for a marketing firm in Texas. Police determined during the early stages of their investigation that she had driven down to Moscow for the weekend in a shiny Range Rover, telling friends she was moving to Austin, where she had already found an apartment. She had recently broken up with her longtime boyfriend, Jack Ducoeur, but the split seemed amicable. She had agreed to go as Dylan's plus-one to a sorority formal. It was a football weekend. Everyone was excited to catch up.

Nothing about Kaylee's homecoming would have seemed unusual on a university campus where end-of-term seniors would be coming and going as they prepared to move on with life. Thanksgiving break was a week away, meaning faculty and students alike were focused on tests and papers. Fall is a particularly busy season in the Greek community, with underclassmen wandering between formals and house parties while the local bars fill up with drinking-age seniors. Police were focused on underage drinkers stumbling home in the early morning hours as the rest of the thirty thousand residents slept. It was just another day.

All that changed, of course, around noon Sunday morning, when Bethany Funke called Whitcom 911 pleading for assistance. From the moment Officer Nunes arrived on scene and stated out loud that Ethan had killed himself, things started to get confusing. It was more than obvious that something almost unimaginable had happened, but for a small-town police department with little experience in crimes of this kind, the who, when, how, and why must have seemed overwhelming. It had been six years since Moscow had experienced even one murder, and now four students lay butchered in a six-bedroom house. From the start, it seemed apparent that robbery was not the motive; there were no signs of rape, and though police knew almost nothing about the killer, the chief did what chiefs do: He held a press conference. He said this was an isolated incident with no immediate threat to the larger community. Nobody bought it.

In reality, law enforcement at that point likely had no idea what was going on, period. They didn't even know where to start until forensic analysis suggested a lone assailant and autopsy reports began to narrow down the targets. Wounds inflicted upon Kaylee Goncalves appeared different in character and scope than those suffered by other people in the house. Xana and Ethan died as a result of edged-weapon attacks, but their injuries were mostly defensive in nature. Maddie died quickly from "stab and incised wounds of the head and neck," the fewest number among the housemates. Kaylee, on the other hand, suffered wounds that seemed to tell a whole different story. She had been asphyxiated to the point of petechia, with burst blood vessels in her eyes and lips. She had been severely beaten with a blunt object that broke out her teeth, fractured bones in her face, cracked her skull.

Forensic analysis suggested this had been a rage-motivated attack on Kaylee, what behavioralists call "overkill." Kaylee's wounds stood out, even from Maddie's, who died in bed beside her.

To try make sense of why Kaylee was singled out and who wanted her dead, detectives quickly moved outside the crime scene to focus on victimology. ISP investigator Joe Lake and his team wanted to know why she had picked that particular weekend to visit, how many people would have known she was coming, which of her interactions Saturday night might have led to an outcome this extreme. We can follow their thinking on Lake's report (Supplemental 110). He wrote:

> On December 14, 2022, I telephonically interviewed Maya Clark. Maya explained she has known Kaylee from Idaho. Although Maya was a couple years ahead of Kaylee in school, they were friends. Maya's sorority little, Kallin Mai, was Kaylee's big within the sorority. Kaylee had two sorority littles, Jayden Smith and Emma Tyger.

Victimologies start broadly with context before moving into specifics. Lake quickly turned his focus to the reasons for Kaylee's visit, details about life on and off campus. He reported:

> Maya has worked for Extreme Networks for the last couple years and at the beginning of the 2022 school year. Maya helped Kaylee obtain an internship with Extreme Networks. Extreme Networks is a small company and during Kaylee's internship she worked within several elements of the company, sales, marketing, etc. Her boss was Jeremiah Shea who is based out of Canada. Kaylee was in the pipeline for a full-time position, but the official offer had not yet been presented. It was known to Maya that Kaylee would be moving to Austin, Texas and working for the company based out of Texas. Maya had not had regular or routine contact with Kaylee, but they did periodically talk over the past couple years. Maya is unaware of any issues related to Kaylee or the murders.

On December 15, 2022, Lake spoke with a woman named Erica Anthony, who is not further identified but claimed to have facilitated Goncalves's "knowledge of salary negotiations but did not directly negotiate her salary." According to Detective Lake, Erica believed Kaylee was in a "full-time paid intern program" at Extreme Networks, earning between twenty and twenty-seven dollars per hour. Some within the department wondered if this was enough income to explain a lifestyle that did not seem to match her means. It seemed plausible to police that Kaylee kept her room at the house on King Road because rent had been written into the cost of her education. It did not particularly bother them that friends said she offered to pay for drinks because it was a big weekend at U of I, and she used her grandmother's card. Besides, she was getting ready to move south to Austin for what promised to be a well-paying job. It did not even concern them that Kaylee told several people about plans for a European vacation.

What got their attention was when she showed up that weekend in a shiny new car—at least one that was new to her. On Wednesday, November 30, 2022, ISP senior detective Gary Tolleson was assigned by ISP detective Gideon Roberts to investigate Kaylee's purchase of a 2015 Range Rover from the AutoNation Subaru in Spokane Valley, Washington. In ISP Supplemental 75, Tolleson wrote:

> I received the Range Rover title information, which showed the vehicle being owned by a Jazmine Danielle Sumner who lived in Spokane, Washington. The lien holder on the vehicle showed Canopy Credit Union of Spokane, Washington. The previous owner to Sumner showed as Mark and Stephanie Stephens of Graham, Washington.

From there, Tolleson determined that Sumner had signed the release of the vehicle's title on October 29, 2022, just two weeks before the crimes, and Kaylee had not yet changed the plates. In fact, investigation at the Idaho Division of Motor Vehicles showed no record that Kaylee actually even owned it. Though this all might sound a bit obtuse, police were focused on motive during the early stages of the investigation, and Kaylee's displays of wealth seemed conspicuous.

Tolleson reported:

> On Thursday December 15, 2022, I drove to AutoNation Subaru in Spokane Valley Washington. I spoke to the salesman who

> sold the Range Rover to Kaylee Goncalves, Samuel P. Shulkin. Mr. Shulkin told me that Kaylee came to the car dealership twice to look at the Range Rover. The first time she showed up with her two grandmothers, the second time she came with her mother and her grandmother. Mr. Shulkin told me he saw no drama or conflicts between Kaylee and her mother or grandmothers during the sale.

According to Shulkin, Kaylee bought the Range Rover for $24,423, with a down payment of $6,500 cash, a charge of $1,000 against her grandmother Cheryl's credit card, and monthly payments for the rest. Tolleson learned from AutoNation's finance manager Tyler Munther that Kaylee's credit application listed monthly income of $3,200 from Extreme Networks, where she worked for the previous five months as an "Operations Manager."

Tolleson determined that Kaylee had good credit and bought the car without a cosigner, but her mother, Kristi Goncalves, called the dealership shortly after the murders, saying she wanted to return the vehicle. After a series of discussions, the Range Rover was returned to the dealership before being handed back to the family once Steve Goncalves decided he wanted to keep it. Tolleson did not indicate how much Kaylee was paying each month to finance her purchase but did obtain a copy of the AutoNation Subaru advertisement offering the vehicle for $24,423. Apparently, she paid the full asking price.

Beyond the Range Rover purchase, Kaylee's life grew less clear. By all accounts, she was a popular and well-loved member of the U of I community, but as Lake's team built their victimology, red flags started to appear. Most of them involved her social interactions with men, but there were also issues of online content that might have been problematic. At first, police talked to as many of Kaylee's friends, family members, and sorority sisters as they could find. Kayla Nguyen, for example, was interviewed November 16 by Officer Jon Rosinsky (LCPA Supplemental 19). He wrote:

> I asked Kayla if Kaylee hung out or associated with anyone with violent tendencies. Kayla said no and expressed she was confused about the incident because of what she saw on the news. Kayla said Kaylee mainly stuck together with her roommates (Xana, Bethany Funke, Madison Mogen, Dylan Mortensen).

He asked if Ethan was into cocaine, and Kayla said she did not know because she didn't know him that well. When specifically asked if drugs were being sold from the house on King Road, Kayla said they were used at parties but not sold. Kayla told him she had never seen and did not know about "any large quantities of drugs at the house."

"I asked Kayla if Kaylee ever mentioned about having a stalker or having concerns about anyone and Kayla said no," Rosinsky reported, before moving on to rumors about a potential predator. "Kayla also said Kaylee never mentioned anything to the girls."

Another question at the top of investigators' lists was early identification of online surveillance video showing Kaylee and Maddie outside a food truck downtown. Rosinsky wrote:

> Kayla asked if we saw the Twitch stream. I asked Kayla what she saw in the stream, and she mentioned there were two guys.

> I asked Kayla if she recognized the two guys and Kayla said she did not. Kayla said her friends Peyton Campbell and Grace were at the Grub Truck and saw Kaylee and Madison. Kayla said Peyton mentioned that the two males were being weird. I asked Kayla if she or anyone recognized anyone from the Grub Truck stream and Kayla said no. I asked Kayla if she was familiar with the fraternity member of Delta Tau Delta and she said yes.

Rosinsky asked Kayla why she referred to the males as "weird," and she told him she thought one of the males nudged the other male, "Like, oh these are your girls, go and get them." Kayla suggested that Peyton Campbell would be worth talking to because she was there at the Grub Truck early Sunday morning with the two victims. Kayla told Rosinsky she did not know if Campbell spoke directly with the two women but mentioned that Zoe McCormick hung out with Kaylee and Madison all night at the Corner Club.

> I asked Kayla if any of the victims had any issues with anyone. And Kayla said that Kaylee was unproblematic and peaceful. Kayla said she can't imagine someone with violent tendencies around her. Kayla said she felt the same way about Madison. Kayla said if anything, maybe Ethan and Xana. I asked if Ethan and Xana associated with violent people. Kayla said that Xana and Ethan were more outgoing and hung out with different friend groups.

In terms of dating and romantic relationships, Kayla said Kaylee dated "a guy named Jack Ducoeur for a couple years" who was "a really nice person," adding that they had been "high school sweethearts." Kayla said she had spoken to her friend a couple of days before the incident, and Kaylee said she met a guy who was already living in Texas, and they were going to be roommates. When asked if Kaylee was still dating Ducoeur while making plans to move in with a new guy, Kayla said no, but she mentioned Kaylee had tried to call Jack around three o'clock Sunday morning. Kayla said her friend Josie told her Jack didn't reply.

When asked how she knew, Kayla said because "Jack told them." When asked if Kaylee "hung out" with any other males, Kayla said Kaylee was "talking to" a guy named Mason Barstow, who was vice president of the Delta Tau Delta fraternity. Rosinsky reported:

> I asked Kayla if there was anyone else she spent time with and Kayla said no, unless Kaylee met someone at the bar that night. Kayla did not know if Kaylee met anyone in particular but heard a male got kicked out for being creepy towards Madison. Kayla said the last time she spoke with Kaylee was about 1700 hours on 11/12/22. Kayla said Kaylee showed up with all of Kaylee's roommates at her apartment at the Whites sometime between 1430 and 1500 hours. Kayla said they left sometime between 1700 to 1800 hours.

Rosinsky told Kayla he was aware of a social media post showing Ethan Chapin and all the King Road roommates pictured together, and Kayla said it was taken outside her apartment.

> I asked Kayla if she has been over to Kaylee's house before. I asked if people used the Wi-Fi, and Kayla was unsure. Kayla

> said they usually leave their doors unlocked and everyone knows it's a Pi Phi house.

When asked about contact with either of the survivors, Kayla said she reached out to Bethany Funke on November 13, but Bethany did not reply. Kayla told the detective Emily Alandt may have reached out to Mortensen or Funke as well, but she was not sure.

> I asked why Kaylee lived in a house with a different sorority, and Kayla said Kaylee and Madison have been best friends for several years and spoke about living with each other.

Reaching further, police fanned out among the U of I community. On November 18, ISP detectives Eric Pesina and Ryan Hoxie interviewed Josephine Tourville, the woman Jack Ducoeur supposedly told about Kaylee's call. Although she was not asked about this particular subject, Tourville said she had known Kaylee Goncalves since freshman year when they pledged the same sorority, and that Kaylee was her "best friend." Josie told him she had seen Kaylee Saturday night around 11:00 p.m. at the Corner Club with Mogen. Josie said her best friend never mentioned any odd interactions with strangers, though she would occasionally take rides "with random people." She said she never saw Kaylee or Maddie Mogen use drugs "but wasn't sure about Kernodle." She suggested police speak with Sophia Whitehead, who had lived in Kaylee's room the year before, as well as a broad circle of friends, including Ashly Couch, Peyton Campbell, and Molly Grate.

Later that same day, Hoxie and Pesina interviewed Parker

Schwers, a roommate and fraternity brother of Jack Ducoeur's, who said he believed Kaylee had been planning a move to "North Carolina or Texas." He told detectives that Jack and Kaylee had been dating since meeting at Lake City High School in Coeur d'Alene but that they had broken up. Pesina reported:

> He thought Goncalves initiated the breakup. There wasn't any turmoil in their relationship, and they were still talking and hanging out together.

Detectives asked about drug use by the victims, and Schwers said he "wasn't aware of any." He told detectives that his housemate Brayden Pollow had heard a dog barking at approximately four o'clock Sunday morning and had reported it to the police. Police checked Schwers for "injuries to his hands, arms, or face," according to the report; they recorded no injuries and left.

That same day, ISP detective James Millar interviewed Ayden McEntee in Meridian, Idaho. McEntee, a former member of Pi Phi sorority, roommate of Sophia Whitehead, and frequent visitor at 1122 King Road, had been at the Corner Club with Kaylee on Saturday night. "There was a weird man at the bar," she told Millar.

> He was pushing her at the bar. MOGEN introduced her to the man. The man was following MOGEN, MCENTEE and GONCALVES while she was there. She spent most of her time at the Corner Club with MOGEN and GONCALVES. She was supposed to go home with them, but she had a weird feeling, so she got a ride home with a freshman Greek life designated driver. She left at approximately 1:15 a.m.

Perhaps the most important detail gleaned from McEntee was that she had grown up with Jack Showalter, knew about speculation regarding the Twitch video of him at the food truck, and had received a text from him at 3:04 a.m. asking "what she was doing." Oddly enough, Millar asked no further questions about Showalter, the text, or her response. He did ask about drug use, which she denied, and the code to the front door of the house, which Mogen had given her. Interestingly, McEntee told Millar "they would often leave their back door open," allowing McEntee and others to "just walk around the back and go in often." She knew Dylan Mortensen from high school, although they were not in the same grade, and Bethany Funke "from Greek life." She told Millar that Kaylee had a previous boyfriend named Jack, but that the "current boy GONCALVES was seeing was Mason BARSTOW."

Within weeks of the murders, police had expanded their victimology beyond King Road to broader areas of Kaylee Goncalves's life. On December 8, ISP detectives Joe Lake and William Adams interviewed a woman named Ava Wood, who "coordinated with the coaches in order to either babysit or get a babysitter for them." Wood told detectives that Kaylee had occasionally worked for Tyler Yelk, a U of I assistant football coach involved in recruiting. Wood said Kaylee babysat for the Yelk family during the summer of 2022, but she did not know how many times. In separate interviews on December 9, police confirmed that Kaylee had earned fifteen dollars per hour providing childcare "five or six times" during the spring semester of 2021.

On November 18, ISP detective Tolleson interviewed a friend of Kaylee's named Natalie Gauss. She corroborated a good deal of what they already knew, including details about Kaylee's employment with Extreme Networks, identification of Showalter as the "Grub Truck guy in the hoodie," and common use of the sliding glass doors into the kitchen. But there was more. Tolleson wrote:

> Saturday night, she went to the Dirty Goat, a local bar. GONCALVES contacted her and wanted her to go to the Corner Club. She met GONCALVES at the Corner Club around 11:00 PM. GONCALVES, MOGEN and a lot of other people were there. She had a small "run in" with a man at the Corner Club.

This was the same man who had been referred to, but not named, by numerous students as a person police should look into. They did, but nothing incriminating was ever found, and he was never a suspect or accused of any wrongdoing.

On December 6, Detective Tolleson handed one of Joe Lake's Adult Victim Background Questionnaires to Malia Jaynes, who said Kaylee was not close with her parents and that she and boyfriend Jack Ducoeur were still on "good terms" after their breakup. She told police Kaylee fully supported herself, paying for all expenses while going to college, and that she worked at a Jitterz coffee kiosk in Coeur d'Alene, among various other jobs. Jaynes told Tolleson that Kaylee was moving to Austin for a job and had lined up an Alpha Phi sister named Jordyn Quesnell as a roommate. It is unclear if Jordyn is the person Kayla Nguyen might have mistaken as male.

That same day, U of I student Taylor Zrno told ISP detectives Brady Walker and Gary Tolleson about campus life as well as family problems they might want to look into. Walker wrote:

> Zrno did not know Goncalves' mother's name. But Goncalves spoke to Zrno about the fights she and her mother had. Zrno described them as average mother/daughter fights, such as Goncalves needing to pay for her own phone. When Goncalves was in her freshman year, she did not get along with her mother. Zrno had not met Goncalves's sisters.

Zrno said Goncalves and Ducoeur had a "very positive relationship."

> When she would break up with Jack she never seemed mad about it and would hang out with the sorority sisters more. Zrno described Goncalves as the most down to earth person with a contagious smile. After Goncalves dropped from the sorority, she started hanging out with Pi Phis more, but their relationship would pick up where it left off when they would see each other.

Zrno said Kaylee drank "the normal average for a college student" and was not into drugs or "abnormally risky behavior." Zrno said Kaylee was studious, a loyal friend who had not "expressed discomfort or fear about anyone." She would never be upset when she and Jack broke up and was always the one to end things because she was bored.

> At one point when she and Jack broke up, she had an interest in Ethan Runge, who is a U of I student and lives in Coeur d'Alene. Zrno did not know anyone who disliked any of the victims.

The mention of Ethan Runge rose to police notice at that point because they had taken a significant interest in Kaylee's dating life and its potential impact on her relationship with Ducoeur. They found her account on Tinder, for example, and discovered, in subpoenaed records, nineteen different interactions. On November 27, ISP detectives Tim Hopkins and Derek Brown interviewed Aldair Rojas, who told them he was at the Corner Club with Kaylee, Maddie Mogen, and his girlfriend, Zoe McCormick, Saturday night. Hopkins wrote in ISP Supplemental 44:

> Everyone was drinking alcohol that night. They were not using recreational drugs. His friend Mason Barstow had been invited to Kaylee's house the night of November 12, 2022, but chose not to go.

On December 3, they interviewed Barstow, who confirmed Rojas's story. As ISP detective Brady Walker wrote in ISP Supplemental 62:

> He and Kaylee started talking about a month prior to the homicide. She would come back with him and stay at the fraternity. They talked on Saturday at the APhi pregame party where Kaylee apologized to him and wanted to go to the game with him. He already had other plans to go to a sorority formal that evening with Mia Darwood. Kaylee texted him that night, but he ignored it. Kaylee was pretty drunk on Saturday. She was probably texting others to hang out as well. The texts were through snap chat. Snap chat deletes after 24 hours.

Police also interviewed Mia Darwood on December 3 and recorded, in the same supplemental, that she corroborated what appeared to be Barstow's story. She did attend the formal with him that Saturday night.

On November 18, ISP detectives David Cortez and Chris Pohanka interviewed Kristen Zoey Wonenberg, who told them she had been a sorority sister of Kaylee's before she dropped out of Alpha Phi because of the cost of dues. Moving quickly to their real interest, Sergeant Cortez asked Zoey if she knew of anyone Goncalves was romantically involved with after Jack. Wonenberg named "Ethan Runge and a Mason Barstow, who are both Delts" but did not know either of the men and did not have any contact information. She said she did not believe either of the men would have had anything to do with the homicide. The report filed by Cortez states:

> Sergeant Cortez asked Wonenberg if Goncalves said anything once her and Jack broke up or if he would want to hurt her. Goncalves described Jack to her as, "Her child," and was not a serious guy. Jack was in Beta Theta Pi Fraternity, and they all hung out together since they lived next door. She described Goncalves and Jack as a "brother and sister" relationship. They shared Murphy the dog. Sergeant Cortez asked her if she thought Jack would do anything to hurt her and she believed he would never do anything to hurt her.

Which brings us back to Ducoeur. He and Kaylee had been dating since high school, they lived less than a block from each other in Moscow, and they shared ownership of an eleven-month-old goldendoodle named Murphy. Of all the people in Kaylee's life, he was almost certainly the one who knew her best.

Due to the complexity of the crimes, police wanted to talk with Ducoeur about Kaylee, although he was never implicated in any wrongdoing or considered a suspect. On November 18, 2022, they started a series of interviews that began with victimology and developed into a full-blown consensual search of his residence. This search included but was not limited to his bedroom, bathroom, laundry room, and common areas of the three-story house at 1127 King Road.

According to police reports, ISP forensic scientist Kerry Hogan and ISP detective Jeff Talbott entered the apartment at 9:17 a.m. on November 18. After searching without a warrant, based solely on Jack's written consent, they found "a drop of possible blood on the wall of the entryway." According to their reports, the sample was collected, along with "what could have been 5 or 6 small drops or runs of blood on a kitchen wall." Nothing is said in the report on any tie to the King Road house.

The search and collection of potential evidence was photographed by forensic scientist Hogan, and "documents related to the consent including the consent form and maps and pictures prepared by Jack were put on a disk and taken into evidence by investigating officers."

Detectives left the apartment at 8:20 p.m. We will return there shortly.

To gain a better understanding of Kaylee's relationship with her ex-boyfriend, Detective Sgt. Michael Van Leuven interviewed Jack S. Ducoeur on three separate occasions. He recorded the first of those conversations on November 15, 2022, and summarized his findings in ISP Supplemental 168. It is here transcribed verbatim:

> I interviewed Jack at the Idaho State Police District 1 office on November 15th, 2022. Jack was the ex-boyfriend of victim Kaylee J Goncalves. Jack had been dating Kaylee since they were in high school and dated on and off for approximately 5 years. Jack said they had broken up approximately 3 months earlier due to her taking a job in Austin and that it had been a mutual decision with no drama.
>
> Jack advised that he was driving a 2010 Volkswagen CC sport sedan gray and silver in color. He said that this vehicle was owned by Kaylee's parents, and they were allowing him to drive the vehicle.
>
> Jack advised that he lived at 1127 King Road, Apartment 1 in Moscow with a number of roommates. Jack listed his roommates as Adam Lauda, Jack Granger, Nathan Royce, Brayden Jensen, Parker Schwers, Brayden Paulo, and Michael Lyons. I noted that the location of Jack's apartment and the crime scene were near each other. I noted that Jack and his roommates were all members of Beta Theta Pi fraternity.
>
> I asked Jack to describe his whereabouts and events leading up to the time that the homicides occurred. On November 12th, Jack advised that he was at work at the Moscow Brewing Company between 2:30 p.m. and 10:30 p.m. working mostly in the kitchen. Jack drove home to the duplex and went upstairs

where he found roommates Parker Schwers, Brayden Paulo, and Michael Lyons. Also present was a friend who was not a roommate named Alex Linzaman. Jack went downstairs, changed into a sweatshirt, got a beer, and waited for a sober driver, who was a Beta Theta Pi freshman, to come pick them up. Jack said that the sober driver arrived in what he thought was a black Nissan Xterra and took him, Nathan Royce, Parker Schwers, and Alan Linzaman to the Corner Club.

Jack said they arrived at the Corner Club around 11:00 p.m. He said the club was packed and that they were admitted in because his roommate Adam Lauda was working at the club and let them in.

Jack said he saw Kaylee at the club that night. It was not uncommon for Kaylee to be at the club. Jack said that he thought Kaylee was accompanied by Laura Lynch, Natalie Gauss and Zoe McCormick who was Rojas's girlfriend. Jack said he left at approximately 1:00 a.m. Jack said he, Nathan Royce and Jack Granger were picked up from the club by Peyton Rossi, who was president of Beta Theta Phi fraternity, and returned to their apartment. Jack said he had consumed two beers, two shots of tequila, one shot of Rumple Minze, and a 32-ounce tub of beer. Jack said after returning to the apartment he hung out with his roommates for a period of time, tried to throw up but couldn't and went to bed.

Jack said he woke up around 11:30 a.m. the next day, Sunday, November 13th, 2022. Jack said Michael Lyons, Nathan Royce, Brayden Jensen came into the apartment and talked about cops being down the street near Halley's [sic] house. He tried to call Kaylee on the phone, but no answer. Jack said he walked down the street where Kaylee's apartment was and saw Hunter Chapin, who was Ethan Chapin's brother. Jack said he asked one of the officers on scene to tell him what was going on and told an officer that his ex-girlfriend lived in the house. Jack said the police put him in the back of a patrol car for about 45 minutes. Also present sitting with Hunter Chapin was another Alpha Phi, Ava Wood. Jack said Ava was a good friend of Kaylee's. At some point the University of Idaho put out a text, university wide, announcing a homicide that occurred.

At my request Jack drew a sketch of Kaylee's apartment and labeled the rooms by the names of the persons he knew to be living in each room. I have attached these drawings to a supplemental and will transfer them to the Moscow Police Department. I also scan these sketches and place the scans on a disk to include the audio recordings of Jack's interviews as well as other documents.

I asked Jack to describe what vehicles the four victims drove. Jack advised Maddie Mogen drove a white Chevy Cruze, Kaylee drove a silver Range Rover, Ethan drove a red Jeep Wrangler and Xana Kernodle drove a blue Honda Civic.

We took a break, and Jack left the room to speak with his mother who was concerned about Jack. Upon returning from speaking with his mother Jack said he did not want to continue the interview without a lawyer being present. We stopped the interview and Jack left.

Jack returned on November 17 accompanied by his attorney, Jed Nixon. After a brief recap of what he had discussed on November 15th, we resumed talking with Jack about his recollections of what had happened on the night the homicides occurred. Jack said that he, Nathan Royce and Jack Granger got back to their apartment a little after 1:00 a.m. He said his bedroom was on the main floor. He said he hung out with his friends for 10 to 15 minutes. Jack advised he was drunk. I asked him to estimate on a scale of 1 out of 10 how drunk he was. Jack said he would put his level of intoxication at an 8 out of 10. Jack advised he had never experienced memory lapses, had never walked in his sleep and had never acted while asleep. Jack advised he went to bed at approximately 1:20 a.m. Jack said that when he woke up the next day, he noticed that he had a number of missed calls from both Kaylee and Maddie. There was approximately 7 from Kaylee and 3 from Maddie. Jack said that he had no argument with Kaylee the night before, and that there was no dispute and no one was upset about anything.

I noted in looking at phone records that there had been several text messages the night before between Jack and Kaylee. The last text message was from Kaylee to Jack at 2:15 a.m. telling him that she had his vape and that he could come pick it up at her house. I advised Jack that there appeared to be a telephone call at 2:26 a.m. between Jack and Kaylee that lasted approximately 17 minutes the night before. Jack said he did not recall the phone call and cannot explain it. Jack said maybe in his sleep he thought it was an alarm, and he pushed the side button of the phone to turn the ringer off.

Jack said that he had been missing more classes than normal and that the breakup with Kaylee had been bothering him. He talked about her going to Texas and the fact that she initiated the breakup.

I asked Jack directly if he had committed these murders,

he stated clearly that he did not. Jack consensually gave a DNA sample at my request. He also consensually gave his cell phone to be downloaded. I later took the DNA samples and transferred them to the custody of the Moscow Police Department. I took thumb drive containing the download from Jack's phone and transferred that to the custody of the Moscow Police Department. Jack signed consent forms for both his DNA and for the download of his phone. Jack has never been implicated or named as a suspect in any of the crimes.

On November 18, 2022, Jack consented to a search of his room, bathrooms, common areas and downstairs laundry of his apartment in Moscow. Forensic scientist Kerry Hogan, Idaho State Police Detective Jeff Talbott and I entered the apartment at 21:17 on the 18th. After searching the areas Jack had consented to, we found a drop of possible blood on a wall of the entryway. A sample of this was collected. We also noticed what could have been 5 or 6 small drops or runs of blood on a kitchen wall. Samples were also collected. This search and collection of possible bullet drop samples was documented through photographs by forensic scientist Hogan. We left the apartment at 20:20.

None of this has ever been tied to any of the crimes.

Despite significant interest in Kaylee, police initially focused on Maddie as the target of the attacks. The first two murders had occurred in her bed on the third floor of a hard-to-navigate house. The killer had bypassed other potential victims on his way upstairs—specifically Dylan Mortensen, whose room would have been closest to the point of entry. Detectives reportedly found the now infamous KA-BAR knife sheath partially lodged beneath Maddie's thigh, which, like the rest of her body, seemed to have been posed. She suffered signature wounds to her throat and shoulder. She was the only person in the house who had lived there the year before.

Beyond this, nothing really stood out. At the end of the day, Madison May Mogen was a twenty-one-year-old marketing major at a small university, an Idaho native, born and raised in Coeur d'Alene. She was a member of the Pi Beta Phi sorority, where she had served as Bethany Funke's "big." She held a regular job at a well-known local eatery, maintained good grades, had a steady boyfriend of two years who lived three hours away in Boise. Friends described her as the head of the house, as did police who usually talked to her when responding to noise complaints during parties. She maintained a strong social media profile presenting what appeared to be the ideal college life: a youthful exuberance expressed via happy faces posing for an endless stream of selfies.

Most of what police learned about Mogen can be summarized in a handful of reports. On November 15, ISP detectives Jake Schwecke and Hugh Powell looked into her employment history, interviewing Jackie Fischer, owner of Mad Greek restaurant, where Maddie waited tables part-time. Fischer said Maddie had worked there for two years and was a "reliable employee who was well liked." The following day, a coworker named Anthony Lopez told investigators that either Maddie or Xana Kernodle once told him they had a stalker, but he could not remember which. A waitress named Jera Taylor told Detective Powell she did not know Maddie but was friends with Xana, who had grown up in a "rough environment" and "used alcohol, Adderall, and Molly (Ecstasy)." On November 22 police interviewed a Mad Greek waitress named Isabell Baunach, who had no information about Mogen but felt suspicious of a maintenance man, who she said gave off "a creepy vibe and asked her an inappropriate question." When police talked to the worker, Powell reported that he "took off his sweatshirt, rolled up his sleeves and showed us his bare arms." He had no visible injuries. He was never publicly named as a suspect or implicated in the crimes.

Beyond the workplace, investigators determined that Maddie's father, Benjamin, and mother, Karen, had divorced and remarried. As an only child, Maddie had no siblings to be interviewed, but there was a long list of friends, sorority sisters, and associates, so on November 18, 2022, ISP detectives drove to Desert Sage Elementary School in Boise to interview a 2021 U of I graduate named Kaylee McConkey. McConkey, twenty-five, had graduated in May of the previous year but was a member of Pi Phi with Maddie, whom she referred to as her "best friend." McConkey told detectives she knew Kaylee Goncalves through Mogen, had met Ethan once through Xana, and had socialized with Bethany and Dylan on occasion.

"She received a FaceTime call from MOGEN the night of the homicides at approximately 1:50 AM, Boise time," Detective Millar wrote in ISP Supplemental 16, filed nine days after the crimes. This would have made McConkey one of the last people to speak with Maddie alive.

> MC CONKEY was drunk at the time of the call; MOGEN appeared to be also. The call only lasted approximately one

> minute. McConkey was with Ruby SIMPSON and Sophia WHITEHEAD during the call at a bar in Boise. MOGEN was with GONCALVES at the Corner Club in Moscow during the call.

According to McConkey, she had run into Maddie's boyfriend, Jake Schriger, at a bar called the Amsterdam Lounge in Boise. She told Millar she took a picture with Schriger, Simpson, and Whitehead at approximately 1:15 a.m., and sent it to Mogen, which Detective Millar confirmed, according to his report. She told Millar she had seen Mortensen and Funke in the days after the homicides, specifically, Monday, November 14, when the two survivors arrived back in Boise. McConkey said Bethany Funke's parents met her there, and she "went home with them." The detectives did not indicate why the Funkes would meet in Boise when they lived in Reno, but it makes sense that Bethany would leave Moscow as soon as possible.

Millar wrote in the report:

> The last social media post MC CONKEY had seen with any of the victims was a picture of MOGEN on GONCALVES Snapchat story. They were at the Grub Truck together.

At this point in the investigation, investigators were still trying to build portraits of their victims and timelines surrounding events, both before and after the murders. Millar's report represents both sides of the investigation, and some of what they gathered had immediate impact.

"She knew the person in the video at Grub Truck was Jack SHOWALTER," McConkey told detectives.

Everyone from Moscow police to the FBI was looking into all aspects of his life, as well as the lives of the people around him.

Millar reported:

> She did not know him well. SHOWALTER had a girlfriend the whole time MC CONKEY was going to school at University of Idaho. She knew SHOWALTER's girlfriend, Meghan SINGH, better than him. SHOWALTER and that girlfriend are not dating anymore. SHOWALTER lived at the brown apartments near the victims.

It should be noted here that Showalter was never charged with or implicated in any crime and denied any involvement.

McConkey told investigators she had not actually been inside the house at 1122 King Road since December 21 of the previous year, but that she had stopped by on homecoming a month before the murders. She was familiar, however, with each of the rooms inside the house and told police she knew where each person slept. Interestingly, McConkey told detectives her friend Whitehead, who was also on the FaceTime call with Maddie Sunday morning, actually paid rent on the vacant first-floor bedroom, down the hall from Bethany. And even though Boise is almost three hundred miles south of Moscow, McConkey knew a great deal about events surrounding the crimes. She told police Bethany and Dylan had called Emily Alandt and Hunter Johnson Sunday morning, that Johnson had walked upstairs and witnessed the aftermath of the crimes. She knew that Alandt and Johnson were in Mexico at the time she was being interviewed by the ISP. Millar wrote:

> She thought Funke and Mortensen called ALANDT and JOHNSON, because they were a little worried. Their other roommates weren't answering. MORTENSEN thought she had heard someone in the house the night before and wasn't sure if that person was still in the house. During MC CONKEY's time living in Moscow, it wasn't uncommon for someone to walk into the wrong house drunk or to hear people up and moving around, in which case you might call someone you know instead of the police.

According to McConkey, Mortensen told her she heard Goncalves playing music at approximately four o'clock in the morning. Dylan said she ended up going down to Funke's room because Funke was the only one who answered her phone.

> They had all been drinking all day the day before and MORTENSEN was a little freaked out that someone might be in the house.

McConkey went on to tell detectives that sometime after the homicides, Funke and Mortensen recounted the story about Mogen and Goncalves going to WinCo for groceries. While in the store, Goncalves apparently felt that someone was "following her or lurking around."

> This freaked Goncalves out enough to go get back in the car and lock the doors immediately. A man then tried to open the door. This happened approximately 2 to 3 weeks prior to the interview.

Perhaps the most important statement McConkey made to police was that Kaylee Goncalves's sister told her Jack Ducoeur woke up the morning after the homicides with sixteen missed calls from Goncalves and Mogen. According to McConkey, Kaylee had called approximately ten times, and Mogen had called approximately seven times. There were also text messages sent to Ducoeur saying things like "Bro, what the fuck?" and "Wake up."

Millar reported:

> Goncalves was known for calling a lot of times consecutively when she wanted to contact someone. Neither Goncalves nor Mogen would call Ducoeur instead of the police for help. Ducoeur and Goncalves had dated previously. They were currently broken up but good friends.

Revisiting Detective Rosinsky's November 16 interview of Kayla Nguyen, we can see that police were very interested in Maddie's love life, especially a full-time boyfriend. Rosinsky wrote:

> And they called him Schriger and said she thought his first name was Jake. Kayla said they are still together. Kayla said she does not think they had problems and Schriger was a good guy. Detective Dean asked what he looked like, and Kayla said Schriger was short maybe 5–7 and balding. Kayla said he had brown hair and was skinny. Kayla thought he lived in Coeur d'Alene.

Jake Schriger actually lived in Boise, but small details like that do not matter when an entire community erupts in speculation.

Hearsay was rampaging through Moscow at that point, and national media were broadcasting every sordid detail, unredacted. Information gathered about Mogen would do little more than add to the department's already burgeoning files. Though victimology is important, the real search for the killer had turned to cell tower pings and DNA. Once Kohberger was identified as a suspect, every other lead faded away. None of the individuals in this chapter has ever been named as a suspect or implicated in the crimes.

Perhaps this is a good thing, considering Kohberger's eventual guilty plea, but what the world did not know at that point was how fragile the police investigation had become. While Bill Thompson trumpeted confidence in his open-and-shut case, his team likely knew their evidence was not what it seemed. Victimology revealed little; forensics may have shown them even less.

PART 3

ABSOLUTE DEVOTION

10.06.2023

Dear Family,

Together, hand-in-hand and galvanized by the wisdom of the Singular Heart, we triumphantly ascend to new peaks, thus apprehending the beautiful pattern/form of the labyrinthine path taken afore; indeed . . . we have traversed many once-novel territories, finding that, when all else may seem variable/entropic, it is the one constant from which clarity and serenity are ever-accessible . . .

Love always,

Bryan, B.C, Bernn, Buddy, Brother
Bryan C. Kohberger
Latah County Jail

CHAPTER 12

8458 Phone, REDACTED, Palouse River Drive

Bryan Christopher Kohberger first appeared on police radar November 29, 2022, approximately two weeks after the crimes. According to the prosecution's timeline, his white 2015 Hyundai Elantra had just been identified in a search of Washington State University vehicle registrations by Officer Daniel Tiengo. This was the same day MSP officer Mowery obtained a search warrant for Kaylee Goncalves's Tinder account, the victims' cars were towed from 1122 King Road, and Detective Dahlinger transported the KA-BAR knife sheath to the ISP lab. The FBI had arrived on scene; national media were descending in hordes; tip lines were ringing off the hook with promising leads. Things were happening fast.

It did not take long for Officer Tiengo's discovery to help law enforcement home in on Kohberger as the sole focus of their investigation. Within hours, detectives began gathering personal information from the Washington State registrar's office, checking criminal histories, canvassing surveillance video, auditing traffic stops, and obtaining search warrants for records from Google and AT&T to the Pennsylvania DMV. Working together, MPD, ISP, and FBI investigators tagged the twenty-eight-year-old PhD student in criminology as male, white, six feet, with brown hair and blue eyes. They determined that he had arrived on campus June 30, 2022, with his father in a four-door sedan after stopping the previous night in Gardiner, Montana. They obtained credit card and registration records proving the two men spent their first night in town at the Quality Inn, after purchasing groceries at the local Safeway and basic household items, such as a knife set, towels, and a "Utility Cloth" at Walmart. They determined that Kohberger moved into his one-bedroom apartment on July 1, 2022, and obtained a Washington driver's license later that day.

Reaching further, they discovered that the owner of the white Elantra had most recently lived in Albrightsville, Pennsylvania, where he grew up in a two-story white colonial with his dad, Michael; his mother, Maryann; one sister named Amanda; and another named Melissa. They documented that prior to enrolling in Washington State University, Bryan C. Kohberger attended Pleasant Valley schools in Brodheadsville, then Northampton Community College and DeSales University. His high school yearbook showed him doing push-ups in a police cadet uniform; he had lost a lot of weight as a teenager, suffered addictions, loved a dog named Scout. He claimed to be allergic to a broad spectrum of foods, and at one time suffered with a neurological disorder called "visual snow." The WSU teaching assistant lived at 1630 NE Valley Road in Pullman, in a one-bedroom apartment designated 201.

Despite early successes, however, police wanted more. Forensic analysis and autopsy reports clearly indicated that these murders were crimes of rage, yet there was no evidence Kohberger had ever met the victims. Why would a highly intelligent, well-educated man from Pennsylvania enroll in a PhD program at the other end of the country just to commit murder? How would an otherwise law-abiding graduate student with no history of aberrant behavior plan and execute one of the most heinous crimes in Idaho history? How did he know the house well enough to get in, cull victims from survivors, and get out in about four minutes? Where had he met Kaylee and Maddie? When did his studies turn to rage? What could possibly have been his motive?

Police had a lot of questions and very few answers at that point in the investigation, so they started with the man himself, tracing his roots to Pennsylvania. By all accounts, the Kohbergers were a close-knit, middle-class family of modest means with roots in the community. Mr. and Mrs. Kohberger had raised three kids working for the Pleasant Valley School District. They lived in a two-story colonial-style house on a quiet street in a private gated community called Indian Mountain Lake. Most of their extended family lived in Brooklyn, New York.

From the outside looking in, most people would consider Bryan's youth normal. His parents were married on Valentine's Day, 1987, in a small Catholic wedding of about fifty people at St. Patrick's Church in Bay Ridge. Mrs. Kohberger was born and raised in nearby Carroll Gardens, where she attended and then taught Catholic school for eight years. She loved Brooklyn but felt it was too expensive to raise a family, so six years later, they moved west to Pennsylvania, where she obtained public school certification but did not get a job, so she worked most of her life as a paraprofessional with children in fifth and sixth grade.

Bryan, the youngest of three children, was bright, though not very athletic; good-looking in traditional ways, though awkward socially. Police would eventually discover a history of substance abuse and limited social acceptance based on spectrum disorders, but he had no history of violence or interactions with the law. Saying he was close to his family might seem an understatement considering he lived at home until the summer of 2022, when he moved to Washington at the age of twenty-seven. According to friends and family, he loved outdoor activities and baseball, especially the Yankees. He had never had a girlfriend but was particularly close to the family dog.

And though much of what the world first knew about Kohberger came from hearsay gathered by journalists, we now have interview transcripts that paint a much clearer picture of the man we all watched say yes four times when asked if he had committed murder. On December 30, 2022, Bryan's mom, Maryann Kohberger, was interviewed by FBI special agents Jessica L. Mahoney, Matthew Mark Phillips, and Eric Bailey at the Pennsylvania State Police Fern Ridge Barracks in Blakeslee, where she and her husband had been taken while their house was being searched. Those agents filed two FD-302s (FBI reports of investigation) documenting their conversations. The first is labeled 9A-SU-3683464-SCRANTON Serial 35. It states:

> SA Eric Bailey questioned Maryann regarding a conversation which took place prior to Bryan moving to Washington state. Maryann recalled a conversation in which she suggested Bryan

> obtain something to defend himself in the event of a bear attack while Bryan hiked in the western US.

Though the first part of this interview was not recorded, SA Bailey clearly seems interested in a KA-BAR knife police say Bryan purchased with an Amazon gift card while living in Pennsylvania, approximately eight months before the crimes.

> Maryann did not know if Bryan purchased anything for this purpose and was unaware of Bryan specifically purchasing a knife for this purpose.

The second part of the FBI document is a transcription of the larger recorded interview with special agents Jessica Mahoney and Matthew Phillips. At thirty-eight pages, the transcript is too long to reprint here, but some sections provide fascinating glimpses into the man himself. Jurors often want context beyond forensics; they want to know how to reconcile the tall, awkward defendant with 0.16 ng of DNA, cell tower analysis, and grainy video of a four-door sedan. What a mother says about her son can be important.

•

"We supported him," Maryann Kohberger responds to SA Phillips at the beginning of the interview. "Both my daughters are, um, they're both therapists. So, we read a lot of encouragement and a lot of support from them. You know, um . . ."

•

This is followed by a bunch of small talk, which is called "rapport building" at the FBI National Academy where I spent two years as a supervisory special agent within the communications unit. The bureau refers to this block of instruction as interview/interrogation, offering similar curricula to new agents and law enforcement executives alike. The idea is to start off low-key, fostering familiarity and trust before employing techniques like modeling, affirmation, and neurolinguistic programming. In this case, Mrs. Kohberger stands at a significant disadvantage, because she is isolated and emotionally distraught and has no lawyer. No one has Mirandized her, because it is not a custodial interview and she has never been implicated in or suspected of any of the crimes, but anything she says will certainly be used at trial.

•

"You know . . . so we've always, we've always been there, you know," Mrs. Kohberger states well into the interview. "But it was very short-lived."

•

It appears she's said this in response to a question about her son's drug use during his late teens, but there is no transcribed reference to that specific topic.

•

"We were fortunate in that regard because, um, like in our community, a lot of families were not as—as fortunate. It was very ongoing and—and we had a lot of people that we know that lost children to it, so we felt really lucky and very, very fortunate and blessed."

"Well, and even with me," SA Phillips says, trying to play on a mother's love for her son under extraordinarily difficult circumstances. "I've been part of many drug investigations, and you run into people with addiction problems, and you know you see people. They progress or they're people who go the other way. And I've seen people fall victim to that, but um . . ."

•

Empathy can be an effective device in a situation like this and is taught in many police interview/interrogation courses. It should be lost on no one that it is well after midnight at this point, and police are searching the Kohberger home for evidence of murder.

•

"More often than not, really," his partner agrees. "When I hear a success story like this it's—I always say never give up on somebody with a problem like that."

"You know, but here we are," Mrs. Kohberger responds. "You know, so . . ."

•

And then Phillips turns things back to the matter at hand. The interview of Maryann Kohberger is not about consolation.

•

"Well, and that's what, again, not to sound like a broken record, but that's why we're here," he says. "We want to know more about the person. Bryan, okay, and I don't think there's any—"

"He's my angel," the mother tells him.

"There's no better person to tell his story," Phillips prods.

"He's my angel."

•

At this point, rapport building goes out the window. To be clear, it is early in the morning, police are searching the Kohberger house, and Bryan is in police custody under a warrant for murder. The agents want to know about Bryan Kohberger's psychological state when he arrived home in Pennsylvania.

•

"Um, so while Bryan was in the home, did he socialize with any of his friends?" Phillips asks. "Or anything? Or did he just stay home?"

"He doesn't have a big group of friends, no," the mother responds. "He touched base with one of his best friends from Arizona who's still in Arizona. Um, but no he's been mostly home with the family, just chilling."

•

She calls her son a "homebody" and says everything seemed normal when he returned from school. She tells the FBI her son is a regular guy who likes to run but does not "work out," which police already know from half-naked selfies on his phone. Mrs. Kohberger says her son was happy to see Scout, the family dog. She said he calls the dog "his Bubba," affectionately referring to him as "Bleeben."

•

"You say that he's, uh, an angel," SA Mahoney presses. "He's kind, he's your baby. Does he have any anger issues ever?"

•

Mrs. Kohberger says her son is not an angry person, has never exhibited any confrontational behavior, does not hold grudges. Though the FBI's Behavioral Analysis Unit has weighed in with guidance, they were never asked to profile the offender.

•

"Um, girlfriends?" Agent Mahoney asks, probing further. "Boyfriends?"

"He doesn't have any girlfriends right now," Mrs. Kohberger answers, adding later that he's had "a couple, not a lot," in the past.

•

When asked about any potential romantic interests in Washington, she says only that he was "making friends" and that she does not "know the names of a lot of them." She tells SA Phillips she "would feel uncomfortable even mentioning them" but brought up one international student, later identified and interviewed in mainstream media as a WSU colleague. This is not the woman named Haley Wette, who said she went on a Tinder date with Kohberger while he was a graduate student in Pennsylvania.

•

"Yeah, that's a big change, you know, coming from rural Pennsylvania, moving across the country by yourself, and it doesn't sound like he's ever lived on his own," SA Mahoney says.

"No," she answers. "This is the first time."

•

When asked about his adaptation to life alone on the other side of the country, Mrs. Kohberger says her son has adapted well, has seemed happy in regular phone conversations, has checked in almost every day and sent pictures of his new apartment in Pullman.

•

"Would he talk to other family members?" Phillips wants to know.

"Um no," she says. "He would call his dad and, you know, talk to the girls once in a while. But mostly me."

"Mother and son talks?"

"Mother and son talks."

"Did he have any concerns or anything like that about school, or were you concerned about anything?"

"No, he just, um, he just finished the semester with a 3.8."

•

Curiously, Mrs. Kohberger talks about her son's organizational habits. This might have interested behavioralists looking for clues as to how the killer left the house covered in blood without tracking a single cell of DNA to his car or his apartment.

•

"Yeah, he's very organized, so he gets things done. Well, sometimes. Mostly he's organized when it comes to his work. Sometimes at home he would get sloppy with clothing and stuff like that, but, um, no. This is just really weird for me."

8458 Phone, REDACTED, Palouse River Drive

•

She says he has no hobbies, other than an interest in being outdoors, a love for nature.

•

"How about sleep?" Mahoney asks. "Does he sleep? Or is he one of those people who is like a night owl and then sleeps during the day?"

"Um, it depends on what's going on, like if he has things that he has to do during the course of the day, then obviously he's gonna do that, but sometimes he's up at night."

•

This would turn out to be critical later when investigators discovered he had turned his cell phone off from 2:42 a.m. until 4:50 a.m. the morning of the crimes. At one point his defense team argued that he was prone to go out late and stargaze. At least one witness saw him going out after dark to hike up into the mountains near WSU.

•

"Um, how about any concerns of, like, partying out in Washington, or here even, when he was going to school?" SA Mahoney wants to know.

"No, not a party animal," Kohberger says. "No, not a party animal, not a drinker."

•

She reiterates that her son is normal in typical ways, that the two of them share a mother-son bond, and that if he confided anything, it would be to her.

•

"Right," Mrs. Kohberger says at one point, turning the interview specifically to the matter at hand. "What's the story here? What are we looking at?"

"So, the reason we were at the house today was because of the arrest warrant and, um, for the incidents that occurred in Idaho, okay?" Mahoney answers.

"Okay."

•

They talk about the white 2015 Elantra that belongs to her son, the car she and her husband bought for him. Mrs. Kohberger says she's seen reports on the news but wasn't concerned because the car that police have been looking for is a different year of manufacture. She says her son's car looks nothing like the one shown on TV; it has a whole "different front."

•

"What's going through my mind right now is that this is a really, really bad mistake, what's going on, like what's happening here," she says.

"Um, yeah, I—and I sympathize with that because as a mom, I definitely would think the same way," Mahoney says.

"To me, I feel like I know it is," Mrs. Kohberger shoots back, followed by, "We know what our, you know, who our children are, you know."

•

At that point, she tries to turn the conversation toward the search of her house, but the agents say only that the warrant was signed by a magistrate based on an affidavit.

•

"There is a lot of evidence," Phillips tells her. "An arrest warrant was issued, okay? There's a search warrant that was issued. In order for that to happen, there needs to be probable cause to get that, there needs to be a considerable amount of evidence."

•

Agent Phillips confirms that her son has been arrested for four counts of premeditated murder. They tell her that's the whole point in the interview, that they want to "get an idea of how Bryan really is."

•

"So now my son's face is gonna be plastered all across the country?" she asks.

•

As one might expect, the interviewing agents skip over the question, claiming they don't know "how the press release is gonna go."

•

"Never, ever, ever," she says when told that the purpose of the interview is to find out whether she's had any concerns about behaviors that might indicate her son's involvement in the crimes.

"My son would not do this. I will stake my life on that. There's a mistake, something is wrong somewhere. And that's what I believe. And that's what I know in my heart."

•

Mrs. Kohberger lived with her son until he left the family home for Washington. Throughout the interview, she seems both shocked and certain police have mistaken her son for a killer.

•

"This is a nightmare," she says midway through the conversation. It's a mother's emotional reaction to what must seem like a surreal interruption of her family's life. "This is an absolute nightmare." Then, turning to the family dog, who has apparently been in the room during the interview, she says, "No, no, Bubba, come here."

On December 20, 2022, MPD officer Brett Payne filed a probable cause affidavit with the Latah County clerk of courts, seeking a warrant for the arrest of Bryan C. Kohberger on one count of burglary and four counts of murder in the first degree. This one document best summarizes what law enforcement believed about their primary suspect at that point in their investigation. Due to its length, only paragraphs that directly address Kohberger and evidence against him are included.

Exhibit A

Statement of Brett Payne

8458 Phone, REDACTED, Palouse River Drive

The below information is provided by Brett Payne, who is a duly appointed, qualified and acting peace officer within the County of Latah, State of Idaho. Brett Payne is employed by Moscow Police Department in the official capacity or position of Corporal (CPL) and has been a trained and qualified peace officer for approximately four (4) years. CPL Payne is being assisted by members of the Idaho State police and agents of the Federal Bureau of investigation.

As part of the investigation, an extensive search, commonly referred to in law enforcement as a "video canvass," was conducted in the area of the King Road Residence. This video canvass was to obtain any footage from the early morning hours of November 13, 2022, in the area of the King Road Residence and surrounding neighborhoods in an effort to locate the suspect(s) or suspect vehicle(s) traveling to or leaving from the King Road Residence. This video canvass resulted in the collection of numerous surveillance videos in the area from both residential and business addresses. I have reviewed numerous videos that were collected and have had conversations with the other MPD Officers, ISP Detectives, and FBI Agents that are similarly reviewing footage that was obtained.

A review of camera footage indicated that a white sedan, hereafter "Suspect Vehicle 1", was observed traveling westbound in the 700 block of Indian Hills Drive in Moscow at approximately 3:26 a.m. and westbound on Styner Avenue at Idaho State Highway 95 in Moscow at approximately 3:28 am. On this video, it appeared Suspect Vehicle 1 was not displaying a front license plate.

A review of footage from multiple videos obtained from the

King Road Neighborhood showed multiple sightings of Suspect Vehicle 1 starting at 3:29 am. and ending at 4:20 a.m. These sightings show Suspect Vehicle 1 makes an initial three passes by the 1122 King Road residence and then leaves via Walenta Drive. Based off my experience as a Patrol Officer this is a residential neighborhood with a very limited number of vehicles that travel in the area during the early morning hours. Upon review of the video there are only a few cars that enter and exit this area during this time frame.

Suspect Vehicle 1 can be seen entering the area a fourth time at approximately 4:04 a.m. It can be seen driving eastbound on King Road, stopping and turning around in front of 500 Queen Road #52 and then driving back westbound on King Road. When Suspect Vehicle 1 is in front of the King Road Residence, it appeared to unsuccessfully attempt to park or turn around in the road. The vehicle then continued to the intersection of Queen Road and King Road where it can be seen completing a three-point turn and then driving eastbound again down Queen Road.

Suspect Vehicle 1 is next seen departing the area of the King Road Residence at approximately 4:20 a.m. at a high rate of speed. Suspect Vehicle 1 is next observed traveling southbound on Walenta Drive. Based on my knowledge of the area and review of camera footage in the neighborhood that does not show Suspect Vehicle 1 during that timeframe. I believe that Suspect Vehicle 1 likely exited the neighborhood at Palouse River Drive and Conestoga Drive. Palouse River Drive is the southern edge of Moscow and proceeds into Whitman County, Washington. Eventually the road leads to Pullman,

Washington. Pullman Washington is approximatively 10 miles from Moscow, Idaho. Both Pullman and Moscow are small college towns and people commonly travel back and forth between them.

Law enforcement officers provided video footage of Suspect Vehicle 1 to Forensic Examiners with the Federal Bureau of Investigation that regularly utilize surveillance footage to identify the year, make, and model of an unknown vehicle that is observed by one or more cameras during the commission of a criminal offense. The Forensic Examiner has approximately 35 years law enforcement experience with twelve years at the FBI. His specific training includes identifying unique characteristics of vehicles, and he uses a database that gives visual clues of vehicles across states to identify differences between vehicles.

After reviewing the numerous observations of Suspect Vehicle 1, the forensic examiner initially believed the Suspect Vehicle 1 was a 2011–2013 Hyundai Elantra. Upon further review, he indicated it could also be a 2011–2016 Hyundai Elantra. As a result, investigators have been reviewing information on persons in possession of a vehicle that is a 2011–2016 white Hyundai Elantra.

Investigators were given access to video footage on the Washington State University (WSU) campus located in Pullman, WA. A review of that video indicated that at approximately 2:44 a.m. on November 13, 2022, a white sedan, which was consistent with the description of the White Elantra known as Suspect Vehicle 1 observed on WSI surveillance cameras travelling north on southeast Nevada Street at northeast Stadium Way. At approximately 2:53 a.m., a white sedan, which is consistent with the description of the White Elantra known as Suspect Vehicle 1, was observed traveling southeast on Nevada Street in Pullman, WA towards SR 270. SR 270 connects Pullman, Washington to Moscow, Idaho. This camera footage from Pullman, WA was provided to the same FBI Forensic Examiner. The Forensic Examiner identified the vehicle observed in Pullman, WA as being a 2014–2016 Hyundai Elantra.

At approximately 5:25 a.m., a white sedan, which was consistent with the description of Suspect Vehicle 1, was observed on five cameras in Pullman, WA and on WSU Campus cameras. The first camera that recorded the white sedan was located at 1300 Johnson Road in Pullman. The white sedan was observed traveling northbound on Johnson Road. Johnson Road leads directly back to West Palouse River Drive in Moscow which intersects with Conestoga Drive. The white sedan was then observed turning north on Bishop Boulevard and northwest on SR 270. At approximately 5:27 a.m., the White Elantra was observed on cameras traveling northbound on Stadium Way at Nevada Street, Stadium Way at Grimes Way, Stadium Drive at Wilson Road, and Stadium Way at Cougar Way.

On November 25, 2022, MPD asked area law enforcement agencies to be on the lookout for white Hyundai Elantras in the area. On November 29, 2022, at approximately 12:28 a.m., Washington State University (WSU) Police Officer Daniel Tiengo queried white Elantras registered at WSU. As a result of that query, he located a 2015 white Elantra with a Pennsylvania license plate LFZ-8649. This vehicle was registered to Bryan

Kohberger hereafter "Kohberger" residing at REDACTED is approximately three (tenths) of a mile from the intersection of Stadium Way and Cougar Way (last camera location that picked up the white Elantra).

That same day at approximately 12:58 a.m., WSU Officer Curtis Whitman was looking for white Hyundai Elantras and located a white Hyundai Elantra at REDACTED in Pullman in the parking lot. REDACTED is an apartment complex that houses WSU students. Officer Whitman also ran the car, and it returned to Kohberger with a Washington tag. I reviewed Kohberger's WA state driver license information and photograph. This license indicates that Kohberger is a white male with a height of 6' and weighs 185 pounds. Additionally, the photograph of Kohberger shows that he has bushy eyebrows. Kohberger's physical description is consistent with the description of the make D.M. saw inside King Road Residence on November 13th.

Further investigation, including a review of Latah County Sheriff's Deputy CPL Duke's body cam and reports, showed that on August 21, 2022, Bryan Kohberger was detained as part of a traffic stop that occurred in Moscow, Idaho, by CPL Duke. At the time, Kohberger, who was the sole occupant, was driving a white 2015 Hyundai Elantra with Pennsylvania plate LFZ-8649 which was set to expire on November 30, 2022. During the stop, which was recorded via a law enforcement body camera, Kohberger provided his phone number as REDACTED 8458, hereafter the "8458 Phone" as his cellular telephone number. Investigators conducted electronic database queries and learned that the 8458 Phone is a number issued by AT&T.

On October 14, 2022, Bryan Kohberger was detained as part of a traffic stop by a WSU police officer. Upon review of that body cam and report of the stop Kohberger was the sole occupant and was driving a 2015 Hyundai Elantra with Pennsylvania plate LFZ-8649.

On October 18, 2022, according to WA state licensing, Kohberger registered the 2015 white Elantra with WA and later received WA plate CFB-8708. Prior to this time the 2015 white Elantra was registered in Pennsylvania, which does not require a front license plate to be displayed (this was learned through communications with a Pennsylvania officer who is currently certified in the state of Pennsylvania.) Based on my experience and communication with Washington law enforcement, I know that Idaho and Washington require front and back license plates to be displayed.

Investigators believe that Kohberger is still driving the 2015 white Elantra because his vehicle was captured on December 13th, 2022, by a license plate reader in Loma, Colorado (information provided by a query to a database). Kohberger's Elantra was then queried on December 15, 2022, by law enforcement in Hancock County, Indiana. On December 16, 2022, at approximately 2:26 PM, surveillance video showed Kohberger's Elantra in Albrightsville, Pennsylvania. The sole occupant of the vehicle was a white male whose description was consistent with Kohberger. Kohberger has family in Albrightsville, Pennsylvania (learned through a TLO search and locate tool database query.)

Based on information provided on the WSU website, Kohberger is currently a PhD student in criminology at

Washington State University. Pursuant to records provided by a member of the interview panel for Pullman Police Department we learned that Kohberger's past education included undergraduate degrees in psychology and cloud based forensics. These records also showed Kohberger wrote an essay when he applied for an internship with the Pullman Police Department in the fall of 2022. Kohberger wrote in his essay he had interest in assisting rural law enforcement agencies with how to better collect and analyze technological data in public safety operations. Kohberger also posted a Reddit survey which can be found by an open source Internet search. The survey asked for participants to provide information to understand how emotions and psychological traits influence decision making when committing a crime.

As part of this investigation law enforcement obtained search warrants to determine cellular devices that utilized cellular towers in close proximity to the King Road residence on November 13, 2022, between 3:00 AM and 5:00 AM. After determining that Kohberger was associated to both the 2015 white Elantra and the 8458 Phone investigators reviewed these search warrant returns. A query of the 8458 Phone in these returns did not show the 8458 Phone utilizing cell tower resources in close proximity to the King Road Residence between 3:00 AM and 5:00 a.m.

Based on my training, experience, and conversations with law enforcement officers that specialize in the utilization of cellular telephone records as part of investigations, individuals can either leave their cellular telephone at a different location before committing a crime or turn their cellular telephone off prior to going to a location to commit a crime. This is done by subjects in an effort to avoid alerting law enforcement that a cellular device associated with them was in a particular area where a crime is committed. I also know that on numerous occasions subjects will surveil an area where they intend to commit a crime prior to the date of the crime. Depending on the circumstances, this could be done a few days before or several months prior to the commission of a crime. During these types of surveillance, it is possible that an individual would not leave their cellular telephone at a separate location or turn it off since they do not plan to commit the offense on that particular day.

On December 23, 2022, I applied for and was granted a search warrant for historical phone records between November 12, 2022, at 12:00 a.m. and November 14, at 12:00 a.m. for the 8458 Phone held by the phone provider AT&T (approximately 24 hours preceding and following the times of the homicides).

On December 23, 2022, pursuant to that search warrant, I received records for the 8458 Phone from AT&T. These records indicated that the 8458 Phone is subscribed to by Bryan Kohberger at an address in Albrightsville, Pennsylvania, and the account has been open since June 23, 2022. These records also included historical cell site location information (CSLI) for the 8458 Phone. After receiving this information, I consulted with an FBI Special Agent (SA) that is certified as a member of the Cellular Analysis Survey Team (CAST). Members of CAST are certified with the FBI to provide expert testimony in the field of historical CSLI and are required to pass extensive training that includes both written and practical examinations prior to being certified with CAST as well as the completion of yearly certification requirements. Additionally, the FBI CAST USA [United States Attorney] that I consulted with has over 15 years of federal law enforcement experience which includes 6 years with the FBI. From information provided by CAST I was able to determine estimated locations for the 8458 phone from November 12th, 2022 to November 13th, 2022, the time period authorized by the court.

On November 13th, 2022 at approximately 2:42 AM the 8458 Phone was utilizing cellular resources that provide coverage to [REDACTED] hereafter the Kohberger residence. At approximately 2:47 AM the 8458 Phone utilized cellular resources that provide coverage southeast of the Kohberger residence consistent with the 8458 Phone leaving the Kohberger Residence and traveling south through Pullman, WA. This is consistent with the movement of the white Elantra. At approximately 2:47 a.m. the 8458 Phone stops reporting to the network, which is consistent with either the phone being in an area without cellular coverage, the connection to the network is disabled (such as putting the phone in airplane mode), or that the phone is turned off. The 8458 Phone does not report to the network again until approximately 4:48 a.m. at which time it is utilizing cellular resources that provide coverage to ID state highway 95 S to Moscow, ID near Blaine, ID (north of Genesee). Between 4:50 a.m. and 5:26 a.m., the phone utilizes cellular resources that are consistent with the 8458 Phone traveling south on ID state highway 95 to Genesee, ID, then travelling west towards Uniontown, ID, and then north back into Pullman, WA. At approximately 5:30 a.m., the 8458 Phone is utilizing resources that provide coverage to Pullman, WA and is consistent with the phone traveling back to the Kohberger residence. The 8458 Phone's movements are consistent with the movements of the white Elantra which is observed travelling north on Stadium at approximately 5:27 a.m. Based on a review of the 8458 Phone's estimated locations and travel, the 8458 Phone's travel is consistent with that of the white Elantra.

Further review indicated that the 8458 Phone utilized cellular resources on November 13, 2022, that are consistent with the 8458 Phone leaving the area of the Kohberger residence at approximately 9:00 a.m. and traveling to Moscow, ID. Specifically, the 8458 Phone utilized cellular resources that would provide coverage to the King Road Residence between 9:12 a.m. and 9:21 a.m. The 8458 Phone next utilizes cellular resources that are consistent with the 8458 Phone traveling back to the area of the Kohberger residence and arriving to the area at approximately 9:32 a.m.

Investigators found that the 8458 Phone did connect to a cell phone tower that provides service to Moscow on November 14, 2022, but investigators do not believe the 8458 Phone was in Moscow on that date. The 8458 Phone has not connected to any towers that provide service to Moscow since that date.

Based on my training, experience, and the facts of the investigation thus far I believe that Kohberger, the user of the 8458 Phone, was likely the driver of the white Elantra that is observed departing Pullman, WA and that this vehicle is likely Suspect Vehicle 1. Additionally, the route of travel of the 8458 Phone during the early morning hours of November 13, 2022, and the lack of the 8458 Phone reporting to AT&T between 2:47 a.m. and 4:48 a.m. is consistent with Kohberger attempting to conceal his location during the quadruple homicide that occurred at the King Road Residence.

On December 23, 2022 I was granted a search warrant for Kohberger's historical CSLI from June 23rd 2022 to current prospective location information and a Pen Register Trap and Trace on the 8458 Phone to aid in efforts to determine if Kohberger stalked any of the victims in this case prior to the offense, conducted surveillance on the King Road Residence, was in contact with any of the victims' associates before or after the alleged offense, any locations that may contain evidence of the murders that occurred on November 13, 2022, the location of the white Elantra registered to Kohberger, as well as the location of Kohberger.

On December 23, 2022, pursuant to that search warrant I received historical records for the 8458 Phone from AT&T from the time the account was opened in June 2022. After consulting with CAST SA, I was able to determine estimated locations for the 8458 Phone from June 2022 to present, the time period authorized by the court. The records for the 8458 Phone show the 8458 Phone utilizing cellular resources that provide coverage to the area of 1122 King Road on at least 12 occasions prior to November 13, 2022. All of these occasions, except for one, occurred in the late evening and early morning hours of their respective days.

One of these occasions, on August 21, 2022, the 8458 Phone utilized cellular resources providing coverage to the King Road Residence from approximately 10:34 p.m. to 11:35 p.m.

At approximately 11:37 p.m. Kohberger was stopped by Latah County Sheriff's Deputy Cpl. Duke, as mentioned above. The 8458 Phone was utilizing cellular resources consistent with the location of the traffic stop during this time (Farm Road and Pullman Highway).

Further analysis of the cellular data provided showed the 8458 Phone utilized cellular resources on November 13, 2022, consistent with the phone travelling from Pullman, Washington to Lewiston, Idaho via US Highway 195. At approximately 12:36 p.m., the 8458 Phone utilized cellular resources that would provide coverage to Kate's Cup of Joe coffee stand located at 810 Port Drive, Clarkston, WA. Surveillance footage from the US Chefs store located at 820 Port Dr. Clarkston, WA and adjacent to Kate's Cup of Joe, showed a white Elantra consistent with Suspect Vehicle 1 drive past Kate's Cup of Joe at a time consistent with the cellular data from the 8458 Phone.

At approximately 12:46 p.m., the 8458 Phone then utilized cellular data in the area of the Albertson's grocery store at 400 Bridge Street in Lewiston, Washington. Surveillance footage obtained from the Albertson's showed Kohberger exit the white Elantra consistent with Suspect Vehicle 1 at approximately 12:49 p.m. Interior surveillance cameras showed Kohberger walk through the store, purchase unknown items at the checkout, and leave at approximately 1:04 p.m.

Additional analysis of records for the 8458 Phone indicated that between approximately 5:32 p.m. and 5:36 p.m., the 8458 Phone utilized cellular resources that provide coverage to Johnson, Idaho. The 8458 Phone then stops reporting to the network from approximately 5:36 p.m. to 8:30 p.m. That

8458 Phone, REDACTED, Palouse River Drive

is consistent with the 8458 Phone being in the area that the 8458 Phone traveled in the hours immediately following the suspected time the homicides occurred.

On December 27, 2022, Pennsylvania agents recovered the trash from the Kohberger family residence located in Albrightsville, PA. That evidence was sent to the Idaho State Lab for a testing. On December 28, 2022, the Idaho State lab reported that a DNA profile obtained from the trash and the DNA profile obtained from the sheath identified a male as not being excluded as the biological father of suspect profile. At least 99.9998% of the male population would be expected to be excluded from the possibility of being the suspect's biological father.

Based on the above information, I am requesting an arrest warrant be issued for Bryan C Kohberger (DOB) 11/21/1994, for burglary at 1122 King Street in Moscow, Idaho, and four counts of Murder in the First Degree for the murders of Madison Mogen, Kaylee Goncalves, Xana Kernodle, and Ethan Chapin.

I declare under penalty of perjury pursuant to the law of the state of Idaho that the foregoing is true and correct.

Among files accessed by the author are 3,509 text messages sent and received by Bryan Kohberger between June 23 and December 29, 2022. The fact that Bill Thompson's office did not refer to a single one speaks volumes about Kohberger's mind-set and how he interacted with the world around him. Detailed analysis reveals patterns that might have interested behavioral analysts if they had been called in by either side in this case. Statistically, more than 99.9 percent of Kohberger's cell contacts involved members of his family. Of those, roughly 70 percent were back and forth with his mother and father, followed by about 30 percent with his sisters, Amanda and Melissa. Virtually all communications were positive, cheerful, and banal—normal everyday stuff.

The real interest police took in his personal communications, of course, involved state of mind and motive. What they found probably seemed disappointing, considering that his first text, Saturday morning, was sent at 4:11 a.m. to his mother, a JPEG image that was not further disclosed. He continued to text his family at 4:24 a.m. and 4:28 a.m. but sent nothing else until 4:33 p.m. when he reached out to his father asking for a call and got a text in return from his mother. It said, "Bud, sorry! I was exercising and totally out of breath to be able to talk well! I will talk to you later this evening! Finalizing my little routine!"

And while Kohberger was very close to his mother, it would be negligent to overlook his relationship to the man police used to track the KA-BAR sheath DNA. Michael Kohberger spent three days driving twenty-six hundred miles from Pullman, Washington, to Albrightsville, Pennsylvania, with his son shortly after the murders. Perhaps, police likely thought, they had discussed the crimes.

On December 20, 2022, Michael Kohberger was interviewed at the Pennsylvania State Police Fern Ridge Barracks in Blakeslee, Pennsylvania, by agents Jared W. Witmier and Joseph F. Noone of the FBI. It is important to note that at approximately 1:20 a.m., arrest and search warrants had been executed in Albrightsville,

Pennsylvania, at the family home. Kohberger had been detained on-site by the Pennsylvania State Police's Special Emergency Response Team (SERT) but was released from temporary custody by PSP officers once the scene was secured.

According to an FD-302 report of investigation, Kohberger was advised that any conversation with law enforcement would be voluntary, and once he agreed, he was transported by FBI agents to the Fern Ridge Barracks in Blakeslee, a distance of about eight miles. As SA Witmier wrote in his FD-302:

> Upon arrival at PSP Fern Ridge, M-KOHBERGER was accompanied to an interview room where he met with interviewing agents for approximately three hours and 32 minutes. With the exception of travel from M-KOHBERGER's residence to PSP Fern Ridge, the duration of the interview was audio/video recorded. Upon conclusion of the interview, M-KOHBERGER was taken to another waiting room where he met with his wife and daughter.

Nothing Michael Kohberger told the FBI appears to have been mentioned in Bill Thompson's filings. We may surmise that he was not Mirandized, because he was not in custody at the time and has never been suspected of wrongdoing or involvement in the crimes, but everything he said could have been used against his son at trial. It seems reasonable to believe Michael Kohberger told the FBI nothing incriminating about his son.

What may be less known, however, is that other people close to Bryan Kohberger were far more open. On March 1, 2023, Idaho State Police detectives Jake Schwecke and Gideon Roberts traveled about eighty-five miles south of Moscow to the North Idaho Correctional Institute (NICI) in hopes of gaining insights from two inmates who had spent time with Kohberger shortly after his arrest. Roberts wrote in Supplemental 163:

> On March 1, 2023, Idaho State Police (ISP) Detective (Det.) Jake Schwecke and I, ISP Det. and Federal Bureau of Investigation Task Force Officer (TFO) Gideon Roberts interviewed Micah James Demoss (Demoss) and Jesse Eugene Burnett (Burnett) at the North Idaho Correctional Institute (NICI) regarding their interactions with Bryan Kohberger (KOHBERGER). Both Demoss and Burnett had been housed at the Latah County Sheriff's Office Jail with Kohberger after his arrest.

Though the interviews were audio-recorded, only Roberts's report was turned over to the defense. According to Roberts's report, Demoss and Burnett were interviewed separately. After being advised of their Miranda rights and the purpose of the interview, Demoss said he "couldn't remember the exact date, but he believed KOHBERGER had been placed in their pod a few days after New Year's Day."

> After arriving in the pod, KOHBERGER immediately sat down and watched the news about his arrest, watching multiple channels that were covering the story. KOHBERGER said, "Wow, I'm on every channel."

According to Roberts's report, Demoss described Kohberger as quiet and awkward.

> KOHBERGER was highly intelligent and analytic, always trying to figure out what you were doing, but didn't know common knowledge things, i.e. the difference between muscle cars.

Demoss described Kohberger's eyes as "creepy" but said he seemed like "a pretty normal guy" who didn't talk very much and never discussed his case. Demoss also said:

> KOHBERGER would use three standard-sized bars of soap per week due to his hourlong showers and excessive hand washing. KOHBERGER'S hands were red from the amount of hand washing.

Demoss, who was housed with Kohberger for about three weeks, said Kohberger's favorite movie was *American Psycho* with Christian Bale.

Roberts wrote in the second half of his report:

> At about 1:28 p.m., Det. Schwecke and I interviewed Burnett regarding his interactions with KOHBERGER. What follows is not intended to be an exact transcript of the interview. For further detail refer to the audio recording. After being advised of his Miranda Rights, confirming he had not been ordered to talk with us, advised of the purpose of the interview, and that the interview would be recorded, Burnett provided the following information: He was housed with KOHBERGER from early January to February 15, 2023. KOHBERGER enjoyed watching the news about his case unless it began talking about his family or friends, at which point he'd change the channel immediately.

> As time continued, KOHBERGER stopped watching the news related to his case almost completely. KOHBERGER analyzed everything. He wanted to know why people had preferences on anything. He psychoanalyzes everything. They talked about his case sometimes but never KOHBERGER'S case. KOHBERGER spent most of his time on the communication tablet talking with people, typically his sister, who he told to retain an attorney after he had seen her on the news.

Like Demoss, Burnett told investigators Kohberger washed his hands excessively, using three bars of soap per week, showered every day, and wanted new bedding and clothes every day. Roberts reported:

> KOHBERGER was very smart, easy to get along with, but was hard to talk to because he talked over him due to KOHBERGER'S vocabulary and topics of conversation. KOHBERGER also talked about his education a lot. KOHBERGER loved baseball, with the Yankees being his favorite team. KOHBERGER also liked to watch court TV and was very interested in the Murdaugh trial.

Despite the fact that police often try to develop incriminating information from jailhouse informants, nothing of evidentiary value has ever been disclosed.

CHAPTER 13

Othram Laboratories, Ibuprofen, Dylan's Green Jacket

Forensics is a catchall term used to describe just about any scientific test, inquiry, or examination. Police often rely on it in the analysis of physical evidence, such as blood spatter, wound ballistics, and toxicology, but there are other applications too. Detectives in this case used forensic techniques to dissect everything from cell phones and laptop hard drives to social media activity, motor vehicle registrations, cell tower pings, and accounting. They pored over autopsy reports, surveillance camera footage, DoorDash deliveries, text chains, group chats and emails, the bar tabs of Corner Club patrons on Saturday night. After three years and tens of thousands of man-hours building files full of half a million items, the State of Idaho's entire investigation can be grouped into just two categories: a few human cells found in Maddie Mogen's room, and everything else. In very simple terms, the case against Bryan Kohberger seemed to hang on the forensic examination of a KA-BAR knife sheath and a tiny sample of DNA.

For the record, we are talking about a sheath, not the knife itself. No murder weapon has ever been recovered, and the prosecution has never once claimed to know exactly what produced the "edged-weapon" injuries inflicted upon the victims. Though media speculation has tied the sheath and wound characteristics to the KA-BAR's flattop blade, the defense claims evidence of four separate instruments. Yes, prosecution files show the defendant owned a KA-BAR knife, but only because somebody ordered one on Amazon using a gift card and had it shipped to his parents' house in Pennsylvania. Autopsy reports detail various depths of intrusive injuries that are labeled by the coroner as "two-edged," "single edge," and round. Other than the steak knife Hunter Johnson took from the kitchen, no brand, type, or specific item has been named; no crime lab has ever matched them.

Before we start down the long, torturous path of validation, we need to look at what Bill Thompson told us. On July 2, 2025, he stood in Judge Hippler's Ada County courtroom and summarized the state's only physical evidence in two sentences. To this day, no transparent accounting of the DNA's provenance, methodology of testing, or disposition has ever been offered.

> The defendant, as he left that room, for whatever reason, ended up leaving . . . or the sheath for a KA-BAR knife was left on the bed next to Madison Mogen's body. That sheath was tested by the Idaho State Police forensic lab and single source male DNA was found on the snap of that sheath.

This was moments before the defendant changed his plea to guilty, of course, so we will stipulate that months of analysis by the FBI's finest genealogists reduced thousands of data points from hundreds of tests conducted on dozens of exhibits into one plausible conclusion: Bryan C. Kohberger broke into 1122 King Road on November 13, 2022, and killed four strangers in less than four minutes, barely leaving a clue. Only forensics kept this from becoming a perfect crime.

"Perfect crime?" asked Dr. Turvey in a second interview conducted by the author in December 2025. "Let me be clear—there is nothing about these murders that was even remotely perfect. No matter what the prosecution wants you to believe, this thing was a mess. We don't know if that scabbard was found on the floor or in the bed. We don't know who placed it in the bag, so we don't know where the bag went either. Or who handled it. We don't know which sample the FBI actually tested, because it was sent to a private lab in Texas first, and in my view, they appeared to have been fired by the ISP because their results did not match what the prosecution wanted to hear. The truth is, we don't even know how the FBI tied the DNA to Kohberger because it sure as hell wasn't CODIS and it is illegal to use commercial sites. So you tell me, what exactly is it about these crimes that you would call perfect?"

Unpacking this statement will take some time, but we'll get there.

Before we do, it is important to note that much of Turvey's ire is based on terabytes' worth of information that he has seen and we have not. When Kohberger pleaded guilty, he offered no allocution, meaning Bill Thompson's fifty-four-word explanation is all we know about the evidence stacked against him. To this day, it would be extremely difficult to look at piecemeal FOIA disclosures and make sense of diluted bloodstains in the living room and signature wounds inflicted postmortem on Maddie's and Kaylee's carefully posed bodies. Blood spatter analysis makes it nearly impossible to know where Xana was first attacked, why Ethan never got up to defend her, how she fled for her life from the kitchen to her room as the killer tossed Maddie's and Kaylee's blood all over the walls without getting a single drop on the floor.

No one has ever explained why the bloodstains on the top half of Xana's bedroom door look different from those on the bottom. The prosecution has never explained how one killer inflicted more than sixty-five wounds on a woman as she fought for her life just three feet from a six-foot-four boyfriend who never got out of bed. In his statements to the court, Bill Thompson did not mention that Ethan Chapin died with a chunk of hair in his fist that was labeled as "debris" by the lab. Most disturbing, perhaps, is the fact that no one has explained how Ethan's undiluted blood was found at the top of the stairwell leading down to the first floor. The prosecution's own reports show that once attacked, he never left Xana's room.

"You know the biggest travesty in this whole thing?" Turvey asked midway through a conversation about what he felt were the problems inherent in Thompson's case. "When Anne Taylor's office questioned how DNA on the knife was tested, the prosecution fought her, tooth and nail. Look at the Franks hearing transcripts . . . look at her discovery filings and the prosecution's motions to suppress. They fought tooth and nail to keep her from finding out the most basic information about what boils down to their only real exhibit. I've never seen anything like it."

It should be noted that among four expert witnesses interviewed by the author for this book, Dr. Turvey is one of only two who consented to his name being used. Most important, we should consider that without "leaks" from disgusted experts, like Turvey, the public would not have known about possible chain of custody issues with the KA-BAR sheath or apparent discrepancies about where it was found. They would not be aware that Paulette Sutton explained the lack of DNA in the defendant's car by suggesting he shed his blood-soaked clothes and ran around the house naked. They would have no idea that police seemed not to care that the first-floor bathroom had been sanitized and was found completely empty of things a college student might use in day-to-day life, staples like a toothbrush, a hair dryer, floor mats, discarded clothes, towels, makeup, toothpaste, a razor. There was no toilet paper at all.

They would not know about a broken woman's bracelet found on the floor of the empty first-floor bedroom; that it appeared to be stained with blood but was never tested or even seized as evidence. Worse, they would have no idea that police found a green, blood-soaked jacket in that same room or that it was handed to Dylan Mortensen as personal property according to the police report, placed in storage, and only found by Anne Taylor weeks after the fact. They would not know that blood on the jacket was tested by an independent lab called Bode Technology, which found a mixture of DNA they could not analyze further except the part that was Dylan's.

First, we need to discuss the basics of what got defense experts like Turvey so riled up. According to sealed court filings, Anne Taylor's office approached the court requesting a Franks hearing.

This legal proceeding is named after the 1978 Supreme Court case *Franks v. Delaware*, which allows a defendant to challenge the truthfulness of a search warrant affidavit.

To be granted such a hearing, Taylor's office had to make a "substantial preliminary showing" that the law enforcement "affidavit" included a false or misleading statement. Here, the warrant in question involved DNA, and Taylor must have checked prerequisite boxes because the hearing was granted. Taylor's burden was to prove that the affidavit's author "either knowingly, intentionally, or with reckless disregard for the truth" failed in stating probable cause. If she had been successful, evidence obtained under the warrant would have been suppressed.

Spoiler alert: She was not.

At this point, however, that does not matter, because admissibility of evidence is moot when the defendant pleads guilty. What Taylor accomplished when she stood before Judge Hippler on January 23, 2025, was exposure of what, in my opinion, might indicate a pattern of official wrongdoing. Though no jury was ever supposed to hear Taylor's objections, we will review them here. This is what so incensed Dr. Turvey and his peers.

•

"Let's go on the record in *State v. Kohberger*, CR01-24-31665," Judge Hippler says, setting the stage at the beginning of these closed proceedings. "Present in the courtroom today are the defendant with counsel, Ms. Taylor and Ms. Massoth. Is Mr. Logsdon here?"

"Mr. Logsdon is here," Taylor responds.

"For the state we have Mr. Thompson, Mr. Nye, and Ms. Jennings."

"Yes, Your Honor," the chief prosecutor affirms; this is his team.

•

After a few procedural exchanges, Anne Taylor calls her first witness, MPD lead detective Brett Payne. He is sworn in, and things get down to business.

•

"When was the first time you heard Bryan Kohberger's name?" she asks after a series of questions about his job and background. At that point in time, he was a corporal with Police Officer Standards and Training (POST) certification and about seven years on the job. Prior to that he had been military police.

"The first time I heard Bryan Kohberger's name was December 19, 2022."

"And what was that a result of?"

"That was a result of investigative genetic genealogy that was being undertaken by the FBI. We had a phone call that evening, and we were told Bryan Kohberger's name."

"And before that, Mr. Kohberger was not on your radar?"

"No, ma'am."

•

This is a critically important statement because according to MPD reports, no one started looking for a white 2015 Hyundai Elantra until December 26, a full week later, and that was supposedly due to a WSU officer stumbling onto it in parking registrations. According to Detective Payne's sworn statement, Kohberger had "appeared on his radar" well before the FBI revised its analysis of the mysterious white sedan from a Nissan Sentra to a Hyundai manufactured between 2011 and 2013. If we are led to believe the WSU police just happened to spot Kohberger's car a week after the detective in charge of the investigation learned his name, it is a significant stretch of credulity. At what point did experts finally decide they were looking for a 2015 Elantra?

•

"Before December 19, was the FBI CAST team member collocated with you?"

"Yes, ma'am."

•

According to Payne's sworn statement, he somehow learned about Kohberger from an FBI CAST member, not from identification of his car, as has always been believed. If true, this changes the prosecution narrative entirely.

•

"How long had he been collocated with you?"

"I don't remember exactly, but it had been several weeks at that point."

"And was that Nicholas Ballance?"

"Yes, ma'am."

"What other FBI team members were collocated with you?"

"Goodness. A lot. We had Technical Assistant Maria Tyndall, SA Jacobson, and numerous other FBI special agents that were there to assist."

•

For those wondering what this has to do with DNA, remember that the whole point in a Franks hearing is to demonstrate false statements by an affiant in the presentation of a search warrant affidavit. Taylor clearly had a target in mind, and Payne was part of her foundation. Remember, we are looking at the state's only physical evidence: DNA.

•

"Did you have any role in deciding to pursue investigative genetic genealogy?"

"Yes, ma'am. It was a collaborative decision among the command team to go that route, but, yes, I was a part of that."

"Were you a part of the discussions during the process of identification?"

"Yes, ma'am."

"Were you aware that Othram laboratories began the work on the investigative genetic genealogy?"

"Yes, ma'am."

"What kinds of information did you receive from Othram laboratories?"

"I don't remember what was received from Othram directly," he says. "I knew they were conducting their specific type of work. I don't remember exactly what they provided us."

•

And here we stop the presses. What Anne Taylor believed she knew and almost everyone else did not is that police may have identified Kohberger as a person of interest well before they supposedly stumbled onto his car. The lead detective, Brett Payne, had just sworn under oath that he learned about Kohberger from CAST specialists from the FBI. They had decided to "go that route" with genetic genealogy, and they had done it not through the Idaho State Police lab but a private company in Texas.

Remember, according to Bill Thompson at Kohberger's change of plea hearing, the KA-BAR sheath "was tested by the Idaho State Police forensic lab and single source male DNA was found on the snap of that sheath." Though not widely known, records show that police also contacted a Department of Defense representative though the FBI's Salt Lake City Division on December 1, 2022, seeking to determine what would be required to have the KA-BAR sample run through the DOD's repository. It seems clear where Taylor is headed.

•

"Did you receive some documents from them?"

"Yes, ma'am."

"Okay. Do you know how many documents you received from them?"

"I do not."

"Was it one time or more than one time?"

"I don't remember."

•

Detective Brett Payne is the detective in charge of the MPD investigation. This is the defining exhibit in his case. It seems like something he would remember.

•

"Were you part of the discussion to take the work from Othram and go to the FBI?"

"Yes, ma'am."

"Why was that decision made?"

"From my understanding—granted, this is my first encounter with investigative genetic genealogy, so, again, as a collaborative discussion we decided that because the Idaho State Police lab and Othram had essentially exhausted their resources—this is how I understood it—that we would move to the FBI because they had more resources available to pursue this particular avenue."

"Do you know what more resources the FBI had?"

"The only thing I'm privy to was that they had more databases that they could compare the sample to. That was the extent of my knowledge."

•

And though we will return to Payne's testimony in a moment, we need a little context. According to a June 22, 2023, filing by Anne Taylor's office, we know that the Idaho State Police announced on July 28, 2021, that they had received a Bureau of Justice Assistance grant to fund genetic genealogy testing through a company called Othram, a private Texas forensic laboratory. In the press release, the Idaho State Police specifically mentioned that Othram "follows accepted laboratory processes and procedures and complies with the United States DOJ Interim Policy on Forensic Genetic Genealogy DNA Analysis and Searching." This will prove critically important moving forward because Anne Taylor is about to allege that Othram was fired when they developed a single source male DNA "profile" on the KA-BAR sheath but could not match it to Kohberger.

•

"What was your communications with the FBI about the IGG?" Taylor asks after a couple of administrative questions.

•

Remember, IGG stands for "investigative genetic genealogy," a relatively new branch of forensic analysis in 2022. To be clear, Anne Taylor's line of questioning is implying that Brett Payne, the lead detective in charge of the case, knew about the Idaho State Police shopping his DNA evidence in search of a predetermined match. If she is correct, the impact on Thompson's case would have been seismic.

•

"So, our communications were just via telephone," he responds. "The sample was sent to the FBI, I don't remember the date it was given over to them, but after that there were very few conversations; and if they happened at all, they were just telephonic advising us that the process was still in the works and they would let us know when or if they had anything of interest."

•

Again, Anne Taylor has established that the MPD sent the KA-BAR knife sheath, or DNA found on it, to the ISP crime lab for analysis. From there it was sent to Othram, the private lab in

Texas. At some point in December 2022, the ISP discontinued their work with Othram, retrieved the evidence, and sent it to the FBI lab in Quantico, Virginia. According to Payne, the motivation boiled down to "database size." What Taylor wants to prove is that police already believed the DNA belonged to Bryan C. Kohberger but did not have a large enough pool of comparables to prove it. They fired Othram and sent their sample to an agency that did.

•

"Do you know what files or documents went to the FBI from Othram?"

"I do not remember."

•

This is the biggest murder case in Idaho history. Payne is the detective in charge. The sheath is his single most important piece of physical evidence. He testified that he does not remember.

•

"Did you receive documents from the FBI?"

"In relation to the IGG?"

"Yes."

"I believe after the fact, after we received Kohberger's name, we did receive documents, but I don't remember what they were."

•

At that point, Taylor asks what happened once police learned Kohberger's name, and from there things get interesting.

•

"So, the only thing that was given to us was Bryan Kohberger's name; that was it. It was conveyed to us by the FBI that it was to be taken as no more than a tip; that was it. So, once we received his name, we set about doing basically an independent verification of whether or not he was involved in this crime."

•

Oddly enough, Taylor does not follow up with what seems to be the obvious question: In what reality would DNA identification of a killer by the FBI be treated as "no more than a tip"? And how is it possible that Payne had already told her he learned of Kohberger's name from the FBI CAST member, one full week before they "coincidentally" identified his car? Suddenly, the prosecution's entire narrative seems to be crumbling.

•

"I'm going to talk to you about that in a little bit more," Taylor continues. "But do you know why the FBI connected Bryan Kohberger to the case?"

"So, December 20, if memory serves, we had a secondary meeting with the FBI via Teams, if memory serves, and they simply walked us through the family tree, how they did that. Now, I don't remember the details of all that—it was an in-depth conversation that, to be honest, is above my head—but they essentially worked their way through the family tree and arrived at a conclusion that Bryan Kohberger was a person we should look into as a tip. That's the extent of my knowledge of how they did that."

"How was Bryan Kohberger, the name you received as a tip, linked to the case?"

"He wasn't until after December 19."

"What item of evidence did they link Bryan Kohberger to?"

"I'm not sure what you're asking. As far as before December 19, is that what you're referring to?"

"Yeah."

"We didn't have one at that point."

"Why did you become interested in learning the identity of Bryan Kohberger?"

"Not quite sure I understand your question. We were interested in anyone who would have been involved in this. The DNA from the knife sheath was obviously the one thing we had that we thought was a very strong piece of evidence in this case, so it was that particular piece that we pursued as a potential avenue of identifying a suspect."

"Is it your understanding that the FBI's work said that it was Bryan Kohberger's DNA on the sheath?"

"That is not my understanding."

"What is your understanding?"

"My understanding is that the FBI concluded that Bryan Kohberger was a possible source of DNA that we should look into. They did not, to my knowledge, at any point say Bryan Kohberger's DNA is on the knife sheath. That was never conveyed to me."

•

For those unfamiliar with three years of media coverage, this is the lead detective in charge of the case stating plainly under oath that to his knowledge the FBI *never* said they found Bryan Kohberger's DNA on the knife sheath. How is it possible that after three years of assurances from Latah County prosecuting attorney Bill Thompson that the DNA proves guilt beyond a reasonable doubt, his lead investigator states, under oath, that it did not?

To make sense of this, and Anne Taylor's entire line of questioning, we need to go back to predicate motions. On September 1, 2023, Taylor's office filed a document titled *Response to State's Notice of Intent Not to Cross-Examine Defense Witnesses, District Court Decision, and Records to Explain Witness Contact.* Though the heading sounds a bit confusing, the argument is simple: Taylor believed the methodology employed by the FBI was flawed. Despite disclosure mandates provided in *Brady v. Maryland*, she seemed to believe that Bill Thompson's office had deliberately withheld exculpatory information crucial to the defense of her client.

She wanted answers. She wrote:

> Counsel has learned through consultation with experts and sources referenced below that the use of genetic genealogy databases does not necessarily lead to a single individual as a potential suspect. And that reports of these searches often reference multiple individuals for further investigation and DNA testing. In fact, the State acknowledges such in its motion for protective order when it acknowledges . . . "hundreds of relatives . . ." (page 5 motion for protection order).

In very simple terms, Taylor is suggesting that the prosecution's claims may not be true.

> The testing conducted by a private lab is completely different in nature than the testing done by forensic labs. Genetic genealogy labs do not generate a "profile" in the same way that forensic labs do, and there cannot be a direct comparison between the data obtained in this case by the Idaho State Forensic Crime Lab and the private lab. The tests used by private labs are either SNP (single nucleotide polymorphisms) or whole genome sequencing. These tests are similar to the methods used by commercial services such as 23andMe and Ancestry.com.

Based on this, it seems plausible that the defense believed, four months prior to the Franks hearing, that Bill Thompson's office had deliberately misled the public about the KA-BAR DNA. Evidence would suggest he knew about possible problems with the chain of custody, about the Idaho State Police "shopping" results between Othram and the FBI, and that based on IGG methodologies, he would face real challenges tying Kohberger to the sheath at trial.

Most important, Taylor appears to believe that evidence Bill Thompson touted as the foundation of his case may have been misrepresented, mishandled, and hidden from scrutiny by the court's own rulings. While the prosecution trumpeted news that Kohberger's DNA had been found at the scene of the crime, Taylor disputes it.

Though few among us hold PhDs in forensic genealogy, the United States Department of Justice does a pretty good job of explaining Kohberger's defense. In 2011, the DOJ published its *Interim Policy on Forensic Genetic Genealogical DNA Analysis and Searching*, laying out acceptable standards and methodologies in criminal investigations. This is the same document Anne Taylor cited at the Franks hearing, a lucid explanation of where the prosecution might have gone wrong. We will not quote the entire document, but excerpts warrant citation:

> **STR DNA Typing and CODIS**
>
> Forensic DNA typing has historically been used to compare 13–20 STR DNA markers between a forensic sample and one or more reference samples. When a suspect's identity is unknown, a participating crime laboratory may upload a forensic profile into the FBI's Combined DNA Index System (CODIS). CODIS is a law enforcement database that compares DNA profiles derived from forensic samples to those of unknown offenders.
>
> CODIS was created by the DNA Identification Act of 1994. This legislation authorized the FBI to create and maintain a national database comprised of designated DNA indices that are routinely searched against one another. If a CODIS search results in the confirmed match between a forensic profile and a known offender, a law enforcement lead is generated and the name of the matching offender is released. If the search does not result in a confined confirmed match, no lead is generated.
>
> **Forensic Genetic Genealogical DNA Analysis and Searching**
>
> Forensic genealogy is law enforcement's use of DNA analysis combined with traditional genealogy research to generate investigative leads for unsolved violent crimes. Forensic genetic genealogical DNA analysis ('FGG') differs from STR DNA typing in both the type of technology employed, and the nature of the databases utilized.
>
> FGG examines more than half a million single nucleotide

polymorphisms (SNPs), which replace the STR DNA markers analyzed in traditional forensic DNA typing. These SNP's span the entirety of the human genome. This allows scientists to identify shared blocks of DNA between a forensic sample and the sample donor's potential relatives. Recombination or reshuffling of the gene genome is expected as DNA from each generation is passed down, resulting in larger shared blocks of identical DNA between closer relatives and shorter blocks between more distant relatives. Due to predicted levels of recombination between generations, it is possible to analyze these blocks of genetic information and make inferences regarding potential familial relationships.

Limitations

If the search of an FGG profile results in one or more genetic associations, the GG service typically generates and provides the service user with a list of genetically associated service user names along with an estimated relationship and (in some cases) the amount of DNA shared by those individuals. A genetic association means that the donor of the (forensic or reference) sample may be related to a service user. However, information derived from genetic association is used by law enforcement only as an investigative lead. Traditional genealogical research and other investigative work is needed to determine the true nature of any genetic association.

A suspect shall not be arrested based solely on a genetic association generated by a GG service. If a suspect is identified after a genetic association has occurred, STR DNA typing must be performed, and the suspect's STR DNA profile must be directly compared to the forensic profile previously uploaded to CODIS. This comparison is necessary to confirm that the forensic sample could have originated from the suspect.

Case Criteria

Investigative agencies may initiate the process of considering the use of FGGS when a case involves an unsolved violent crime and the candidate forensic sample is from a putative perpetrator, or when a case involves what is reasonably believed by investigators to be the unidentified remains of a suspected homicide victim (unidentified human remains). In addition, the prosecutor, as defined in footnote twenty of this interim policy, may authorize the investigative use of FGGS for violent crimes or attempts to commit violent crimes other than homicide or sexual offenses (while observing and complying with all requirements of this interim policy) when the circumstances surrounding the criminal act(s) present a substantial and ongoing threat to public safety or national security. Before an investigative agency may attempt to use FGGS, the forensic profile derived from the candid forensic sample must have been uploaded to CODIS, and subsequent CODIS searches must have failed to produce a probative and confirmed DNA match.

In the interest of full disclosure, it should be noted that the author of this book worked as chief advocacy officer for a Colorado company called ANDE, developing use of "rapid DNA" technology in criminal investigations. I have lobbied at both state and federal levels for legislation expanding use of DNA technology, and I have worked extensively with former FBI colleagues seeking private access to CODIS. That said, the problem with using DNA for identification is that what you get out is only as good as what you put in. It gets confusing.

The primary issue is that scientists match genetic material using two primary methodologies. One is available to regular people who are looking to build family trees on commercially accessible sites like Ancestry.com. The other is limited to law enforcement trying to match evidence found at a crime scene to the person who left it. That kind of forensic DNA identification is the domain of the FBI via submission to its CODIS database. Based on information gathered by Anne Taylor, and probed at the Franks hearing, she believed police had tried to identify her client through CODIS, and when that failed, they may have violated DOJ policy by using two private databases: GEDmatch and MyHeritage. This is what is referred to as investigative genetic genealogy.

Returning to the Franks hearing, I believe that she was right.

•

"Will you please state your name for the record?" Anne Taylor asks. She has just called her second witness.

"Rylene, R-Y-L-E-N-E," the witness states, "Nowlin, N-O-W-L-I-N."

"I think you've done this before."

"A few times."

•

Rylene Nowlin is next up, after Brett Payne, who just testified under oath that the FBI never said they found DNA from Lake's client on the KA-BAR sheath.

In January 2025, Nowlin worked as a forensic manager at the ISP Forensic Services (ISPFS) laboratory in Meridian, Idaho. She had worked there for twenty-three years, originally hired as a scientist in the Biology DNA Unit based on formal education and training in genetics, molecular biology, biochemistry, and statistics. She completed the ISPFS specialized training program in biology screening, DNA, and DNA database analysis. She was a member of the Northwest Association of Forensic Scientists, the American Society of Crime Laboratory Directors, and the National Technology and Validation Implementation Collaborative. Suffice to say she is smart, accomplished, a leader in her field.

•

"Would investigative genetic genealogy be a new technology?" Taylor asks.

"That is one of the technologies," Nowlin answers. "However, our group refers to it as FIGG, forensic investigative genetic genealogy."

"FIGG, okay," Taylor responds. "I'll try to remember that. That's the one I want to talk about today. So, your group is talking about best practices for FIGG; is that right?"

"That's one of our areas of focus, correct."

"Are you doing that because there are practices that are important in that discipline?"

"We are doing that because it's a new technology coming into the forensics world and not every laboratory manager has a background in DNA."

•

You do not need a law degree or years in law enforcement to see where this is going. Anne Taylor has staged this hearing because she has specific information regarding the prosecution's assertions that her client's DNA was found in Maddie Mogen's bed.

•

"Tell me what CODIS is, briefly," Taylor asks after a few setup questions.

"CODIS, Combined DNA Index System, is essentially a national DNA database. It exists on three levels: There's a local level, your county sheriff's office, local PDs; there's a state level, which is typically the state laboratory, it is limited to public laboratories; and then the national level."

•

Biometric identification has evolved past the 1980s when the FBI kept three-by-five-inch fingerprint cards in file cabinets to be searched by hand. CODIS is an extraordinary resource.

•

"In Idaho," Nowlin continues, "the Idaho State Police Forensic Services lab in Meridian is the only DNA lab in the state, so there are no local labs in the state of Idaho. And the database contains different indices: There's a forensic index; those are profiles obtained from items of evidence. There's an offender index; those are samples from those convicted of qualifying offenses in your state as determined by your state legislation. If your state legislature allows arrestees, there's an arrestee index. There's also a missing persons index for remains."

•

Taylor asks a few more questions, establishing that Nowlin previously served as Idaho's alternate CODIS administrator. She's laying the groundwork for a bomb everyone sees coming.

•

"For CODIS, DNA that goes into CODIS, what kind of profile is used?"

"If I'm understanding the question correctly," Nowlin answers, "there's different types of DNA profiles, and what goes into CODIS is known as an STR profile or short tandem repeat."

"What kind of information is in short tandem repeat or STR?"

"So, DNA is a substance that's found in the cells of our body," Nowlin explains. "It acts as a blueprint; it tells our bodies what form to take and how to function. Between individuals it is over 99 percent the same, that is why we all have the same basic structure and our bodies function in basically the same way. In forensics and in STRs we are targeting that less than one percent that is unique to an individual, with the exception of identical twins; and so, areas of DNA that vary widely between individuals don't code for anything typically, so it doesn't tell us anything about a person. When I look at an STR profile, I can tell you if that person is genetically male or genetically female and that is all."

"Do you know what a SNP profile is?"

"I do."

"What is that?"

"A SNP profile is a single nucleotide polymorphism, so you're looking at a single nucleotide, whereas the STR is a series of repeating nucleotides, a specific repeat that we're looking for."

"The SNP, then, is that a closer look at a person's genome?" Taylor asks.

"I would like to state that I'm not an expert in SNPs, I'm not qualified in the SNP technology and have not ever been qualified in the SNP technology. With STRs, depending on the chemistry, you're looking at anywhere from thirteen to twenty-five-plus locations. With SNPs, my understanding is in general you're looking at a minimum of ten thousand."

•

At that point the prosecution objects to something about expertise but Hippler overrules them. What might seem needlessly academic is actually the lynchpin of the prosecution's case.

•

"You mentioned that there's four indexes and you talked about a forensic index."

"Correct," Nowlin answers.

"What is that one used for?"

"The forensic index is where profiles generated from items of evidence can be uploaded. There are rules about what can be uploaded, though. It cannot match someone known to be the victim of a crime; it cannot match someone whose DNA should be in a place outside of a crime being committed; it cannot be anything taken directly from a suspect of a crime where you would reasonably assume their DNA would be present; it must be related to a crime, and it must be believed to be from the putative perpetrator of that crime."

"So, if I understand it, you use DNA, get an STR, and only

under certain circumstances can you use CODIS. Do I understand that right?"

"Correct."

•

And here she lights the fuse. Taylor asks Nowlin about her role in using investigative genetic genealogy and puts the lab manager on record as saying she developed the contract's "scope of work," determining who "won the bid."

•

"Did Idaho State Police forensics have a contract with this laboratory, Othram?"

"They were the winning bid through that process, and so they were under contract with the Department of Purchasing, correct."

•

Taylor asks a number of questions about administrative matters and obligations between the State of Idaho and the lab. But it all comes down to this: Anne Taylor knows that Othram labs obtained the DNA profile from the KA-BAR sheath that was ultimately touted by the prosecution as Kohberger's. Anne Taylor knows that police had already identified her client as a suspect in the case and believed the DNA on the sheath would come back to him. She knows that as a private laboratory, Othram could not query CODIS under the rules Nowlin previously stated. Further, she knows they did not have access to a public database large enough to match the sample with Kohberger. She knows that when the Idaho State Police figured this out, they took the evidence back and sent it to the FBI.

•

"Were you aware that Othram was just stopped from doing any further work at some point?" Taylor asks, going directly to the point.

"I was aware of that."

"And was this before they produced any result?"

"No. We received a preliminary report. I recall receiving that because that's how I know I can approve payment of the invoice, so I know we received that prior to them being told they were stopped."

•

Taylor is establishing that the ISP lab sent the KA-BAR sheath DNA to Othram, that Othram produced a preliminary report, and that shortly after, their work was discontinued. According to files reviewed by the author, it appears it was discontinued only in this particular case.

•

"Does the forensics lab continue to contract with Othram?"

"Yes."

•

Laying further foundation, Taylor asks Nowlin if she was made aware of a "trash pull," the one we now know occurred December 27, 2022, at the Kohberger home in Pennsylvania. Nowlin states that she was aware of the warrantless search and that she recalled being asked by detectives which items might be most likely to yield usable samples.

•

"The discussion was a person of interest had been developed and to analyze the items from the trash to determine if they could be inclusive of the DNA profile that was developed from the knife sheath, Unknown Male A," Nowlin explains.

•

Unknown Male A, of course, was Bryan Kohberger. Everyone involved in the case knew it at that point. They had him and his family under surveillance.

•

"What date was it that you received the trash?"

"The trash was received into the laboratory on December 28 of 2022."

•

Taylor asks more questions about process. The lab manager seems to dodge them.

•

"Okay. When you got the trash to go through in the lab, you knew that you were looking for a male, right?" Taylor asked.

"Correct."

"And you knew that the male and his family members lived in a house that produced the bag of trash; is that right?"

•

The implication, at this point, is clear. According to Detective Payne's testimony, police had identified Bryan Kohberger as a suspect from an FBI CAST member. They had used that information to narrow their search of white sedans from a Nissan Sentra to a 2011–2013 Hyundai Elantra, then to his 2015 model. According to Payne, Kohberger must have been under investigation by December 19 because CAST was tracking his phone. It seems impossible that the detective in charge did not know Kohberger's name until then; something was not adding up.

Which brings us to Anne Taylor's third witness at the January 23 hearing. His name was Matthew Gamette, and he was a laboratory system director with the Idaho State Police Forensic Services division, overseeing administrative matters like procurement, contracts, and human resources. He had worked in that role for about ten years.

•

"Let's talk about Othram being involved in the case that winds up being why we're here today," Taylor asks well into a series of questions laying foundation that Gamette was fully knowledgeable of and involved with the lab. "What communication did you have with Othram on the early end of that process?"

"So, to my recollection, our early communication on this case was providing them with DNA that they would be able to develop, hopefully, an investigative lead for us on a case. After that sample, to my knowledge, had been—that we had followed our processes through and that we had put a sample into CODIS, that we had not received any hits off of CODIS, and then we would proceed with the next step of testing. We did have a contractual relationship with them since early in, I believe, 2021, and so we did have a contract with them in place."

"How did they get the DNA?"

"The DNA sample itself?" Gamette clarifies. "That DNA sample was delivered by Moscow Police Department in person to them at Othram labs."

According to ISP Supplemental 56, Corporal Chad Willerford transported the KA-BAR sheath from Moscow to the state police crime lab in Meridian, Idaho, on November 16, 2022. (On the "Chain of Custody" form, his last name is, for some reason, spelled *Willerfonn.*)

"Did you have any role in that?" Taylor asks.

"I accompanied the officer from Boise down to Houston and down to the Othram laboratory. I didn't have possession of the sample, but I was with the investigator that did."

The evidence was transported to Othram on November 22.

"And when were they notified to stop work?"

"I believe the notification, the official notification was on December 10, if I remember correctly."

The two talk back and forth about operational logistics and procedures, using language of the trade like SNPs, Y-STRs, and "wet work," defined as "anything that would be done in the physical laboratory."

"So after that, they have a recommendation for you?" Taylor asks.

"Their recommendation, to my memory, to my recall, was that they had several individuals that had the potential to be of interest in this investigation. They ask us if—to further their family tree building—if we could be in contact with individuals and see if they were willing to contribute information into the database that they were using in order to further the family tree building and further the geological [sic] work."

•

For the record, Gamette is telling Taylor that the Othram lab had identified several individuals based on DNA analysis of the KA-BAR sheath found in Mogen's room.

•

"And we're in a closed setting here, so I'm going to ask you to give me the last name."

"I don't recall the last name," Gamette says. "I'm sorry."

"Was it your understanding that these were four brothers?"

"Yes."

"Okay. What did you do in relationship to these four brothers?"

"So, we did some cursory work, just looking in publicly accessible information, literally Google searches and things of that nature. What our approach was is we didn't want to be approaching people, especially with an investigation of this nature, that really had nothing to do with anything. We just wanted to make sure there was some reason why Othram laboratories was asking us to go and ask these individuals to put their DNA into the database that law enforcement can search. So, we just did some work to build just very cursory family trees to see what connection these individuals might have and to verify these individuals were indeed brothers, things of that nature."

"Did you verify they were four brothers?" Taylor asks.

"I don't know that we would use the word verify, but we believed that the information was reliable that they had given us based on the publicly accessible information."

"Now, I know you said you can't remember the last name of these brothers," Taylor says. "We're here today and Bryan Kohberger's name has been on the news for two years; you know his name. That wasn't the last name."

"That was not the last name," Gamette says.

•

Taylor takes great pains to verify, for the record, that the first genetic profile developed by a state-contracted laboratory based on DNA found on the thumb snap of the KA-BAR sheath was not Bryan Kohberger's. She asks what happened next, and Gamette tells her they contacted one of the four brothers, who said he wanted nothing to do with the investigation. After that, things happened quickly.

•

"There was a meeting, to my knowledge," Gamette testifies. "And I don't remember exactly when but probably the morning of December 10, when we had a meeting, telephonic meeting is my memory, with representatives from Moscow Police Department, I believe FBI had representatives on the phone call, ISP, I believe, myself, ISP legal counsel, and I believe that the colonel of state police was on that phone call."

"What happened on that phone call?"

"In that phone call we were asked to turn over any kind of investigative records that we had, any kind of information that we had, to the FBI team. They provided me with an email address to be able to provide what they were requesting from us, which was—to my memory it was the two—the login information essentially, and it might have been other things I'm not aware of, like packets and things. I'm not aware of the technical terms, but basically they were asking us to provide that information to the FBI investigators."

•

Taylor asks Gamette what they turned over, and he mentions database information.

•

"When you say two databases, do you mean the two genetic genealogy databases that allow law enforcement search?"

"Yes," Gamette affirms. "To my knowledge, these samples were searched in two genealogical databases that allow searching by law enforcement. GEDmatch and FamilyTreeDNA, I believe, were the two that were searched, and we were asked to provide those credentials, that information, to the FBI."

•

Gamette confirms that Othram provided what is called a "preliminary report," which contained no notes or work product, and they were then told to "terminate the testing." It should be noted that law enforcement agencies may be given access to CODIS but not private DNA databases.

•

"Why was the decision made for the FBI to take this over and not let Othram finish?"

"I don't know," Gamette says. "I can't speak to that."

•

And this is where Anne Taylor's line of questioning moves from the ridiculous to the sublime. She has already secured sworn testimony from Lead Detective Brett Payne that the FBI never told him they found Bryan Kohberger's DNA on the sheath. She has put former lab director Nowlin on the record stating that Othram was a state-approved vendor. She has put Gamette on the record saying Othram obtained a profile from DNA found on the KA-BAR sheath and traced it to four brothers who were not named Kohberger. She has established that virtually everything Latah County prosecuting attorney Bill Thompson has said about his only physical evidence is false.

•

"Okay," Taylor asks. "Did you ever take a look at the two profiles, the FBI's SNP profile and Othram's SNP profile? Have you ever looked at those?"

"Did we look at those or did I look at those?"

"Did you?"

"I did not, no," Gamette states.

"Have you seen them?"

"No."

"Would it surprise you to know the FBI profile was over twice as big as Othram's?"

"Again, I have no knowledge of what the FBI did or didn't do," Gamette answers. "I had no knowledge, or . . . yeah."

•

One last thing before Lorenz's butterfly fully becomes a storm. Taylor has just documented that Thompson's Brady disclosure included almost no documentation of Othram's work. It did not mention the DNA profile they generated, the interview of the unidentified brothers, or the December 10 interagency phone call, which seems not to have been recorded or documented in written reports.

•

"Any of the work that Othram did in getting the DNA sample all the way down to SNP profile, where are they?" Taylor asks.

"Where is the documentation of that?" Gamette responds. "I do not have that documentation. That was not provided to us, to my knowledge. And I don't know everything that was provided back to the laboratory potentially, but to my knowledge we were not provided with that information."

"Would Othram have it?"

"Potentially. I don't know."

"The work that they did to come up with a name to give you for further investigation, where are those documents?"

"I don't know."

•

Nor does anyone else, it seems. Anne Taylor's office never received additional information about how DNA found on the KA-BAR sheath was initially used to identify four brothers whose names have been lost to history. All testimony recorded and transcribed in 175 pages of property filed by clerks was sealed from public scrutiny by Judge Hippler, right before he denied the defense's pleas to suppress.

CHAPTER 14

Dark SUV, Loud Exhaust, 12 ng/mL

There is no way to properly analyze this case without addressing the issue of how the killer actually got to and escaped from the house. Based on widely available door camera video, we all know about the white four-door sedan police have identified as an Elantra and tied to Bryan Kohberger. We know, from this same video, that DoorDash driver Molly McMichael was there as well. She can be seen walking up and down Queen Road with a flashlight just minutes before the crimes, and based on police reports, we know she claims a light-colored sedan drove next to her as she was walking.

As Detective Payne wrote in LCPA Supplemental 157, documenting his November 23 interview with McMichael:

> During the time McMichael was in the area of the King Road residence, the white Elantra can be seen via the 1112 King Road camera driving back and forth on Walenta Drive and

> then enter the King Road/Queen Road loop at approximately 0356 hours.

The DoorDash driver said she first parked behind the house, based on GPS, but then got out and walked around front, trying to verify the address.

> McMichael said she started to walk down the road which runs north/south immediately to the east of the residence. McMichael stated a tan sedan drove next to her while she was walking.

For some reason, police did not trust her recollection.

> At that point McMichael pulled into the front parking lot before she dropped the order off, the Elantra pulled in behind McMichael's vehicle (a Gray Subaru Forester) and then exited the King Road at approximately 0358 hours. McMichael did not mention seeing the white Elantra behind her at any time.

Perhaps she did, but it appears that police did not believe her.

> Subsequent investigation of video footage and cellular data showed the "tan sedan" McMichael saw was likely a light-colored SUV which left the area.

Those who view the 1112 video for themselves will see that an unidentified SUV did arrive at 3:46:07, but that is almost certainly McMichael arriving in her gray Forester. She can be seen walking with a flashlight at 3:51:42, time-stamping her presence in front of the house, and we can see from the video that no other vehicle drives down King Road until 3:53:38, when a light-colored sedan leaves via King Road toward Taylor. At 3:56:24, a white sedan enters the neighborhood and passes King to Queen, out of sight, only to return at 3:58:19. McMichael's Subaru is seen leaving the area at 4:00:38, making it impossible that she saw an SUV.

Why, one might ask, is this important? The single least-debatable fact in this entire case is that a white four-door sedan traveled in and out of the neighborhood numerous times until 4:20:45, when it leaves at a high rate of speed and disappears southeast up Walenta.

Bill Thompson made it a part of his evidentiary testimony at Kohberger's change of plea hearing.

"At approximately 04:20 that morning," he said, "defendant's car is seen on a surveillance camera for 1112 King Road leaving the area at a high rate of speed. The evidence would show that following that, the defendant in his Elantra drove south of Moscow. We know that he drove on the back roads because there are surveillance cameras on the main highways, Highway 95, that would've picked up the defendant's car if he'd gone that route."

What no one has yet publicly discovered, however, is that there is another vehicle that presents compelling questions about who might have gone in and out of that house Sunday morning. Oddly enough, this mystery starts with Dylan Mortensen. She told police she saw a dark truck passing the house just after the crimes.

In order to place this vehicle in context, we need to return to her November 17, 2022, interview with ISP detective Vickie Gooch and MSP detective Dustin Blaker. Though we have covered the written summary of this discussion (ISP Supplemental 0003), the author has obtained the actual audio recording, which had not been released to the public at the time of this writing. This interview was conducted at Mortensen's residence in Boise, with her lawyer, Robin McPherson, present via video feed from the Sullivan Law Offices in Moscow.

•

"Can you think of anything else right now?" Gooch asks at the 1:26:28 mark.

"No . . . oh so this is something else that I remember, um . . . cars do come by a lot, but I remember looking out the window, I just remember, I think it was a black truck, I don't remember . . . I don't know for sure, but like that is normal for cars to go by but like I don't know if that could be something, just a car driving past our driveway."

"What time was that at?" Gooch asks.

"That was right when I went down to see Bethany, so I don't know exactly when that was."

"Was it moving? Was it in movement?"

"It was moving, it wasn't stopped at all, it was moving and like, people drive by our driveway like around this side um housing neighborhood a little bit, like we hear cars go by all the time, that's not weird but I—"

"But when you were making your way to Bethany's room—"

"That's not when I . . . it was when I got into Bethany's room. I don't know why I looked out the window, but I saw a car drive by, and I believe it was a . . . I shouldn't say I believe because I don't know for sure, but I think it was a black truck. But I don't know for sure, it could have been it was dark and I just thought it was a black truck."

•

As luck would have it, one can actually document her statement via the 1112 door cam recording. At 4:23:49, a dark full-size SUV passes in front of 1122 King Road with a distinctive audio signature, caused by what appears to be very loud exhaust. Unlike the white sedan, this dark SUV turns right on Taylor Road instead of left on Walenta. We know this because of the "dumpster video," which clearly shows it passing eastbound on Taylor at 4:25:17.

Things start to get interesting, however, when the dark SUV returns to King Road at 4:28:49, as documented by the 1112 camera. Review of the "dumpster video" verifies it returning along Taylor Road, meaning it left the neighborhood just five minutes after the white Elantra, then returned about four minutes later.

What really stands out, however, is a third set of images captured by widely known footage referred to as the "Linda Lane" video. This is the same camera police relied upon to document travel of the white Elantra before and after the crimes. Careful review of footage shows the boxy SUV parked nose in, facing the camera. At 4:23:17, an unidentified subject carrying a backpack can be seen walking from the direction of 1122 King Road, across the parking lot toward the truck. They appear to open the tailgate of the SUV, which triggers the interior dome light, then climb in through the driver's side door.

Here is where things start to get weird.

The SUV leaves its parking spot near Linda Lane, passes down Queen, turns right on Taylor, and returns by the same route approximately four minutes later. Instead of returning to its original parking space, however, it stops in front of 1122 King Road. We know this because the Linda Lane video shows that it did not return, and the distinctive sound of its exhaust is recorded by the door cam at 1112. Based on the recording, and the SUV's distinctive exhaust, it seems clear that the vehicle stops in front of 1122, idles there for about thirty seconds, then shuts down its engine. You can hear a door close.

Although the 1112 camera did not provide visual evidence, a witness did.

According to police, a neighbor named Nick Makowhich contacted them November 18 to report hearing the loud engine Sunday morning around four thirty. ISP detective Hugh Powell documented the call in ISP Supplement 196, noting that Makowhich lived at 1106 King Road. Powell wrote:

> After going to bed, he had been asleep for approximately an hour when he was awoken by a vehicle with loud exhaust speeding away down the street past his house.

Makowhich said he did not actually see the vehicle, but a different neighbor did. On February 16, 2023, Detective Payne interviewed a man named Jeffrey Manning. He wrote in LCPA Supplemental 147:

> Manning started by stating he lived at 1868 Conestoga Drive in Moscow and had called in a tip early on in the investigation

> about seeing a vehicle drive by his house at approximately 04:25 to 04:30 on the morning of November 13th, 2022. Manning told me he was out in front of his house at that time placing items into his recycling and trash bins.

Manning told Payne he could not describe the vehicle other than its headlights, teardrop-shaped taillights, and unusually loud exhaust. He believed it was an SUV. Payne reported:

> Manning also told me the vehicle was going faster than usual but did not seem to be driving erratically or dangerously. Manning told me it was quite unusual for anyone to be driving in the area at that time and said he had not seen many cars driving at that time since the morning of November 13, 2022.

It seems that the police were not the only ones aware of this SUV.

"Manning stated he was contacted by someone from the Kootenai County Public Defender's Office who asked him about the dark SUV he caught on security camera," Payne wrote, adding that Manning did not have any surveillance footage to give them.

Perhaps not, but fortunately, the camera at Linda Lane did. At 6:23 a.m. the mysterious SUV returned to its original parking spot to the east of 1122 King Road, near Linda Lane. It appears that the same person who entered the vehicle at 4:23 exits the driver side door with a backpack and walks west back toward 1122 King Road.

For the record, this is the dark SUV with the same distinctive exhaust that is documented leaving and returning approximately four minutes after the crimes by three witnesses and three separate cameras. This is the vehicle that left Linda Lane only to park for two hours in front of the crime scene and return to its original parking spot two hours later. The camera at 1112 King Road provides no indication that the vehicle started or moved during that time.

For those wondering what might have happened inside the house in the eight hours after the crimes, who might have cleaned up the common areas of the second floor, and where all those blood-soaked materials might have gone, the dark SUV prompts compelling discussion. To this day, no one has identified the distinctive-looking vehicle with the easily identifiable exhaust. Why did someone walk out to it at four thirty in the morning, put something in the back, and drive away, only to return four minutes later and park in front of the house, only to re-park in its original spot two hours later?

As with so many unanswered questions, now that Kohberger has admitted to the crimes, no one seems to care.

Retired FBI special agent Christopher Holland is a forensic criminologist engaged by the defense to evaluate certain aspects of the prosecution's case. Based on thousands of Brady disclosure files, he composed a behavioral evidence analysis "seeking to establish and understand the role of victim psychodynamics and their contextual vulnerability with relation to the crimes." Relevant portions of his thirty-eight-page report are here excerpted verbatim:

IDAHO v. BRYAN C. KOHBERGER

Case Number CR01-24-31665

Holland Felony Analysis, LLC

MEDICO-LEGAL FINDINGS

Victim autopsies were completed on 11.16.2022 by VEENA D. SINGH, M.D., M.P.H., Chief Medical Examiner for Spokane County, Washington. The following are extracts from the autopsy reports. (Note, there was no evidence that any of the victims were sexually assaulted.)

Kaylee Goncalves: Investigative reports indicate that this 21-year-old female was found deceased in her shared home at 1122 King Road, Moscow, Idaho. Postmortem examination showed a well-developed adult female with stab and incised wounds of the scalp, face, and neck (24+); stab and incised wounds of the chest (11); and stab and incised wounds of the upper extremities (3). Associated injuries included punctures of the outer table of the skull; injuries to the teeth and tongue; perforations of the subclavian artery and vein; and hemorrhage into the chest cavities. Blunt force injuries included scalp laceration, bleeding around the brain, and nasal fracture, as well as scrapes on the nose and cheeks, bruising around the eyes, and patterned bruises extending across the lower face. Petechial hemorrhages were present in the eyes and mouth. There was no evidence of natural disease that would have caused or contributed to death.

***Postmortem toxicology testing showed a blood alcohol concentration of 0.107 g/100 mL. The cause of death is multiple sharp force injuries. Blunt force injuries of the head and asphyxia injuries were listed as significant contributors to death.*

Madison Mogen: Investigative reports indicate that this 21-year-old female was found deceased in her shared home at 1122 King Road, Moscow, Idaho. Postmortem examination showed a well-developed adult female with stab and incised wounds of the scalp, face, and neck (13); stab wounds of the chest (5); and incised wounds of the upper extremities (10). Associated injuries included wounds of the lung and liver as well as perforations of the subclavian vein, subclavian artery, and blood vessels of the chest wall. There was no evidence of natural disease that would have caused or contributed to death.

***Postmortem toxicology testing showed a blood alcohol concentration of 0.282 g/100 mL. The cause of death is multiple sharp force injuries.*

Xana Kernodle: Investigative reports indicate that this 20-year-old female was found deceased in her shared home at 1122 King Road, Moscow, Idaho. Postmortem examination showed a well-developed adult female with stab and incised wounds of the scalp, face, and neck (23); stab wounds of the chest (7) and abdomen (4); incised and puncture wounds of the back (3); incised wounds of the upper extremities (25); and incised wounds of the lower extremities (5). Associated injuries included punctures of the outer table of the skull; perforations of the jugular vein, heart, lung, and pulmonary blood vessels; hemorrhage into the chest cavities; and wounds exposing the bones of the hand. Additional injuries included scrapes and bruises on the face, torso, and extremities. There was no evidence of natural disease that would have caused or contributed to death.

***Postmortem toxicology testing showed a blood alcohol concentration of 0.229 g/100 mL and an amphetamine level of 12 ng/mL. The cause of death is multiple sharp force injuries.*

Ethan Chapin: Investigative reports indicate that this 20-year-old male was found deceased in a shared home at 1122 King Road, Moscow, Idaho. Postmortem examination showed a well-developed adult male with stab and incised wounds of the scalp, face, and neck (4); a stab wound of the upper chest (1); incised wounds of the upper extremities (6); and stab and incised wounds of the lower extremities (6). Associated injuries included perforations of the jugular vein, subclavian vein, and subclavian artery. There was no evidence of natural disease that would have caused or contributed to death.

***Postmortem toxicology testing showed a blood alcohol concentration of 0.122 g/100 mL and an amphetamine level of 260 ng/mL. The cause of death is multiple sharp force injuries.*

VICTIMOLOGY

Kaylee Goncalves was a senior at the University of Idaho, 21 years of age. She was born in Coeur D'Alene, Idaho, and graduated from Lake City High School in 2019. She enrolled in the University of Idaho at Moscow, majoring in general studies at the School of Arts, Letters, and Social Sciences. She reportedly intended to be a school teacher. She had completed her studies, and moved back to Coeur d'Alene, living with her parents. She returned to Moscow that weekend to attend the home coming football game and begin preparations for her move to Austin, Texas, where she planned to share an apartment with a female friend (Jordan) and an (unidentified) male she met online. The week prior to her murder, she purchased a Range Rover in conjunction with the anticipated move.

Kaylee is described as unproblematic and peaceful and "having it together." Kaylee was active on social media, and her posts garnered a significant number of responses, though there is no indication she sought to be a social influencer.

Kaylee was best friends with Madison Mogen, whom she had known since they were in 6th grade. She had a boyfriend—Jack DeCouer—whom she had known since high school. He was also in attendance at the University of Idaho. At the university, they shared ownership of a dog named Murphy. Their relationship had ended in the weeks preceding the murder. She reportedly had a relationship with a fraternity member at Delta Tau Delta, with whom she would occasionally "hook up." In the weeks prior to the murders, Kaylee had reported to friends that she thought she was being stalked.

During the evening and early morning hours of November 12/13, 2022, Goncalves consumed drugs, including Adderall, and alcohol, which would inhibit the ability to think and react. She was in a residence with other individuals who had been drinking heavily, creating the potential for harm to occur. Persons who did not live at the residence had access to the combination to the cypher lock on the first floor, creating a risk of an intruder. At the time of her death, Goncalves' Blood Alcohol Content (BAC) was 0.107 g/100 mL.

(Based on potentially harmful environmental elements and behavioral factors impacting Goncalves' day-to-day life, she is assessed a **medium** "lifestyle exposure." Based on actual vulnerability to harm, she is assessed a **medium** "situational exposure.")

Madison Mogen was a popular member of Pi Beta Phi sorority and the "big" of Bethany Funke, who also lived at 1122 King Road and survived the attacks. Mogen moved into the King Road residence in 2021. Friends considered Mogen a strong and thoughtful person. She worked part time at the Mad Greek (a Moscow restaurant) where Xana Kernodle also worked. She was a marketing major and had begun using those skills in a media campaign for the restaurant and interned with an insurance company.

During an interview with police, one friend described first meeting Mogen when she was walking around "without any clothes." The friend said she "got her clothes" and walked Mogen back to Pi Beta Phi, where she lived at the time. Mogen regularly posted photos of an "influencer" nature, with her friends and sorority sisters, at various college events, as well as posts with her boyfriend, Jake Schriger. One of her posts solicited a response from Peach Perfect scouts who appeared to be looking for online influencers and brand ambassador recruiters.

Mogen had an Instagram account with the user name *maddiemogen* and display name, *madison may mogen*. The account profile stated, "Backup, Onlyfans, DM me for any information, My 18+ content here onlyfansmaddiemogen." Madison Mogen consumed alcohol and used drugs recreationally. Any use of illegal drugs requires interaction with someone who is potentially dangerous. Mogen had an account on OnlyFans, which could potentially draw attention to her. The incident of another student finding her without clothes suggests she was inebriated in public or high on drugs, either of which would increase her lifestyle exposure.

Mogen's postmortem toxicology showed a Blood Alcohol Content (BAC) of 0.282 g/100 mL. This is sufficient to cause impairment of speech and movement, and therefore could have affected her ability to react when she was attacked. At the time of her death, she was living in her own residence. Other persons were present who had been drinking heavily, creating the potential for harm to occur. Persons who did not live there had access to the combination to the cypher lock on the first floor, creating a risk of an intruder.

(Based on potentially harmful environmental elements and behavioral factors impacting Mogen's day-to-day life, she is assessed a **moderate** "lifestyle exposure." Based on actual vulnerability to harm, she is assessed a **moderate** "situational exposure.")

Xana Kernodle was born in Sandpoint, Idaho, and graduated from Post Falls High School. She was a state champion gymnast. Her parents are divorced. Her mother is in prison on drug related charges. She enrolled at the University of Idaho in May 2022 as a marketing major. She enjoyed volleyball. She was a member of Pi Beta Phi, as was victim Madison Mogen and witness Dylan Mortensen, however she had to drop from the sorority due to inability to pay the $1,000.00 membership fees. She was a server at The Mad Greek, where Mogen worked. She was very popular among her peers, with a cheerful, outgoing personality. She had been dating victim Ethan Chapin for about six months. According to police reports, he was alleged to use cocaine on occasion.

Xana Kernodle's postmortem toxicology testing showed a blood alcohol concentration of 0.229 g/100 mL and an amphetamine level of 12 ng/mL. This is sufficient to cause impairment of speech and movement and therefore could have affected her ability to react when she was attacked.

At the time of her death, she was living in her own residence, where other persons had been drinking; some had been using drugs.

(Based on potentially harmful environmental elements and behavioral factors impacting Kernodle's day-to-day life, she is assessed a **moderate** "lifestyle exposure." Based on actual vulnerability to harm, she is assessed a **moderate** "situational exposure.")

Ethan Chapin was the eldest of triplets (one brother, one sister), born in Conway, Washington, and graduated from Mt Vernon H.S., Skagit County, Washington. He was in his sophomore year at the University of Idaho, 20 years of age when he was murdered. He was an avid swimmer and surfer, 6ft 4 inches in height, and 228 pounds. Chapin was a member of the Sigma Chi fraternity but could not live in the residence due to his poor grades. He had been dating Xana Kernodle for about six months. His Facebook page had an open list of 140 friends, with few posts from 2021. He was athletic, calm by nature. According to police reports, he consumed alcohol and was a recreational drug user.

At the time of death, Chapin was at the residence of Xana Kernodle where other persons had been drinking heavily, and some had been using drugs, creating the potential for harm to occur. Persons who did not live at the residence had access to the combination to the cypher lock on the first floor, creating a risk of an intruder. His postmortem toxicology testing showed a blood alcohol concentration of 0.122 g/100 mL and an amphetamine level of 260 ng/mL, sufficient to cause impairment of speech and movement.

(Based on potentially harmful environmental elements and behavioral factors impacting Chapin's day-to-day life, he is assessed a **moderate** "lifestyle exposure." Based on actual vulnerability to harm, he is assessed a **moderate** "situational exposure.")

POSSIBLE EVIDENCE OF TWO OFFENDERS

1. Kaylee Goncalves was found dead in a full-sized bed, directly adjacent to Madison Mogen. Autopsy reports show that she suffered three defensive wounds to upper extremities, indicating she was surprised and overwhelmed by her attacker. Cast-off blood on the walls of the bedroom where she died indicates her attacker climbed onto the bed and slashed at her from right to left. Wounds she sustained to the top of her skull are consistent with an assailant mounting her upper body and striking downward. While choking, beating and stabbing Goncalves, it would have been extremely difficult for a single offender to simultaneously control Mogen and prevent her from fleeing the open side of the bed. The mechanism, brutality, and chronology of these two murders strongly indicate the presence of two or more offenders.
2. Ethan Chapin's undiluted blood was found at the top of the stairway leading from the 2nd floor to the 1st.

According to the State's own experts, there is no evidence that Ethan Chapin left his bed after being attacked. According to statements by surviving witness, Dylan Mortensen, the man in the black balaclava made his escape, moving directly from Xana Kernodle's bedroom to the sliding door in the kitchen, and never went near the stairway. If Mortensen is correct, the man she saw could not have transferred blood to that location. The presence of Chapin's blood on the stairwell necessitates transfer from a second offender.

3. Xana Kernodle sustained 64 wounds, while Ethan sustained 11 wounds. Wounds to Chapin's lower extremities are evidence that he awoke after being attacked and reacted to the assault by pulling his legs up into a defensive posture. The absence of blood on white socks he was wearing at the time of death proves that he was attacked in bed and never rose to assist Xana Kernodle as she was fighting for her life on the floor beside him. Based on the nature and extent of wounds inflicted upon Chapin, it is impossible to believe that he slept through the attack on Kernodle, and it is illogical that Kernodle stood in her bedroom and waited for the offender to kill Chapin before killing her. The only possible explanation is that the two were attacked and killed simultaneously by more than one assailant.
4. When let out of the house at 0230 hours, Murphy (the dog) ran away, as evidenced by Bethany Funke's statements to police. Brayden Pollow, residing at 1127 King Road, stated that Murphy was the only dog in the

neighborhood, and Pollow awoke sometime after 0400 to the sound of Murphy barking. The barking continued until almost 0500, when it stopped abruptly, as if he had been let inside. As of 0430, Funke and Mortensen were the only persons known to be in the residence, and according to statements by both women, they never left Funke's 1st floor bedroom, until approximately 1154. The only explanation is that a second offender was still in the residence at 0500 and that the offender opened a door, allowing Murphy back into the house.

5. The floor in Xana Kernodle's room was covered with blood, which should have resulted in bloody footprints in the hallway outside. The lack of footprints in the hallway indicates that the floor was cleaned sometime between 0415, when the murders occurred, and noon when police arrived. Police reports document cast-off blood in the common areas of the second floor, which had been "diluted with an unknown substance," indicating efforts to clean up after the murders. In statements to police, Mortensen said she observed a masked man in black clothes walking from the direction of Xana Kernodle's bedroom, through the kitchen as he exited the house. If this offender left immediately after killing Chapin and Kernodle, a second offender had to have stayed to alter the scene.
6. At 1000, the front door of the residence was observed open by a witness walking his dog. Due to its location at the bottom of the stairs, Mortensen would have noticed the door being open when she relocated to Funke's bedroom at 0430. Had the door stayed open all night, the

first floor would have been cold, but neither Funke nor Mortensen made that observation. Someone else in the house must have opened or closed the door.

METHOD OF ATTACK

Kaylee Goncalves was killed in a "blitz attack," that is, the offenders suddenly and viciously attacked her in her sleep with overwhelming force. Goncalves' cast off blood was found on the ceiling above the bed and on the walls. This indicates great force used in the attack. Goncalves received 38 sharp-edged wounds, with only three being defensive wounds, reflecting complete surprise and an inability to fight back. She sustained blunt force trauma to her face, resulting in fractures, and she was strangled to the point of petechia, which requires a significant amount of time to induce.

Madison Mogen was also assaulted in a blitz attack, in which she sustained 28 sharp-edged wounds, with ten being defensive wounds to upper extremities. Cast off blood on the far walls of the room and the ceiling indicated that great force was used in the attack.

Xana Kernodle suffered a surprise attack, where neither the victim nor the offender was aware of the other's presence until just before the encounter.

Ethan Chapin was murdered in a blitz attack in which the offenders suddenly and viciously overwhelmed him with sharp-edged weapons. He received 11 significant wounds, including the fatal blow to his throat.

EVIDENCE OF PLANNING

These attacks were not spontaneous. The offenders had to select, surveille and prepare for the attacks. The planning was not extensive, however, based on errors made in altering the crime scene and the handling of the dog. Evidence indicates that the offenders were either unaware Ethan and Xana were home or anticipated they were asleep and did not expect to encounter them when they moved to the 3rd floor. At least one offender was dressed in black and wearing a balaclava to conceal their identity. The offenders had knowledge of the house.

OFFENDER TRAITS AND CHARACTERISTICS

Signature Behaviors are acts committed by an offender that exceed what would normally be expected during the crime. These excessive actions suggest a psychological or emotional need that is unique to the assailant at time of the offense. Both Goncalves and Mogen received identical post mortem wounds to the throat and left shoulder. These post mortem wounds represent a compulsion by the offender(s) to disfigure the victims. They indicate an excessively violent behavior associated with rage. Based on these characteristics we can conclude the following:

Kaylee Goncalves was the primary target of these attacks. She had completed her course work and moved from 1122 King Road to her parents' home in Coeur d'Alene, Idaho. She returned to U of I that weekend for the express purpose of attending the homecoming football game and selling furniture she had in her room in preparation for her move to Austin, Texas. The weekend of 11\12–13\2022 would have presented the killers with one last opportunity to kill Kaylee Goncalves. They bypassed persons on the 2nd floor and went directly to the third floor, seeking Goncalves. Goncalves sustained strangulation and blunt force trauma resulting in facial fractures, and 38 wounds inflicted by a sharp-edged weapon(s). Goncalves was strangled, as evidenced by the presence of petechiae hemorrhage. There is no evidence of ligature use, indicating she was strangled by hand, the most personal of all homicidal methods.

Injuries inflicted on Goncalves represent "overkill," in excess of what was necessary to cause her death. One or both offenders had a deep, personal anger against Goncalves. The attack was directed primarily at her face, which was severely disfigured in an effort to destroy her identity. This indicates the offender had a personal and deeply hateful relationship with his intended target.

Madison Mogen sustained 28 injuries from a sharp-edged weapon and was an intended, though secondary, target. The killer's aggression toward Mogen would be described as retaliatory anger, but to a lesser extent than Goncalves, as she sustained far fewer injuries. The act of staging of Goncalves' head on Mogen's shoulder; the identical nature of wounds inflicted post mortem on both victims, and the fact that the killers "tucked them in" beneath the comforter indicate they were aware of and resented the close relationship between Goncalves and Mogen. As Mogen's injuries were less severe than Goncalves, the anger toward Mogen was possibly due to her relationship with or a trait she shared with Goncalves, and not specifically because of something Mogen had done.

Xana Kernodle was murdered to protect the identity of the offenders. Had she been sleeping in her bedroom, it is unlikely she would have been killed.

Ethan Chapin was murdered to protect the identity of the offenders. Had he not awakened, it is unlikely he would have been killed.

If the first two pillars of Bill Thompson's case are DNA and the white sedan, the third and final pillar is the FBI CAST analysis tying Bryan Kohberger's cell phone to the scene. To be precise, no law enforcement document ever places Kohberger's phone anywhere near the scene of the crime between the hours of 2:47 a.m. and 4:48 a.m. If the state is correct in asserting that all four murders occurred in the moments before surveillance cameras at 1112 King Road recorded what sounds like a woman (Xana) screaming and a white sedan speeding away, it could not have tied it to Kohberger's phone, because it was off.

What we know about the prosecution's evidence, in lieu of a trial, begins with what the Latah County Prosecuting Attorney told us at the change of plea hearing.

•

"About 04:48 that morning, the defendant's phone comes back on," Thompson states. "And the evidence will show that that phone was located south of Moscow, likely at a side road intersection with Highway 95."

•

Using the term "likely" might seem conspicuously effete in a death penalty prosecution, but those were his words.

•

"From there, the defendant's phone activity tracks a heading back north towards Pullman, Washington, where the defendant lived. About 05:26, starting approximately 05:26, various surveillance cameras in Pullman, Washington, pick up the defendant's vehicle as he enters Pullman from the south and heads north and slightly west towards his apartment where he arrived at approximately 05:30 in the morning."

•

According to reports the FBI CAST team prepared for trial, the words "towards Pullman" mean absolutely nothing. Cell tower analysis shows that it was impossible to track Kohberger's phone to less than a ten-mile radius. Yes, he could have been traveling toward Pullman—or anywhere else north of Nevada. But there's more. Based on Brett Payne's December 20 arrest warrant affidavit, we know all about what prosecutors believed at that time. We will recall that police referred to Kohberger's AT&T cell by the last four digits in his number.

•

"A query of the 8458 Phone in these returns did not show the 8458 Phone utilizing cell tower resources in close proximity to the King Road Residence between 3:00 a.m. and 5:00 a.m.," Payne wrote.

•

While many would conclude that this was due to the phone not being anywhere near that location, recall that Payne extrapolated, based on his experience, that "individuals can either leave their cellular telephone at a different location before committing a crime or turn their cellular telephone off prior to going to a location to commit a crime. This is done by subjects in an effort to avoid alerting law enforcement that a cellular device associated with them was in a particular area where a crime is committed."

Based on CAST analysis and data obtained from a December 23, 2022, police report, it was determined that Kohberger's cell "utilized cellular resources that provide coverage to ID state highway 95 S to Moscow, ID near Blaine, ID (north of Genesee)." They claimed that between 4:50 a.m. and 5:26 a.m., his phone traveled south on 95 to Genesee, then west toward Uniontown, then north back into Pullman.

"At approximately 5:30 a.m., the 8458 Phone is utilizing

resources that provide coverage to Pullman, WA," Payne wrote, "consistent with the phone traveling back to the Kohberger residence."

Though this all makes sense on its surface, Payne did not mention the FBI's specific analysis or the fact that the only way to verify cell tower pings was to match them with what they claimed to be their suspect's white Hyundai Elantra. Bizarrely, Payne noted in his affidavit that FBI analysis did show Kohberger's phone connecting to a cell phone tower providing service to Moscow on November 14, 2022, but for some reason, did not believe "the 8458 Phone was in Moscow on that date." No explanation was offered regarding this obviously troublesome fact.

On July 8, 2024, the FBI provided Bill Thompson's office with a colorful and animated thirty-one-page Historical Mobile Device Location Analysis, completed by Special Agent Nicholas Ballance. Page 1 of this Cellular Analysis Survey Team (CAST) report states that the MPD requested assistance with three "target cell phones," which need not be printed here, though they are obviously tied to the murders. One, of course, is Kohberger's, and for reasons not yet explained, the other two belong to victims. The report offers basic information about methodology, which amounts to matching a phone with the tower it pings, and notes that locations are denoted in latitude and longitude, using "mapping software" that is not further described.

Page 2 of the report shows a map graphic depicting tower locations in the area surrounding Moscow, photographic depictions of sample towers, including a simulated evergreen tree, a flagpole, and a cactus. Page 9 of the report lists "Locations of Interest" as the crime scene at 1122 King Road and Kohberger's apartment at

1630 Northeast Valley Road, Apartment G 201 in Pullman. The following page maps two AT&T network towers in Moscow, seven in Pullman, and two along Route 270, the primary route connecting the two towns. The report lists Kohberger's phone information, with a 509 prefix, a billing address in Pennsylvania, and an activation date of June 23. From there, the CAST report uses maps, legends, and graphic representations to track Kohberger's phone based on where and when it pinged on the closest adjacent towers. Although Bill Thompson made bold claims about what these analyses show, a thorough review of the CAST report leads to very different conclusions. Since this document is animated with highlights, diagrams, and graphics full of information, it appears obvious that it was built for courtroom presentation, specifically to bolster expert testimony.

"509-xxx-8458 had no network interactions on November 13, 2002, between 2:54:45 a.m. and 4:48:40," page 14 proclaims. This we already knew.

After 4:48, the CAST report shows tower connection south of Moscow, as the prosecution has alleged. Based on a legend at the bottom of the page graphic, it appears that Kohberger's car could have been as far away as twenty-five miles from the crime scene at that time. Between 5:20 and 5:27 a.m., it appeared to have pinged towers south and east of Kohberger's apartment in Pullman. Between 6:13 a.m. and 8:03 a.m., he placed three calls to two different family members, received a fourth call from one of them, and received one text. Notably, one of the calls (6:17:15 a.m.) lasted more than thirty-six minutes, while a second (8:03:10 a.m.) lasted almost fifty-five. All five of the communications pinged a tower within two thousand feet, according to the report.

At 9:00 a.m. and 9:03 a.m., Kohberger's phone pinged a tower south of his residence from two different directions, implying travel, and nine minutes later interacted with a tower in Moscow. From there, the CAST charts show Kohberger's phone pinging towers over a broad stretch of Latah and adjoining counties, as far as Sweetwater, which is almost fifty miles south. While one could certainly see how Bill Thompson's office used these charts to link Kohberger to the crime scenes, it is just as easy to use the same graphs to argue that microwave geometry makes it impossible to pinpoint locations within a range of more than ten miles.

For reasons that are not immediately obvious, the CAST presentation tracks certain cell communications for Maddie Mogen. A chart on page 27 shows her phone receiving incoming calls at 4:19:58, 4:21:55, and 4:28:42. Clearly these document calls Dylan Mortensen and Bethany Funke say they made shortly after the murders, but there is no information in the report to indicate origin, type of transmission, or length or connection.

The last two pages of the CAST report document Kohberger's phone pinging a tower "providing coverage to within 100 meters" of 1122 King Road twenty-three times between July 9, 2022, and November 7, 2022. The report notes that all twenty-three connections occurred between 10:00 p.m. and 4:00 a.m., implying, perhaps, that Kohberger cased the house late at night. What they do not state is that none of the residents had even moved into the house at that point, and that while the tower in question could have tied a user to "within 100 meters" of the crime scene, it could not, in fact, prove they were closer than ten miles.

As for the science and methodology behind cell tower analysis,

Anne Taylor had hired an expert named Sy Ray. According to an April 2024 defense filing, the former police officer and founder of ZetX Corporation planned to refute the FBI CAST analysis based on missing information and incomplete data.

•

"Kohberger's mobile device was south of Pullman, Washington and west of Moscow, Idaho, on November 13, 2022," Taylor's office wrote, seeking discovery of additional information from police. "Bryan Kohberger's mobile device did not travel east on the Moscow-Pullman Highway in the early morning hours of November 13th and thus could not be the vehicle captured on video along the Moscow-Pullman Highway near Floyd's Cannabis shop."

•

Sy Ray actually testified to misgivings during a pretrial hearing.

•

"Because of piecemealing of the data, because of the missing data, because of the data I'm reviewing that is incredibly inaccurate, everything that is missing is absolutely in benefit of the defense right now," he said. "There are other reports that are missing that I can't tell you are benefiting of Mr. Kohberger or the state."

•

Although Ray has remained outspoken about what he perceives to be flaws in the FBI's methodology and conclusions, there will be no trial. He will not get the chance.

CHAPTER 15

Drunk or Not, Death Row, the New Normal

No one knows what really happened inside that house early Sunday morning—but we all know what did not.

We know the killer did not stop at Dylan Mortensen's room on his way upstairs toward his intended targets. We know the assassin did not, by himself, asphyxiate, beat, stab, and hack away at Kaylee Goncalves while Maddie Mogen lay quietly in bed beside her without fighting back or running away. We know that a complete stranger would not take the time to slice each of their throats twice, postmortem, before suggestively posing their bodies in an assault that Bill Thompson himself said was not sexual in nature.

We know that Dylan Mortensen did not apparently hear the extreme violence of the attacks though her bed was directly beneath Maddie's in a house where she told police, "You can hear everything." We know, despite Bryan Kohberger's admissions of guilt, that police have not produced a shred of evidence linking him to any of the victims or the two survivors. There is no indication in the terabytes of investigation that he ever visited or stepped inside the house.

In terms of means, motive, and modus operandi, we know the killer premeditated his crimes, wearing black clothing and a balaclava to the scene, though we don't know why. We know he left blood transfers on the walls and flat surfaces in the stairwell but not on the floors. We know he did not interact with Murphy, because the dog was lying on Kaylee's bed when police arrived with no signs of injury and not a drop of blood on his fur. We know from Bethany, neighbors, and Ring cam audio that Murphy was barking outside the house forty-five minutes after the murders, but we do not know how he got back inside.

Moving downstairs, we know that the killer did not stop at Dylan Mortensen's room on his way out. We know the killer attacked Xana in or near the kitchen, chasing her across the living room as she screamed so loudly it was picked up on a Ring camera down the street, but we do not know why no one heard her in the house. We know from lab reports that the killer splashed Maddie's and Kaylee's blood on the living room walls, but we do not know how every droplet was found to have been "diluted with an unknown substance." We know blood was found on the floors of both murder scene bedrooms, but we don't have a clue how the killer walked through the house without tracking anything around on his shoes.

We know police found a beer pong table blocking the path of what would have been Xana's frantic escape toward Ethan, but we cannot explain its apparent lack of displacement. We know what the table looked like in cell phone pics Lakelynn McComas took around 1:15 a.m., but not why things changed by the time Nunes arrived. We know they found Xana's blood spatter on one side of the table, and Maddie's and Kaylee's on the knee wall at the far end, but we have no clue what physics police used to make sense of the trajectories. We know police found Hunter Johnson's steak knife near bloodstains within plain sight of Xana's body, but not why they dismissed it. We know Bethany told police she woke up to a loud bang and the sound of the beer pong table moving and cups falling.

Moving down the hall toward Ethan's mutilated body, we know police found it covered with a blanket, but not why or when or how. We know that Dylan Mortensen told police she saw Xana's body on the floor, moments after coming face-to-face with a man clad in black, wearing a mask, but not why she assumed her housemate was sleeping. She said she could see the top of Xana's head, though her head was pointing the other way, and that Xana was wearing a hoodie and underwear, but we don't know how she missed the giant pool of blood.

Moving down to the first floor, we know detectives found Ethan's undiluted blood above the railing, but we have no idea how it got there.

We know Dylan went down to Bethany's room where the two women waited eight hours before calling 911, but not why they called Emily and her boyfriend, Hunter, first.

We know the front door was closed when Hunter arrived, but not why a witness swore it was open between nine o'clock and eleven o'clock that morning while he walked his dog.

We know that both women claimed they went immediately to sleep after all the ruckus, but not why records show they were up texting and using social media. We know they claimed they did not leave their room "even to go to the bathroom," but not why Dylan's Apple Watch showed physical movement at five o'clock that morning, the exact time Murphy stopped barking.

We know police found the downstairs bathroom scoured and completely empty of what one might expect to find in college housing, but not why they disregarded that as normal. We know they found a blood-soaked green jacket in the empty first-floor bedroom and that it tested positive for DNA mixtures that could not be "deconflicted," except for one, which was Dylan's. We know they found a broken woman's bracelet on the floor of that same room and that photographs suggest the bracelet was stained with blood, but there is no record stating why it was ignored.

While on the subject of suspicious oversights, we know Spokane County medical examiner Dr. Veena Singh found "trace evidence" in Ethan Chapin's hand that later turned out to be human hair. We do not know why it was tested for type and color but not for DNA.

We know the notorious KA-BAR knife sheath was found either on the bed or on the floor, but not why nobody seemed to care. We know about potentially devastating issues with chain of custody and about the state firing Othram laboratories, seemingly at the same time that they tied sheath DNA to four brothers "whose name was not Kohberger." We know about the sample being twice as large when it arrived at the FBI lab in Quantico, though at 0.168 ng/ul, it was submitted to CODIS but deemed too small to be tested for Y-STR. We know Anne Taylor's office went to great lengths trying to determine how the knife sheath DNA was tested and by whom, but not why none of the evidence was suppressed.

Finally, we know that Bryan Christopher Kohberger admitted to being responsible for the crimes behind every one of these questions, but not why he chose to keep the answers to those questions secret. We know he pled guilty to one count of burglary and four counts of premeditated murder, but not how he committed the crimes—or, most important, why.

Perhaps none of this matters, because justice is blind, and according to the State of Idaho, justice has been served. Using the language of lawyers and courts, affiants have presented probable cause in affidavits, based on evidence gathered in accordance with rules of criminal procedure. Warrants have produced vast tranches of information that would not have seemed imaginable just a decade ago, digital records most people would not imagine government could so easily gather.

Forensic experts have swabbed and processed crime scenes gathering biological traces so small they are measured in nanograms and cells. Gone are the days of fingerprint examination, replaced by DNA analysis—a whole new language of forensic science full of terms like *single tandem repeats*, *single nucleotide polymorphisms*, and *investigative genetic genealogy.*

Even with the change of plea, properly certified and duly appointed attorneys have carried out their responsibilities, arguing via Franks hearings and motions of limine which evidence is exculpatory, admissible, and unfairly prejudicial. The judge, in this case Hippler, has exercised years of experience applying constitutional guarantees and case law precedent, using jurisprudence to weigh the best interests of an ordered society against those of the accused.

Bryan C. Kohberger is doing life without the possibility of parole for heinous crimes he admitted to committing. But is it not reasonable to look at the facts of this case and wonder if justice has been served? In this era of crowd-sourced inquiry, is it not our obligation to point out gaping holes in the prosecution's narrative, and in lieu of a trial, look deeper?

If so, it seems easy to imagine how the whole thing might have played out at the Ada County courthouse. Criminal trials always begin with opening statements, with the prosecution going first because they bear the burden of proof. In this case, Latah County prosecuting attorney Bill Thompson would have approached the jury, detailing the gruesome nature of the murders, the legal elements of the crimes, the facts of the case based on what the evidence would show. On behalf of the State of Idaho, he would express confidence that Bryan C. Kohberger was the only person responsible.

We already know the basics of his presentation because he made it at the change of plea hearing.

•

"The state submits that the evidence would show that on November 13th, 2022, Mr. Kohberger entered the residence at 1122 King Road in Moscow, Idaho. He did that with the intent to kill. We will not represent that he intended to commit all of the murders that he did that night, but we know that that is what resulted, and that he then killed intentionally, willfully, deliberately, with premeditation and with malice and forethought, Maddie Mogen, Kaylee Goncalves, Ethan Chapin, and Xana Kernodle. Thank you."

•

When he was finished, Anne Taylor would have stood and offered firm but heartfelt confidence that fair and impartial consideration of the facts would prove her client innocent of all charges. She would have reminded the jury that the state's burden is proof beyond a reasonable doubt. She would have done her best to sound resolute, measuring her tone with conviction and compassion, while trying to keep jurors from staring at her sometimes disturbingly awkward client.

When she was done, Judge Hippler would have told Mr. Thompson to proceed, and the prosecution would have begun building its case by calling its first witness. We do not know who that would have been, exactly, but based on what we heard in July, the State of Idaho's three-pronged narrative comes down to the KA-BAR knife sheath, video imagery of a white sedan, and cell tower analysis performed by the FBI.

Due to the complex science involved in all three types of evidence, they would have called everyone from MPD officers like Nunes and Payne to ISP detectives like Mowery and Gooch. They would have summoned FBI agents from Pennsylvania, Salt Lake City, headquarters, the Operational Technology Division, the Cellular Analysis Survey Team, the Critical Incident Response Group's Behavioral Analysis Unit in Quantico, and various other offices. Experts like Paulette Sutton would have been called to the stand, bolstering her findings with statistics and math.

And though we know most of the players, at this point, trials can be as theatrical as they are strategic. At some point, non-technical experts would have been called to the stand to lay out context, timeline, and foundation. Hunter Johnson would have been prominent among them, testifying to how and when he found the bodies. Anne Taylor likely would have cross-examined recollections about whether he touched the bodies, who went upstairs with him, where he found and left the knife. Both sides would have called friends and Greek life associates to the stand, looking to establish who might or might not have come into contact with the defendant. It is possible that Bill Thompson would have summoned Molly McMichael to the stand, establishing when she dropped food at the door. It is just as possible that Anne Taylor would have called her to introduce exculpatory statements she made regarding the driver of the tan sedan who looked nothing like the defendant. Perhaps Lakelynn McComas would have testified about what she remembered as one of the last people in the house prior to the murders, or Emily Alandt, who was one of the first to return.

It is possible that the prosecution would have called Bethany Funke. As one of two survivors, she could testify to what she heard or observed during the commission of the crimes. The prosecution might have used her to establish events leading up to the murders, like where she last saw Kaylee upstairs, when she and Maddie took Murphy outside, what time she went to bed. It is just as possible that Thompson would not have called her due to significant issues with her statements about the eight hours between Dylan running down to her room and the call to 911.

It is difficult to believe that the prosecution would not have called Dylan Mortensen, despite her role as the only eyewitness. Based on her four statements, Dylan's testimony would have been cannon fodder for the defense. No matter how important her eyewitness testimony would have been in identifying Kohberger's bushy eyebrows, I believe that little of what Dylan Mortensen has ever told police would have stood up at trial. In four interviews conducted between noon the day of the crimes and 1:54 p.m. on December 20, she made what seemed to me to be innumerable contradictory statements about what she saw and heard, including who she heard running down the stairs, who was crying in the bathroom, and basic information about the man she saw leaving the house.

No matter what Bill Thompson, online sleuths, and media opine about the veracity of her claims, no one can truly comment until they hear her actual words. The two-hour-and-seven-minute audio recording of her interview with Gooch and Blaker is, to me, appalling.

•

"I don't, I don't know if my mind's like making up stuff like at that moment when everything was happening," she states with regard to Kaylee Goncalves running down the stairs with Murphy. "I don't know how much I make stuff up so that I can remember, like . . . I just don't know. It just doesn't make sense to me, and I don't know how to fully explain it I guess."

•

Though not mentioned in Gooch's ISP summary, every single statement Mortensen made about what she saw, heard, felt, or did between 3:10 a.m., when she and Bethany went upstairs to Kaylee's room, and the moment police arrived, is qualified with "I don't know," "I'm not sure," or "I don't remember."

This is not an exaggeration or a generalization. After carefully and repeatedly listening to the interview, I can state, for the record, that in 127 minutes of recorded statements, Dylan Mortensen expressed doubt about her recollection 62 times. Perhaps that's not surprising, since her roommates had just been brutally murdered, but it bears mentioning.

•

"Yeah, this is all stuff that I . . . this is what I remember from that night," she says when asked about her interactions with the killer and events that followed. "Again, it's something I don't know if it was real or what happened. This is what I remembered, something that could be real, some of it could be not. I don't know, this is what I think, I don't remember."

•

It did not help that Mortensen blamed much of her confusion on being drunk when other witnesses found that confusing. On December 1, for example, a woman named Yesenia Rajo called police from the Delta Zeta sorority to report that she saw Mortensen the night of November 12, and Dylan was not drinking. Rajo told police she had heard from friends that Dylan was "too drunk to know what happened," but that could not be correct because she had talked to her friend about being completely sober.

Based on seemingly wild disparities in her accounts, it is just as likely that Anne Taylor would have called Dylan to the stand as a witness for the defense.

While at it, Taylor would have called any number of the dozen or so experts she hired to poke holes in the prosecution's case. Criminologists like former special agent Chris Holland would have stated that police found zero physical evidence of the crimes in Kohberger's apartment; found zero evidence in a storage unit; zero evidence in his Elantra, which they disassembled completely. Other experts would have testified that police found no personal or social media connections between Kohberger and Kaylee Goncalves or Maddie Mogen, the targets of these premeditated attacks. Behavioralists would have pointed to overkill and signature wounds as proof of rage as a motive, something no one could tie to a stranger.

The defense would certainly have called Dr. Steven Turvey to attack Paulette Sutton's testimony with vigor and zeal. Based on what he has stated here in this book, it seems likely the veteran of seventy-three multiple homicide trials would have capitalized on Sutton's possible mistakes, parading a laundry list of apparent stumbles past the jury. Among them he would have highlighted the likely missteps matching photos to exhibits, drawing conclusions without examining actual physical evidence, opining that Kohberger could have escaped the crime scene without tracking blood to his car if he was naked.

There is no way to guess how closing arguments would have gone, because a trial this complex could have taken ten weeks or more, and based on what we know—and we don't know much—there would have been plenty of drama and surprises. That's the way these things go.

In the end, it would all have gone to the jury, and at that point, one guess is as good as another. Everyone knows a grand jury will indict a ham sandwich, but as Mark Twain once quipped, "A jury consists of twelve persons chosen to decide who has the better lawyer."

In this case, there was no Johnnie Cochran.

But none of this matters, of course, because regardless of what we believe or think we know about what happened around 4 a.m. on November 13, 2022, at 1122 King Road, one thing is certain: On July 2, 2025, Bryan Christopher Kohberger stood in front of Judge Steven Hippler and pleaded guilty to one count of burglary and four counts of premeditated murder. After nearly three years of steadfast denial, he changed his mind and took a plea.

The only question that remains is why.

Why would a man confess to something he may not have done, knowing he was going to spend the rest of his life in prison with no possibility of parole? Only two people know the answer: Kohberger and his attorney, Anne Taylor.

As luck would have it, we have firsthand insights into her thinking.

•

"She called it the new normal," a source told me during a face-to-face interview in October 2025.

"She said it was exhausting working with Kohberger to make a decision once the actual offer came in from Bill Thompson's office. She said the whole thing was like getting ready at an amusement park for a giant roller coaster, and then getting pulled out of line just before getting to the gate."

In July 2025, approximately one week after Kohberger changed his plea to guilty, Anne Taylor consented to a call with one of the two dozen criminologists and mitigation experts she had hired to poke holes in the prosecution's case. This individual felt strongly that information gathered by the defense was far too compelling to warrant waiver of a trial and wanted to know what had changed.

He agreed to discuss recorded conversations with Taylor, but only in general terms, and requested that his name not be used, for professional reasons.

"Before we get into the reasoning behind Kohberger's change of plea, let me say I found out just like you and everyone else. I want to make that clear up front. I started to get all these texts from colleagues telling me this case was getting a plea, and I'm like, 'what?' We'd all just had a meeting that previous Wednesday where everyone got together to discuss the case, how everything was coming together. As far as we knew, we were proceeding toward trial."

It should be noted that both forensic criminologists, Dr. Brent Turvey and Christopher Holland, expressed shock at the sudden change in direction. Neither had any suspicion of a plea agreement until it was announced in the media.

"This stuff happens, especially in larger cases," the source said, referring to last-minute deals. "But I couldn't believe it, because this wasn't just reasonable doubt; it was overwhelming. I have worked dozens of cases like this during my career, and I was shocked. I think the common impression was that the prosecution had real problems with chain of custody on the KA-BAR sheath, inconsistencies in DNA testing, holes in Paulette Sutton's analysis, evidence of a second offender."

The source said he was so convinced the case was going to trial, he had left a bag full of clothes in Taylor's office.

"She told me it happened right after the *Dateline* leak," he said. "I had been told that the judge had gotten involved as a mediator between the two parties. In my opinion that's completely inappropriate, so I told her so, but she said once the offer came in from the prosecution, things happened quickly with no back and forth. She said he told her not to let it out, that she couldn't talk about it with anyone except her client."

This explained the cloak of silence, but not the reasoning for Kohberger's change of heart.

"She said there was no clear-cut answer, just that they had fought their asses off and filed every motion under the sun. So, I asked her directly if she had talked to him, her client, if she had asked him if he had done it, if she had asked him for any details whatsoever that would explain what happened inside that house. And I'll tell you exactly what she said. She said, 'There was . . . there was nothing.' She had no idea whether he actually did it or not."

The source stated that he was led to believe Kohberger had been taken to death row to see where he would stay pending execution of sentence, but that Taylor refuted this. She told him that another lawyer in her office and a mitigation expert toured the prison, and they explained things to Kohberger as he made up his mind.

"She told me she followed ethical guidelines and talked pros and cons with him, that he read all the reports we had compiled. She told me he talked to the psychologists and his parents leading up to the decision to change his plea but said the decision was his, that he made the choice for himself. And I'm sure this is probably true, but in the end, what bothers me the most is that she never asked him how or why. She seemingly never asked her client for a single detail about these horrific crimes. She allowed him to plead guilty knowing he was not going to explain anything in court, that he was not going to explain anything to the parents of those kids, or the investigators who will never be able to put the loose ends together. In my opinion, she watched him stand up in that courtroom and take the plea, perhaps knowing it was broken."

If justice is the realm of lawyers and courts, where has that left us?

Yes, Bryan Christopher Kohberger will spend the rest of his life in prison for horrific crimes committed in the early morning hours of November 13, 2022. Yes, the prosecution has moved on to other cases, as has the defense. Yes, Moscow police have returned to their rounds, doing their best to protect the community as their bosses grudgingly disclose bits and pieces of a fifty-one-terabyte file so large it may never be adequately probed. Yes, the survivors are left to try to make sense of senseless horror.

The obvious question, of course, is this: Where do we go from here?

Perhaps it makes sense to look back at where we started and agree that while most stories do not begin at the end, we still don't have one. Perhaps we take it upon ourselves to press the people we pay to protect us for answers. Perhaps we gather together our resources and talents to question what the experts have tried to sell as fact.

Perhaps we push forward for truth. Because the system we trusted to prove guilt beyond a reasonable doubt has left us all with plenty.

Acknowledgments

I would like to thank my friend and agent David Vigliano for years of steadfast support.

Thank you to Matt Baugher and his remarkable team at HarperCollins for providing the editorial, legal, artistic, and marketing expertise necessary to turn a bunch of pages into a story worth reading.

Thanks to my wife and first line editor, Dr. Rose Marie Whitcomb, for months of research, weeks of proofreading, and years of selfless commitment. It never escapes me that although my name appears on the cover of this book, we share in its production.

I am grateful for Dr. Brent Turvey, former FBI agent Christopher Holland, and two "unnamed sources" for their courageous and unflinching devotion to truth. Without their expertise, perspectives, and intimate knowledge of the case, details of this terrible story may never have been disclosed.

Finally, I want to acknowledge a new generation of amateur sleuths who labor in obscurity, pioneering innovative new techniques to solve cold case investigations, find missing persons, and right wrongful convictions. May this book spur your advances.

About the Author

Christopher Whitcomb is a writer, entrepreneur, and former FBI agent with business and operational experience in more than thirty countries.

He is the bestselling author of *Cold Zero: Inside the FBI Hostage Rescue Team,* the novels *Black* and *White*, and the memoir *Anonymous Male: A Life Among Spies.* He has written for numerous outlets, including *The New York Times*, *GQ*, Netflix, CBS Films, and HBO.